TWAYNE'S WORLD AUTHORS SERIES
A Survey of the World's Literature

Sylvia E. Bowman, Indiana University

GENERAL EDITOR

SPAIN

Gerald Wade, Vanderbilt University
Janet W. Diaz, University of North Carolina, Chapel Hill

EDITORS

Mira de Amescua

TWAS 449

MIRA DE AMESCUA

By JAMES A. CASTAÑEDA

Rice University

TWAYNE PUBLISHERS

A DIVISION OF G. K. HALL & CO., BOSTON

Copyright© 1977 by G. K. Hall & Co.
All Rights Reserved
First Printing

Library of Congress Cataloging in Publication Data

Castañeda, James A.
  Mira de Amescua.

  (Twayne's world authors series; TWAS 449 : Spain)
  Bibliography: p. 195–205.
  Includes index.
  1. Mira de Amescua, Antonio, fl. 1600.
  2. Dramatists, Spanish—17th century—Biography.
PQ6413.M7Z59   862'.3 [B]   77–1956
ISBN 0-8057-6285-X

MANUFACTURED IN THE UNITED STATES OF AMERICA

In loving memory of my grandparents

James Matthew Sincock
(1879–1968)

Ada Richards Sincock
(1882–1970)

Contents

About the Author

James A. Castañeda is Professor of Spanish at Rice University, where he has served as department chairman (1964-72), Master of Will Rice College (1969-76), and assistant baseball coach (1961-present). For eight years he was Executive Secretary of the South Central Modern Language Association. He was named *Miembro Titular* of the *Instituto de Cultura Hispánica de Madrid* in 1972, he was appointed to membership of the American Committee of the Modern Humanities Research Association in 1975, and he has served as President of the Indiana Chapter of the American Association of Teachers of Spanish and Portuguese, of the Institute of Hispanic Culture of Houston, and of the National Federation of Modern Language Teachers Associations.

Following receipt of the B.A. *summa cum laude* from Drew University, Professor Castañeda had a brief career as a professional baseball player. A recipient of Danforth and Fulbright fellowships, he obtained the M.A. and Ph.D. degrees at Yale University and also studied at the University of Paris and the University of Madrid. He started his teaching career at Hanover College and has been a visiting professor at the University of Southern California, Purdue University, the University of Notre Dame, the University of North Carolina, Western New Mexico University and, for the academic year 1976-77, he was Florence Purington Visiting Professor of Spanish at Mount Holyoke College. His publications include a critical edition of Lope de Vega's *Las paces de los reyes y Judía de Toledo* (Chapel Hill: University of North Carolina Press, 1962; Madrid: Anaya, 1971), *Agustín Moreto* (Twayne, 1974), and several articles on Lope de Vega, Góngora, Mira de Amescua, Moreto, Calderón, and Sor Juana Inés de la Cruz. A member of the "Comediantes," Professor Castañeda is a contributing author to *Lope de Vega Studies, 1937-1962* (Toronto, 1964), *Calderón de la Barca Studies, 1951-1969* (Toronto, 1971), and the group's forthcoming annotated bibliography of Tirso de Molina studies.

Preface

Antonio Mira de Amescua (1574?-1644) was one of the many Golden Age dramatists who wrote for the stage while serving in important ecclesiastic positions. There is documentary evidence that his writing enjoyed great popularity and fame during his lifetime and for some time thereafter. In the eighteenth century, however, his renown waned sharply, a process which continued until a revival of interest in his considerable talents began early in the present century. The revival has primarily taken the form of critical editions of Mira's plays; only one comprehensive monograph has been published — in 1931 — and this is currently subject to revision based on the results of scholarly investigation in the intervening years. The goal of this book, therefore, is to provide an up-to-date synthesis of available knowledge on the life and works of this Golden Age dramatist whose talent and literary importance are far greater than is indicated by the scant scholarly comment which has been devoted to him.

Of great significance is the fact that Mira wrote during the dawn of Spanish Golden Age Drama. Although the beginnings of Spanish theater go back to the work of Juan del Encina (1468?-1529), to the contributions of Lucas Fernández (1474?-1542), Torres Naharro (?-1524?), Lope de Rueda (1500?-1565), Juan de la Cueva (1543-1610), and Cervantes (1547-1616), it was the monumental Lope de Vega (1562-1635) who really originated the Spanish *comedia* as we know it. Mira, born less than a decade and a half after Lope de Vega, shows evidence in his plays of having been influenced by the best and the worst of Lope's writing. Indeed, there is a tendency to consider Mira as nothing more than a servile follower of Lope. We do not accept this simplified view, however, and hope to lend support to the theory that Mira is artistically unique in several important ways.

Although he lacks some of the technical perfection and sophistication of dramatic structure which are found in the works of the truly outstanding members of the so-called schools of Lope de Vega and of Calderón de la Barca, Mira frequently exudes a somewhat primitive strength which constitutes the beauty of some of his most successful scenes, if not entire plays. When compared with other members of the school of Lope de Vega, Mira distinguishes himself with great lyric flights in the better moments of many of his *comedias;* in terms of dramatic structure and organization, however, he does not always compare favorably with the illustrious contemporary giants, Lope and Tirso, or with the meticulous craftsman, Alarcón.

Nevertheless, the fact that Mira de Amescua deserves to be ranked immediately behind these three stars of his epoch places him in a category of high distinction. His reputation has been severely hampered by the traditional attribution of several of his better plays to contemporary dramatists of greater renown. When these plays are firmly established in Mira's canon, the fame of this relatively neglected playwright should rise considerably. Although he does not deserve to be placed on a par with Lope and Calderón, the two undisputed masters of Golden Age drama, he does seem to merit admission to the constellation of next greatest magnitude, headed by Tirso and Alarcón, who are closely followed by Moreto and Rojas Zorrilla.

Special thanks are in order to the respective staffs of Rice University's Fondren Library, the British Museum, the Institut Hispanique of Paris, the Bayerische Staatsbibliothek of Munich, and Madrid's Biblioteca Nacional. Christine Womack has skillfully and conscientiously typed the manuscript, which was begun in Madrid during a sabbatical leave generously awarded by Rice University and partially supported by a grant from the Instituto de Cultura Hispánica de Madrid. My colleague John E. Parish has read the manuscript carefully and offered many valuable suggestions. The translations into English are the author's. Although space limitations preclude acknowledgment by name, to all of the individuals who have so kindly collaborated in this project through cooperation, advice, encouragement, and criticism go the deep appreciation and heartfelt gratitude of the author, who holds himself exclusively responsible for whatever shortcomings may be present in this volume.

JAMES A. CASTAÑEDA

Rice University

Chronology

1574? Antonio Mira de Amescua is born in Guadix.

1580 September 17: Francisco de Quevedo y Villegas is born in Madrid (d. September 8, 1645).

1581 Birth of Juan Ruiz de Alarcón in Mexico City.

1592– Mira begins the study of canon law in Granada.
1595

1598– Receives the doctorate in theology.
1600

1600 January 17: Pedro Calderón de la Barca is born in Madrid (d. May 25, 1681).

1600 September 4: Fernando del Pulgar, *corregidor* of Guadix, names Mira his lieutenant and *alcalde mayor* (mayor) of the city and its jurisdiction.

1601 May 8: Mira is sent by the Bishop of Guadix to settle a dispute over the priorate of Baza.

1602 Lope de Vega and Mira de Amescua meet in Granada.

1604 August 4: Lope de Vega reports in a letter having seen Mira's *La rueda de la fortuna* presented in Toledo.

1605 Mira's first published work, a poem on the sack of Cádiz by the English in 1595, appears in Pedro Espinosa's *Flores de poetas ilustres.*

1605 Cervantes' *Don Quixote* (Part I) is published in Madrid.

1606 Mira takes up residence in Madrid.

1609 The *moriscos* (Spanish Moslems) are expelled from Spain.

1609 September 1: Mira is named by Philip III to the chaplaincy of the Royal Chapel in Granada. (He takes possession of this charge in 1610.)

1609 February 9: Mira grants ecclesiastic approval to Bernardo de Balbuena's heroic poem *El Bernardo.*

1610– Residence in Naples, in the service of the Viceroy, don
1616 Pedro Fernández de Castro, Count of Lemos. Mira's invitation had been recommended by Lupercio Leonardo de Argensola, secretary to the Count.

1615 Cervantes, in the prologue to his *comedias,* praises Mira as an "imitator and disciple" of Lope de Vega.

1615   *Don Quixote* (Part II) is published in Madrid.

1616   April 23: Cervantes dies in Madrid.

1616   Having returned from Naples, Mira again resides in Madrid, neglecting his religious duties.

1621   March 31: Death of Philip III; ascension to the throne of his son, Philip IV.

1622   *Décimas* by Mira win first place in the poetry competition held in conjunction with the *fiestas* held to celebrate the canonization of San Isidro.

1622   Mira is a contestant in the *certamen* (poetry contest) organized by the Colegio Imperial to celebrate the canonization of Saints Ignatius Loyola and Francis Xavier.

1622–   Mira serves as chaplain of the infante don Fernando de
1631   Austria, in Madrid.

1624   October 5: Mira approves the *Parte veinte* of Lope's plays and compares Lope favorably with Menander.

1627   May 23: Death of the controversial baroque poet Luis de Góngora (b. July 11, 1561 in Cordova).

1631   Guillén de Castro dies in Madrid (b. 1569 in Valencia).

1631   Mira is proposed as archdeacon of Guadix; appointment is approved on September 13, 1631, but Mira does not take possession of the office until June 16, 1632.

1632   Mira's *La jura del príncipe* is one of the *autos* presented as part of Madrid's Corpus Christi celebrations.

1633   Mira is reprimanded for two incidents in which he lost control of his temper among his fellow priests.

1635   August 27: Death in Madrid of the creator of the modern Spanish theater, Lope de Vega (b. 1562 in Madrid).

1639   August 1: Death of the Mexican-born dramatist, Ruiz de Alarcón, in Madrid.

1640   February 4: inauguration of the *Coliseo,* court theater in Madrid's Buen Retiro.

1641   Mira's *auto, Ronda y visita de la cárcel,* is presented in Madrid's Corpus Christi celebrations.

1644   September 8: Mira dies in Guadix, in whose Cathedral he is buried.

CHAPTER 1

Biographical Sketch

M OST of our meager documentary knowledge concerning Antonio Mira de Amescua's biography derives from the *prueba de linaje* (proof of lineage) assembled from July to September, 1631, in support of his candidacy for the position of archdeacon of the cathedral church of Guadix. Although the full text of this document has never been published, extensive excerpts provided by Fructuoso Sanz in 1914[1] constitute the best available source for many details concerning Mira's life. Brief biographic sketches may be found in the work of Nicolás Antonio (1672),[2] Mesonero Romanos (1852 and 1858),[3] Barrera (1860),[4] Tárrago (1864 and 1888),[5] Rodríguez Marín (1907 and 1918),[6] Díaz de Escovar (1911),[7] and Valbuena Prat (1926).[8] To these may be added the extensive study of Cotarelo y Mori (1930 and 1931)[9] and the concise but comprehensive studies provided by Karl C. Gregg, first in the introduction to his 1968 edition of *La mesonera del cielo*[10] *(The Innkeeper of Heaven)* and then, slightly revised, in 1974 in a separate article.[11]

Born in Guadix, a small Andalusian city in the Province of Granada, Antonio Mira de Amescua was the illegitimate son of Melchor de Amescua and Beatriz de Torres.[12] Melchor's grandfather, Juan de Mira, was a soldier of noble birth who fought in the victorious forces of Fernando and Isabel which conquered the city of Baza in 1489: his reward for participation in the conquest consisted of land grants in Guadix and Baza. He chose to settle in Baza, where his wife, Mariana Páez de Sotomayor, gave birth to Antonio Mira, grandfather of our dramatist. Fruit of Antonio's marriage to Luisa de Amescua were Isabel, María, and Melchor. The poet's mother, Beatriz de Torres, was one of four offspring of Francisco de Heredia and Francisca de Morales. Her father, a captain, was killed by the *moriscos* on Christmas Eve, 1567, during

13

their uprising in Berja. Following the death of her father, Beatriz left Berja and came to Guadix to live with her uncle-in-law and aunt, Doctor Matías Figueras and Constanza Vázquez del Oso. Antonio's father, who reversed his surnames and chose to call himself Melchor de Amescua y Mira, had by this time also settled in Guadix where his status was that of a gentleman of considerable distinction. Melchor never married, but he did live for a period of time with Beatriz and, from this union was born, possibly in 1574,[13] Antonio Mira de Amescua. Soon after birth, Antonio was brought to Melchor's house, where he was apparently reared by his father and two aunts, Isabel and María de Amescua. Antonio's mother seems to have played a very small part in his upbringing. Although Melchor and Beatriz are said to have intended to marry, they apparently never did.

The poet's name appeared in many forms in the seventeenth century: Mescua, Amezcua, Mezqua, and even the combined form Mirademescua. We use the form which Mira preferred for his own signature, a copy of which has been published by Rodríguez Marín.[14] Although information concerning Mira's adolescence is extremely sparse, it appears that he began his studies in Guadix and that he was confirmed on January 30, 1593, by the Bishop of Guadix, Juan Alonso de Moscoso. At some time between 1592 and 1595, he enrolled in the Colegio Imperial de San Miguel in Granada where he studied *cánones y leyes* (ecclesiastical law). Subsequently, he studied enough theology to be ordained as a presbyter upon the award of his doctorate, which he received between 1598 and 1600.

After completion of his studies, Mira returned to Guadix. On September 4, 1600, don Fernando de Pulgar, *corregidor* of Guadix, named Mira his lieutenant and *alcalde mayor* (mayor) of the city and its jurisdiction and delegated to him full authority for carrying out the duties of this important position.[15] Although we do not know precisely how long Mira held the post of *alcalde mayor,* we do know that he had ceased to hold it by June 9, 1607, at which time a document from the Archives of Simancas classifies him as a resident of Madrid.[16] On May 8, 1601,[17] Juan de Fonseca, Bishop of Guadix and Baza, sent Mira to the latter city to see to it that the priorate of the church of Baza be given to Francisco de Solórzano. Juan Ortega de Grixalua had been instructed to obtain the post for Francisco de Solórzano, but the parish priest and the municipal council had refused to relinquish it to him. Bishop Fonseca delegated great power to Mira for this undertaking, including instructions to depose the vicar general and himself serve in that high position should any resistance to the bishop's instructions be met.

In 1602 Mira is known to have been in Granada, where he met Lope de Vega during the latter's visit to that city. They met, according to Rafael Carrasco,[18] in literary sessions hosted by don Pedro de Granada Benegas. Lope later complained of the cool reception proffered by the literary figures of Granada with the sole exception of Mira, to whom he dedicated a sonnet that same year in *La hermosura de Angélica (Angelica's Beauty)*. Favorable reference to the dramatic production of Mira de Amescua in the 1603 *Viaje entretenido (Entertaining Journey)* of Agustín Rojas proves that Mira's literary career had already been successfully launched prior to that date. We have an example of his nondramatic poetry written as early as 1596.

The death of Mira's father occurred sometime between 1601 and 1605 and, newly independent, the young lawyer, priest, and writer journeyed to Madrid in 1606 to seek a place in the court. For the next few years, Mira occupied himself with his developing literary career, a fact attested to by the appearance of his poems in several volumes, the completion of some *comedias,* including his delightful *La Fénix de Salamanca (The Phoenix of Salamanca)*, in 1607, and his installation as censor. On February 9, 1609, he wrote the *aprobación* for Bernardo de Balbuena's heroic poem *El Bernardo*. Cotarelo assumes that Mira's request in 1607 for a copy of the document by which he was named *alcalde mayor* of Guadix[19] is evidence that Mira intended to utilize his studies to obtain a position in one of Madrid's civil or ecclesiastical tribunals.

On September 1, 1609, Philip III ordered the chaplaincy of the Capilla Real de Granada to be turned over to Mira, a replacement for the deceased Dr. Pedro Martínez de Espinosa.[20] Although the royal document mentions the need for traditional *pruebas de linaje y limpieza,* no records of any such examination are known to us. Also in 1609, the Count of Lemos was appointed Viceroy of Naples. The Count of Lemos, who was to become a patron of Cervantes in 1613, was the most prominent Maecenas of the time, having previously patronized such notable literary figures as Lope de Vega, Vicente Espinel, Bartolomé Leonardo de Argensola, and Cristóbal de Mesa. Applications flowed in for places in the Count's entourage. According to Otis Green, "Cervantes undoubtedly

sought a place ... receiving instead promises ... that they would
send for him as soon as possible. His protest at their failure to do so
fills a much quoted page in the *Viaje del Parnaso*."[21] Among other
literary notables disappointed at not being invited were Góngora,
Suárez de Figueroa, and Cristóbal de Mesa. Those eventually
chosen were Mira de Amescua, Gabriel de Barrionuevo, Antonio
de Laredo, Francisco de Ortigosa, and Gabriel Leonardo de
Albión, son of the elder Argensola. Mira seems to be the only
genuine poet of this group. He left Madrid for Naples with the
Viceroy's entourage on May 17, 1610, and he is thought also to
have returned with the Count of Lemos, who had already departed
for Spain by June 24, 1616.[22]

Luis Pérez Cardader, last of the witnesses of Guadix, affirmed
that, while in Italy, Mira was almost named bishop and that he in
effect did serve as an administrator in an Italian bishopric.[23] Although this claim was reported by Sanz, he doubted it as well as the
assertion that Mira actually did accompany Lemos to Italy.[24] Otis
Green, however, has discovered documentary evidence that Mira
actually did assume the stewardship of the bishopric of Tropea;[25]
but he doubts that Mira belonged to the famous Accademia degli
Oziosi, which was founded on May 3, 1611, under the protection of
Lemos and the guidance of his secretary, Lupercio Leonardo de
Argensola.[26] That this foreign residence had a profound effect on
Mira is indicated by the large number of Italian settings and histori-
cal references which are found in his dramatic production subsequent to 1610.

Ruth Lee Kennedy perceptively notes the literary climate of
Madrid upon Mira's return from Naples: "Between 1616 and 1621
the greatest talents of Spain were being drawn to Madrid as though
by a magnet, some of them after long years abroad."[27] Edward
Wilson also notes that Mira was one of several dramatists who were
ordained priests, the most widely known of this group being
Lope, Tirso, Calderón, Godínez, and Montalván.[28] Among these
great talents, Mira became active as a censor, as attested by several
aprobaciones which bear his signature.[29] In 1619, he was named
chaplain of the infante don Fernando, son of Philip III who, on
July 29, at the age of ten, had just been granted the cardinalate of
Toledo.

On October 30, 1619, Mira, absentee chaplain of the Capilla
Real in Granada, and Dr. Bartolomé de Llerena, a recently ap-

pointed canon in the cathedral church of Guadix, submitted a joint request that they be allowed to exchange their ecclesiastic appointments.[30] On August 31, 1621, Jorge de Tovar, the king's secretary, informed the Bishop of Guadix that Mira had explained his refusal to obey orders to return to his chaplaincy in Granada by referring to the long-pending transfer which he had requested. It is suggested that the documents for the transfer had already been signed and that Llerena had been instructed to take his new position in Granada within thirty days. The reply, dated September 12, 1621, shows a perceptive understanding of Mira's delaying tactics. In it, the Bishop of Guadix assumes that Mira will stop at nothing to stay in Madrid, in whose literary milieu he must have been very happy. In a letter from Philip III to Martín Fernández Portocarrero, president of the royal tribunal and chancellery of Guadix, dated March 23, 1622, it is revealed that the transfer of Mira and Llerena was finally approved but that Llerena's retirement kept it from being implemented. Mira then proposed as a candidate for the chaplaincy in Granada one Diego de Bracamonte, a native of Guadix, currently canon of the cathedral church of Palencia. In exchange for his position, Mira would receive an annual pension of 200 *ducados* from a benefice held by Bracamonte. Portocarrero informed the king of the acceptability of Bracamonte on April 12 and commented on the joy occasioned by his appointment "because of the remedy it provides for the lack of residence of Dr. Mira de Amescua whom we have not been able to persuade to come here in ten years."[31]

Meanwhile, the theatrical winds were shifting.[32] In a letter to the Count of Lemos, dated May 6, 1620, Lope de Vega states that he finds himself "competing in plots (*enredos*) with Mesqua and don Guillén de Castro over which of us handles them best in his *comedias.*"[33] In 1617, Mira had been commissioned by Philip III to plan and produce dramatic and musical festivities in a palace courtyard.[34] In 1620, he was called on again, this time for the important task of producing a dramatic presentation as part of the festivities held in conjunction with the celebration of the beatification of San Isidro. Pérez Pastor provides the text of the presentation and a detailed enumeration of the elaborate costumes requested by Mira.[35] Probably because of his heavy administrative assignment, Mira was apparently unable to submit any poetic entries of his own for the competition held under the direction of Lope de Vega. During the

ceremonies of San Isidro's canonization which took place in 1622,
Mira was awarded first prize for the *décimas* which he submitted
for a similar competition. In the same year Mira was also a prize-
winning contestant in the competitions held in conjunction with
celebrations of the canonization of Saints Francis Xavier and Ignatius Loyola.

It was Lope also, who in *La Filomena* (Madrid: Viuda de Alonso
Martín, 1621) provides one of the few references to Mira's physical
characteristics. In describing a portrait of the dramatist, painted by
the famous Heredia el Mudo, Lope tells us that:

> El divino pincel del mudo Heredia
> (que entera no pudiera) al doctor Mira
> de su figura retrató la media.[36]

> The divine brush of the mute Heredia
> (in entirety he couldn't) of Dr. Mira
> portrayed half his body.

In August of 1623, special ceremonies were planned in Madrid to
celebrate the visit of Charles Stuart, Prince of Wales, who had
come to Spain to negotiate marriage with the Spanish princess,
María of Austria. The dramatist Juan Ruiz de Alarcón was commissioned to write a poetic description of the events. Legend has it
that the uninspired Alarcón sought help from Mira and a few other
poets. The resultant poem, composed of seventy-three *octavas,* was
cruelly and satirically criticized in a literary academy or *tertulia* attended by Góngora, Lope, Quevedo, Montalván, Tirso de Molina,
Castillo Solórzano, and Mira, to name only the most well-known.
Each in attendance composed a burlesque *décima* criticizing
Alarcón's poem; some cruelly added references to his grotesquely
hunched back. These *décimas* were first published by Alfay in
1654,[37] and then by Hartzenbusch in 1852 and again in 1860.[38]
Mira's, which exhibits the anomaly of containing eleven lines, does
not criticize the poem, but it does demand from Alarcón half of the
money received for its composition, since Mira claims to have been
the one who invented "el componer de consumo" (collaborative
writing). Hartzenbusch took this to be a boast by which Mira took
credit for the initiation of collaboration in dramatic writing, a prac-
tice much abused and one which has few outstanding results to its
credit. In view of the fact that the collaborative monstrosity,

Algunas hazañas del Marqués de Cañete (Some of the Many Exploits of the Marquis of Cañete), obviously engineered by Luis de Belmonte, was published in 1622, it seems more likely that Mira is here saying simply that he suggested collaboration for this particular poem.

Mira's name was once again linked to Alarcón's later the same year in connection with the première of the latter's *El Anticristo*. A flask which released a vile odor was placed in the theater the night of the first performance of Alarcón's play. The poet Góngora, in a letter dated December 19, 1623,[39] informed the famous priest and orator, Hortensio Paravicino, that Lope de Vega and Mira were first arrested as the guilty parties, but then released when one Juan Pablo Rizo was found with the ingredients used to produce the infernal smell.

Throughout the remainder of the decade Mira remained in Madrid, neglecting his ecclesiastic duties. The investigation of Mira's ancestry lasted from July 20 to September 13, 1631, on which date the findings were approved by the Bishop of Guadix and a dispensation was obtained for the poet's illegitimacy.[40] Mira did not journey to Guadix to take possession of his new appointment until June 16 of the following year, when he presented his credentials to the municipal council of Guadix and was officially invested as archdeacon. It is generally agreed that Mira ceased to write for the theater after assumption of his new ecclesiastic duties in Guadix in 1632. Very little is known of the remaining years of his life, although two incidents found documented in the archives of the Cathedral of Guadix by Rodríguez Marín[41] have probably been responsible for the general imputation to Mira of an irascible character. On June 7, 1633, Mira stormed out of a council meeting and slammed the door after vehemently protesting that the candidate he proposed for a minor position had not been appointed. For such uncomely behavior he was banned from council meetings for a year and fined ten ducats. Anything but chastened, Mira became involved the very next day in a dispute with the *maestrescuela* (schoolmaster) at the entrance to the cathedral. He was again fined and the two were briefly interned in the church until June 17, by which time their tempers had cooled. The same document speaks in general of constant problems caused by Mira. It is undoubtedly on this document that Valbuena Prat bases his contention that Mira was wild, arrogant, and neurasthenic.[42]

Mira's literary inactivity in Guadix explains his absence from the list of eulogists whose poetic tributes comprised the *Fama póstuma* (1636) in memory of Lope de Vega. Contributors to that volume are a multitude of followers and friends of Lope de Vega, among whom we would certainly expect Mira to be represented had he not withdrawn from literary activity. The only remaining published document on Mira's life, dated August 27, 1638, contains a report of instructions which he laid down four days previously for the cathedral musicians and choir.[43] George Ann Huck reports having found in Guadix documents which reveal that Mira showed signs of failing health which caused him to be absent from his duties in March and June of 1642.[44]

Until Rodríguez Marín published Mira's death certificate in 1907,[45] scholars speculated on dates ranging from 1635 to 1645,[46] some basing their conclusions on the assertion by Pedro Suárez, historian of Guadix and Baza, in a volume published in 1696, that Mira had died some fifty years prior to that date.[47] The death certificate reveals that Mira died on September 8, 1644 and that he was interred in the Cathedral of Guadix.

Karl Gregg has compiled the following chart, which helpfully summarizes the major periods in Mira's life:

Guadix	1574? — 1592/95
Granada	1592/95 — 1600
Guadix	1600 — 1606
	(visit to Granada, 1602)
Madrid	1606 — 1610
Naples	1610 — 1616
Madrid	1616 — 1632
Guadix	1632 — 1644[48]

Mira's death came quietly in Guadix and evoked no known reaction from his contemporaries. As we will show in a later chapter, he enjoyed a place of high esteem among them, a reputation which suffered slow erosion through the ensuing years. A single short tribute was paid to this important dramatist on the fourth centenary of his birth,[49] and, as we roamed the narrow byways of his provincial Guadix in 1968, we noted a single, unpretentious street named after Mira de Amescua. In our opinion, he deserves much more renown than has been his lot to date. It is our hope that the tribute to Mira de Amescua represented by this volume will in some way help to restore his well-deserved reputation as one of Spain's most outstanding dramatists.

CHAPTER 2

Mira de Amescua's Literary Production

I Mira's Place Among His Dramatic Contemporaries

ALTHOUGH critics are virtually unanimous in assigning Mira to the school of Lope de Vega (1562–1635), Pfandl casts a dissenting vote in placing him in the school of Calderón (1600–1681), in spite of the fact that he assigns to Lope's school two dramatists who lived beyond the date of Mira's demise: Tirso de Molina (d. 1648 and Montalván (d. 1649).[1] In support of Mira's affinity to Lope, Mesonero Romanos notes that, in the selection of themes, in plot structure, and in character portrayal, "one notes the indubitable influence, or rather the tyranny of Lope."[2] Rodríguez Marín finds Mira "very close to Lope in style, although more lyrical and high-flown."[3] In the words of Menéndez Pelayo: "The style of Mira de Amescua is closer to Lope's than that of any other of our dramatists; but the poet from Guadix usually shows himself to be more exuberant and overadorned with lyric pomp than the Madrilenian."[4]

Margaret Wilson also offers a perceptive comparison of Mira with his contemporary dramatists: "Mira preaches the essential neo-Stoic lesson, the need for equanimity in the face of all vicissitudes . . . , and in this shows how deep was his sense of his country's decline. Lope ignores it; Tirso and Alarcón make their political attacks, but seem to presuppose that an improvement is possible. Only Calderón, among the other dramatists, resorts like Mira to a philosophy born of despair."[5] Parallel techniques which relate Mira and Calderón have been noted by Sloman, who declares: "Calderón's plays also show a clearer subordination of characters to the protagonist. Their parts are conceived in terms of his, their qualities and behaviour throw his into relief. The foil technique was of course used by Calderón's predecessors, and it has been taken

21

even to be a distinctive feature of the plays of Mira de Amescua."[6]

Our personal view places Mira in the school of Lope de Vega. In the succeeding pages, however, we shall enumerate a number of characteristics and emphases which attest to Mira's originality within the genre and which establish him as an important transition between the schools of Lope and Calderón. We also believe that the reassignment to his canon of several important works long associated with other dramatists qualifies Mira for a place of distinction among Golden Age dramatists. If not the equal of the giants of the period, Mira should be ranked with Moreto and Rojas Zorrilla as the best of the playwrights after Lope, Tirso, Alarcón, and Calderón.

II *Language, Themes, and Attitudes*

Mira de Amescua is, in many ways, truly a transitional author. It is easy to detect in his *comedias* the heritage bequeathed to him by Lope de Vega, founder of modern Spanish theater, but documentation is also available to prove the debt to Mira, in terms of language and themes, of such well-known contemporaries as Tirso de Molina and the later dramatists, Moreto and Calderón.

In many ways which do not require elaboration here, Mira was typical of his age. He frequently used such stock figures as women in male disguise, abandoned infants of noble parentage reared in rustic surroundings, and cowardly servants. Several of his heroines, in varying degrees of protest against paternal domination, express by word and deed their conviction that a woman should have some say in the choice of her husband. Mira also is fond of parodying the at times pathologic power exerted on society by the rigid contemporary honor code. Witchcraft and magic are also treated in Mira's theater, although not frequently.[7] In these and in other areas, Mira was not unique.

Considered on a universal level, Mira has enjoyed through the years a reputation for richness of invention and facility in constructing intrigue, although Anibal has documented several instances in which he repeats himself or in which he reworks an earlier play of his own.[8] Unevenness is another characteristic of Mira's theater. Mesonero Romanos finds in his plays "great beauties beside frequent and lamentable disorder; some passages and scenes full of passion, truth, and comic strength, and others enshrouded in that cloud of hyperbole and metaphor of Gongoristic taste or of the style labeled *culto.*"[9] The same critic elsewhere finds in Mira "unlikely scenes, fragments of exaggerated and pompous style which obscure and deform even his best plays."[10] Duncan Moir has provided a provocative comment on Mira's "Incoherence of action" which, he claims, "may be deliberate, in order to provoke speculation on the playwright's motive in creating it; and incoherence in action may also be an invitation to seek underlying coherence of theme."[11]

Virtually all scholars have agreed, however, that Mira's strength lies in lyricism. It is not unusual to find passages of great lyric flight imbedded in *comedias* of negligible dramatic worth. At times he is Gongoristic in his plays, but never to the same extent that he reflects such baroque tendencies in his nondramatic poetry. Indeed, Duncan Moir may have dealt with Mira's "incoherence in action" too kindly; for while one could agree with Pfandl that Mira frequently "searches for balance through contrasts between people, events, and emotions,"[12] it seems quite obvious that some of his less happy creations are marred by the presence of superfluous subplots, many of which the dramatist never even bothers to resolve.

For the analysis of specific techniques and devices which seem to be distinctive characteristics of Mira de Amescua, we are indebted to the critiques of Vern Williamsen and Claude Anibal. *Cuentos,* or *cuentecillos* ("little stories") were a stock device of Golden Age playwrights. Williamsen[13] has convincingly shown, however, that while most dramatists use interpolated stories for ornamentation or for didactic purposes related to the specific scene in which they appear, Mira's *cuentos* underscore the play's thesis, foreshadow the conclusion, and serve as a unifying device.

A number of scholars have traced the famous first monologue of Segismundo in Calderón's *La vida es sueño (Life Is a Dream)* to sources in Mira's theater. Williamsen summarizes and augments that scholarship in documenting passages from ten of Mira's plays which show a subtle progression in thought and technique toward the masterful expression attained in *La vida es sueño.*[14]

In 1925, Anibal propounded his theory that the device he terms "voces del cielo" (voices from heaven)[15] is used distinctively by Mira de Amescua. According to Anibal, characters in Mira's plays, upon hearing a voice, of which no rational explanation is evident, will take the words spoken as admonitions of conscience. "The words ... are by no means directed to the character that hears them, but in each case they so aptly fit in with his thoughts that they are inevitably taken as something of a divine message."[16] Margaret Wilson claims that "moral seriousness" is Mira's most distinctive quality, as she recalls the comment made by him in his 1620 approbation of Lope's *Parte XX* in which he "states that the purpose of drama is to teach moral and political virtues."[17]

Perhaps, however, the single most distinctive feature of Mira's dramatic production is his obsessive interest in the inconstancy of fortune, especially as manifest in the theme of the fallen *privado* (royal favorite). The theme of Fortune and the inexorable turns of her wheel was commonplace centuries before Mira's birth and plays on the theme of the fallen *privado* abounded in the first decades of the seventeenth century. Nevertheless, we feel certain that our analyses of Mira's *comedias* will give the clear impression of the inordinate importance which these topics held for him. Although our system of classification precludes a separate grouping of all of the *comedias* in which this theme is central, it will be readily seen that the theme is a constant in all areas of Mira's dramaturgy.

Cauvin has devoted her 1957 doctoral dissertation to the subject: "The *comedia de privanza* in the Seventeenth Century." Basing much of her theory on groundwork laid by Ruth Lee Kennedy in 1948,[18] Cauvin explains the vogue of the fallen *privado* theme as the result of three major factors: the phenomenon of historical *privanza* in the court of Philip III, numerous contemporary writings which focused attention on *privanza,* and the fact that *privanza* had been a familiar theme in Spanish ballads and chronicles since the late Middle Ages.[19] She states that the turn of the seventeenth century marked the beginning of a half century of prominence enjoyed by the *privado* plays. Although one important figure in this cycle of plays, the historical Álvaro de Luna, was beheaded as early as 1453, contemporary interest in the fallen *privado* was generated by the tragic fate of several early seventeenth-century *privados*. Lerma was dismissed in 1618 and died in exile in 1625. Osuna was arrested in 1619 and died in prison in 1624. Rodrigo Calderón was arrested in 1619 and beheaded in 1621. Uceda, Lerma's son, fell from power in 1621 and died in prison in 1624.[20] Cauvin postulates that many plays written between 1605 and 1635 had as their purpose a protest against excessive administrative power which had been delegated by the monarchy to royal favorites.[21]

III *Mira's Dramatic Canon*

If the study of certain periods of Mira's biography is plagued by lack of documentary evidence, the study of his literary production is complicated by the difficulty of establishing an accurate canon for dramatic works of an age classified as golden partly because of the profusion of superior plays which it fostered. Mira de Amescua is the only Golden Age dramatist of stature not to have had published at least one *parte* (volume) of his own *comedias*. He did, however, have the posthumous honor of having one of his plays, *Lo que puede el oír misa (What Hearing Mass Can Do),* included in 1652 in the first volume of the famous *Escogidas*[22] series, as well as several other titles in subsequent volumes.

Mira de Amescua was famous enough to have had attributed to him in printed collections some plays which he did not write. The opposite problem, however, has long been the major obstacle to the conclusive establishment of Mira's canon. Several famous plays now thought to be Mira's were originally published under the names of such giants as Lope de Vega and Tirso de Molina, from whom it has been most difficult to wrest titles of high quality for the purpose of awarding them to a dramatist of only secondary importance. Since there is not even one volume of Mira's collected work, we have but scant data for establishing his canon. An early attempt at cataloguing Golden Age plays is the 1735 Medel list[23] of plays available for sale in the compiler's bookstore. Medel lists 46 *comedias* and 10 *autos* attributed to Mira, of which several have subsequently been excised from his canon. Fifty years after Medel, Vicente García de la Huerta published in his famous *Theatro hespañol*[24] a similar list of plays attributed to Mira which, he admits, represents but a corrected and expanded version of the Medel list. With the reawakening of interest in Spanish Golden Age drama which took place early in the nineteenth century, lists of titles proliferated, but the authors of most of the lists reveal only the most cursory acquaintance with the works themselves and propose many capricious attributions. In 1852, Mesonero Romanos lists 52 dramatic works, including *comedias* and *autos,* attributed to Mira.[25] Barrera, in 1860, provides another catalogue of Mira's dramatic works.[26]

Although the aforementioned contributions to the establishment of Mira's canon are of value, for our present knowledge on the subject we are most indebted to Emilio Cotarelo y Mori who, in 1931,[27] provided the first book devoted exclusively to Mira's life and overall literary production. Most subsequent classifications of Mira's plays lean heavily on Cotarelo.

In 1925, in the prefatory remarks to his edition of *El arpa de David (The Harp of David),* Claude Anibal remarked that "only seven of [Mira's] plays, together with his portions of two others written in collaboration, have been conveniently accessible."[28] Prior to 1925, the only critical edition of any of Mira's plays was Buchanan's edition of *El esclavo del demonio (The Devil's Slave).* The remaining "conveniently accessible" titles were all included in volumes of the *Biblioteca de Autores Españoles.* In addition to the five edited in volume XLV by Mesonero, *La Judía de Toledo (The Jewess of Toledo),* attributed to Diamante, which appeared in volume XLIX (1859), is really but a transcription of Mira's *La desgraciada Raquel (The Unfortunate Rachel). Polifemo y Circe (Polyphemus and Circe),* in which Mira collaborated with Montalván and Calderón, had appeared in BAE, XIV (1850), and the chaotic collaboration of nine dramatists, *Algunas hazañas de las muchas de D. García Hurtado de Mendoza, Marqués de Cañete,* appeared in volume XX (1852).

Since Anibal's excellent edition, however, there has been an increase in the number of modern editions of Mira's plays, although it is disappointing to note that Anibal himself was never able to fulfill the promise that *El arpa de David* would be "the first of a series of critical texts of *comedias* and *autos* of Mira de Amescua that I shall prepare largely from hitherto unpublished manuscripts now existing in the Biblioteca Nacional of Madrid."[29] Although Anibal himself was not able to follow through on this ambitious project, several students of his at Ohio State University did edit *comedias* by Mira for masters theses or doctoral dissertations (see Selected Bibliography). Furthermore, several of Mira's plays have been published since Anibal's 1925 lamentation. Ángel Valbuena Prat published *El esclavo del demonio (The Devil's Slave)* and *Pedro Telonario* in 1926, as also *La Fénix de Salamanca (The Phoenix of Salamanca)* and *El ejemplo mayor de la desdicha (The Greatest Example of Misfortune)* in 1928. In 1939, Charles H. Stevens published an edition of *El palacio confuso (The Confused Palace),* which he attributed to Lope de Vega. Twenty-one years then elapsed before the publication, in 1960, of two editions of the same play, *La adversa fortuna de don Álvaro de Luna (The Adverse Fortune of don Álvaro de Luna),* by Nellie Sánchez-Arce in Mexico, and by Luigi de Filippo in Florence. Sánchez-Arce published the companion Álvaro de Luna play in 1965. Other editions which appeared in the sixties are: Francisca Moya del Baño's *Hero y Leandro (Hero and Leander,* Murcia, 1966) and Edward Nagy's *Galán, valiente y discreto (Gallant, Valiant, and Discreet), for Clásicos Ebro* (Zaragoza, 1969). In 1970, Vern G. Williamsen published his 1968 doctoral dissertation, a critical edition of *No hay dicha ni desdicha hasta la muerte (There Is Neither Happiness nor Misfortune Until Death).* In 1972, Bella made available *La mesonera del cielo (The Innkeeper of Heaven)* and *La jura del príncipe (The Oath to the Prince)* in a third *Clásicos Castellanos* volume devoted to Mira, and in 1973, William Forbes published his 1971 doctoral dissertation, a critical edition of *Galán, valiente y discreto.* Williamsen's edition of *La casa del tahúr (The House of the Gambler)* also appeared in 1973.

In any attempt to establish the canon of a Golden Age playwright, one runs the risk of erring both in claiming doubtful titles for a particular author and in excising titles from those tenuously attributed to him. The monumental *Chronology of the Comedias of Lope de Vega,* published in 1940 by Morley and Bruerton,[30] scientifically applied findings concerning strophic distribution in Lope's immense dramatic corpus to the task of resolving hundreds of problems concerning authenticity and chronology. The validity of their method was doubted by a few traditionalists who claimed that such objective criteria should not be employed in an area which required subjective judgment. Morley and Bruerton were triumphantly vindicated by the discovery and publication, in 1945, of the invaluable Gálvez list[31] and by the scant revision required for the 1968 version in Spanish of their *Chronology.*[32] Studies of Mira's theater have not yet had the benefit of versification studies comparable to those of Morley and Bruerton, but Vern G. Williamsen has informed us in a letter dated July 25, 1975, that he is preparing a study entitled "The Versification of Mira de Amescua's *Comedias* and Some *Comedias* Attributed to Him." Williamsen's results may solve some of the perplexing problems related to Mira's canon.

Associated with the name of virtually every Golden Age dramatist are titles of doubtful attribution. In many cases we are unable to solve with any degree of certainty these perplexing problems, but with regard to Mira's theater, the *comedias* which have already been reclaimed for his canon are sufficient in number and quality to justify an upward adjustment in his ranking as a Golden Age dramatist. There remains, however, one mysterious play of immense literary value which has been associated with Mira's name, *El condenado por desconfiado (Condemned for Lack of Faith)*. If it could be conclusively shown that this monumental work is Mira's, a further drastic reassessment of Mira's place among Golden Age dramatists would be in order. *El condenado por desconfiado* was published in Tirso's puzzling *Parte II*, in whose preliminary pages Tirso affirms that only four of its twelve *comedias* are his.

In support of a Tirsian attribution, Alan Paterson has argued that *El condenado* was previously published in a now-lost *Primera parte* of Tirso's plays.[33] Most of the testimony, however, which is based on versification and internal evidence, tends to deny Tirso's authorship. In 1905[34] and again in 1914,[35] Morley's versification studies indicated that Tirso was probably not the play's author. As early as 1881, Menéndez Pelayo had the following to say on this matter: *"El condenado* not being Tirso's, if we should verify that it was written by Mira, the only one of the authors of second rank capable of something similar, it would be necessary to place him for this play alone among our most outstanding dramatic poets."[36] In 1925, Claude Anibal called attention to the use in *El condenado* of the name Lisardo, a pseudonym associated with Mira, and promised to present his "major arguments" in support of Mira's authorship at a later date.[37] To our knowledge, the promised study was never published. Lidia Santelices, in 1936, found suggestive analogies between *El condenado* and Mira's *El esclavo del demonio* and proposed Mira as the probable author of the disputed work.[38] M. A. Zeitlin has wavered on attribution to Mira.[39] Such contradictory opinion has done little to resolve this most important issue, which commands strong interest in contemporary criticism. The distinguished Ruth Lee Kennedy has embarked on a series of studies whose goal it is to discover more concerning the interrelationship of Mira and Tirso de Molina, primarily to resolve the question of the authorship of *El condenado por desconfiado*.[40]

Williamsen, in 1970, found that the play's versification was not typical of Tirso and announced that he too is studying the possibility of its attribution to Mira.[41]

Several titles at one time·or another attributed to Mira have been convincingly excised from his theater by Cotarelo. In this category are *Los celos de Rodamonte (Rodamonte's Jealousy), El negro del mejor amo (The Black's Best Master), El Marqués de las Navas (The Marquis of Las Navas),* and *El pleito que tuvo el diablo con el cura de Madrilejos (The Dispute Between the Devil and the Priest of Madrilejos).*[42] Other titles, such as *La fe de Abraham (Abraham's Faith), Los mártires de Madrid (The Martyrs of Madrid),* and *El rico avariento (The Avaricious Rich Man),* although listed by Cotarelo as apochryphal titles,[43] are probably alternate titles for identifiable *comedias.* Medel[44] attributes *El duque de Memoransi (The Duke of Montmorency)* to Mira but, although a *suelta* of the play in the Buchanan Collection[45] supplies the same attribution, Barrera correctly excises the title from Mira's canon and assigns it to Martín Peyrón y Queralt.[46] Mira had already retired to Guadix by 1632, date of the historical decapitation of Montmorency which is recounted in the play's dénouement.

Much has been written on individual plays since these early efforts to establish Mira's canon. We have attempted to reflect in the classification which we propose an up-to-date scholarly view of the canon of Mira de Amescua, realizing full well that canons of Spanish dramatists of the Golden Age are not frequently definitive. It is hoped that forthcoming scholarly discoveries and interpretations will bring us ever closer to an accurate and full acquaintance with all extant plays of Mira and of his contemporaries.

A Classification of Mira's Theater

I. SECULAR THEATER
  A. *National History and Legend*
    1. *Algunas hazañas de las muchas de don García Hurtado de Mendoza, Marqués de Cañete (Some of the Many Exploits of don García Hurtado de Mendoza, Marquis of Cañete)*
    2. *El caballero sin nombre (Knight No-Name)*
    3. *El conde Alarcos (Count Alarcos)*
    4. *La desgraciada Raquel (The Unfortunate Rachel)*

5. *Las desgracias del rey don Alfonso el Casto (The Misfortunes of King Alfonso the Chaste)*
6. *La hija de Carlos Quinto (The Daughter of Charles V)*
7. *No hay dicha ni desdicha hasta la muerte (There Is Neither Happiness nor Misfortune Until Death)*
8. *Obligar contra su sangre (Obligations Against One's Blood)*
9. *La próspera fortuna de don Álvaro de Luna (The Prosperous Fortune of don Álvaro de Luna)*
10. *La adversa fortuna de don Álvaro de Luna (The Adverse Fortune of don Álvaro de Luna)*
11. *La próspera fortuna de don Bernardo de Cabrera (The Prosperous Fortune of don Bernardo de Cabrera)*
12. *La adversa fortuna de don Bernardo de Cabrera (The Adverse Fortune of don Bernardo de Cabrera)*

B. *Classical and Foreign History and Legend*
   a) Classical:
      1. *Hero y Leandro (Hero and Leander)*
      2. *El hombre de mayor fama (The Man of Greatest Fame)*
      3. *La manzana de la discordia y robo de Elena (The Apple of Discord and Abduction of Helen)*
      4. *Polifemo y Circe (Polyphemus and Circe)*
   b) Foreign:
      1. *Los carboneros de Francia (The Charcoal Burners of France)*
      2. *La confusión de Hungría (The Confusion of Hungary)*
      3. *El ejemplo mayor de la desdicha (The Greatest Example of Misfortune)*
      4. *Las lises de Francia (The Lilies of France)*
      5. *Lo que le toca al valor, y el Príncipe de Orange (Pertaining to Valor, and the Prince of Orange)*
      6. *Nardo Antonio, bandolero (Nardo Antonio, Brigand)*
      7. *El primer conde de Flandes (The First Count of Flanders)*
      8. *La rueda de la fortuna (The Wheel of Fortune)*

C. *Plays of Intrigue and Novelesque Interest*
1. *La adúltera virtuosa (The Virtuous Adulteress)*
2. *Amor, ingenio y mujer (Love, Wit, and Woman)*
3. *Los caballeros nuevos (The New Knights)*
4. *La casa del tahur (The House of the Gambler)*
5. *Cuatro milagros de amor (Four Miracles of Love)*
6. *Examinarse de rey (Examination in Kingliness)*
7. *La Fénix de Salamanca (The Phoenix of Salamanca)*
8. *El galán secreto (The Secret Suitor)*
9. *Galán, valiente y discreto (Gallant, Valiant, and Discreet)*
10. *Lo que es no casarse a gusto (What It's Like Not to Be Happily Married)*
11. *Lo que puede una sospecha (What Suspicion Can Do)*
12. *No hay burlas con las mujeres, o casarse y vengarse (Women Cannot Be Tricked, or Revenge Through Marriage)*
13. *No hay reinar como vivir (There's No Reigning Like Living)*
14. *El palacio confuso (The Confused Palace)*
15. *La tercera de sí misma (Go-Between for Herself)*
16. *La ventura de la fea (The Good Fortune of the Ugly Girl)*

II. RELIGIOUS THEATER — *Comedias*
A. *Biblical*
1. *El arpa de David (The Harp of David)*
2. *El clavo de Jael (Jael's Nail)*
3. *El más feliz cautiverio, y los sueños de Josef (The Happiest Captivity, and the Dreams of Joseph)*
4. *Los prodigios de la vara, y Capitán de Israel (The Prodigies of the Rod, and Captain of Israel)*
5. *El rico avariento (The Avaricious Rich Man)*

B. *Devotional*
1. *El amparo de los hombres (The Protector of Men)*
2. *Lo que puede el oír misa (What Hearing Mass Can Do)*
C. *Hagiographic*
1. *El animal profeta (The Prophetic Animal)*
2. *El esclavo del demonio (The Devil's Slave)*
3. *El mártir de Madrid (The Martyr of Madrid)*

   4. *La mesonera del cielo (The Innkeeper of Heaven)*
   5. *El santo sin nacer y mártir sin morir (The Saint With-
       out Birth and Martyr Without Death)*
   6. *Vida y muerte de la monja de Portugal (Life and Death
       of the Nun from Portugal)*

III. TEATRO MENOR
   A. *Autos de nacimiento*
       1. *Coloquio del nacimiento de Nuestro Señor (Colloquy
           of the Birth of Our Lord)*
       2. *Los pastores de Belén (The Shepherds of Bethlehem)*
       3. *El sol a medianoche, y estrellas a mediodía (The Sun
           at Midnight and Stars at Noon)*

   B. *Auto Mariano*
       1. *Nuestra Señora de los Remedios (Our Lady of
           Remedies)*

   C. *Autos Sacramentales*
       1. *El erario y monte de la piedad (The State Treasury
           and Mount of Piety)*
       2. *La fe de Hungría (The Faith of Hungary)*
       3. *El heredero del cielo (The Heir to Heaven)*
       4. *La jura del príncipe (The Oath to the Prince)*
       5. *La mayor soberbia humana de Nabucodonosor (The
           Greatest Human Presumption of Nebuchadnezzar)*
       6. *El pastor lobo (The Wolf Shepherd)*
       7. *Pedro Telonario*
       8. *El Príncipe de la Paz (The Prince of Peace)*
       9. *Las pruebas de Cristo (The Examination of Christ)*
      10. *La santa Inquisición (The Holy Inquisition)*
   D. *Entremés*
       1. *El entremés de los sacristanes (Interlude of the
           Sacristans)*

IV   Nondramatic Poetry

Mira's muse, although favoring almost exclusively dramatic
poetry, has received wide acclaim for its lyric qualities. Several of
Mira's lyric flights which are anthologized are simply passages extracted from his *comedias.*[47] This fact corroborates the conclusions

of the many critics who, like Adolfo de Castro, claim that "all of the *comedias* of Mirademescua are full of lyric verses of extraordinary merit. No one has imitated the simplicity and tenderness of Lope with more success than this felicitous wit."[48] Barrera, after praising Mira's lyric production, notes: "We may infer that he did not preferentially dedicate himself to that genre, since, in addition to the considerable number of laudatory poems which he contributed to the introductory pages of books, and those which he composed for literary contests, we know only three poems of his which are the fruit of spontaneous inspiration."[49] A few more of Mira's lyric compositions have been discovered since Barrera penned these words in 1860, but not enough to invalidate the claim that he never fully exploited a genre in which he was so obviously talented.

In speaking of Mira's poetic qualities, Valbuena Prat notes "a tendency toward the new and exotic styles of his time, and a vacillation between the simple manner of Lope and the overdone and lavish manner of Góngora and Calderón."[50] While these baroque tendencies may be perceived from time to time in Mira's dramatic production, they become more pronounced and more heavily concentrated in his separate poems. Adolfo de Castro states that "Mirademescua did not allow himself to be carried along by the current of the bad taste of his century, with the exception of those instances in which he wrote for literary contests. Then, the desire to win the prize led him to imitate to a certain point the language of the *poetas cultos,* so much to the liking of the judges who rendered the verdict."[51]

Mira's earliest known poem is a *canción,* "España, que en tiempo de Rodrigo" ("Spain, in Rodrigo's time"),[52] written to commemorate the sack of Cádiz by the English fleet in 1595. It was published first by Pedro Espinosa in the *Primera parte* of his famous *Flores de poetas ilustres* (Valladolid, 1605), where it is attributed to "Doctor Mescue." Both Cotarelo[53] and Rafael Carrasco[54] are harsh in their judgment of this poem, unfairly so in our opinion. While not fully subscribing to Díaz de Escovar's opinion that it is a "bellísima poesía,"[55] we find in this youthful patriotic effort a moving and forceful lyricism still unencumbered with the baroque heaviness which will characterize Mira's later poems. Not surprisingly, the proud nationalism and disdain for heresy which Mira enunciates here are distinctive characteristics found in his full-length *comedias* and his *autos*, as well as in his lyric poetry.

The second of the three poems of spontaneous inspiration alluded to by Barrera is the *Canción real a una mudanza*[56] (*Royal Song to Change*), "Ufano, alegre, altivo, enamorado" ("Proud, joyful, haughty, in love") which was published under Mira's name in the volume of *Poesías varias* compiled by José Alfay (Zaragoza, 1654), but whose first strophe had already been published by Gracián as an example of a poetic technique in his *Agudeza y arte de ingenio* (*Wit and the Art of Ingenuity,* Huesca, 1648–49).[57] The poem was critically edited in 1907 by Foulché-Delbosc,[58] who bases his text on a collation of six manuscript and printed versions. The theme of this poem, which was anthologized by Buchanan in 1942,[59] is the instability of life, a variant of the inconstancy of fortune theme which so obsessed Mira in his dramatic production. Buchanan praises it in the following terms: "The poem is remarkable for its symmetrical construction, each stanza being a dramatic allegory describing a sudden change or peripetia of fortune (the first three referring to animals, the last three to persons)."[60]

A Biblioteca Nacional codex (M. 82),[61] dated 1622, contains the third of the poems mentioned by Barrera, *Acteón y Diana,*[62] "Coronado de paz y de blasones" ("Crowned with peace and glory"), a baroque rendition in fifty-eight *octavas* of the mythological story of Actaeon, who was trained by Chiron to be a finished huntsman. For having dared to watch while Diana bathed, he was changed by her into a stag and torn to pieces by his own hounds. Barrera remarks that *Acteón y Diana,* with the *Canción real a una mudanza,* "are enough to insure [Mira] a distinguished place among our best lyric poets."[63]

John J. Reynolds, in 1969,[64] called attention to another little-known poem by Mira, "Príamo joven de la Gran Bretaña" ("Young Priam of Great Britain"), comprised of twenty *octavas* addressed to the Prince of Wales, which is not mentioned by Barrera, Adolfo de Castro, or by José Simón.[65] Neither is it listed in Jenaro Alenda y Mira's *Relaciones de solemnidades y fiestas públicas de España* (Madrid, 1903). Cotarelo does make brief reference to some "Octavas al Príncipe de Gales," found in the index of the library of the Marquis of Jerez de los Caballeros,[66] but he is forced to wonder if these may not be the *octavas* composed in co-operation with Alarcón and other poets (see p. 18). Reynolds, in whose article the poem is published in its entirety, has shown that these *octavas* have no relation whatsoever to those commissioned to Alarcón on the occasion of the visit made to Madrid by Charles

Stuart, Prince of Wales, in 1623 to undertake arrangements to marry María de Austria, sister of Philip IV.

Mira's poem, stiffly baroque in its praise of Charles Stuart, and staunchly in support of the royal marriage which never materialized, has, as Reynolds reports, provided forty-six complete and ten partial verses for the opening scene of Act II of Quevedo's play entitled *Cómo ha de ser el privado (What the King's Favorite Should Be).*[67] Quevedo's play, which may belong to the period 1627–28, is a panegyric of the Count-Duke of Olivares which "develops against the background of Charles Stuart's fruitless visit to Madrid and María de Austria's eventual betrothal to Ferdinand III of Hungary."[68]

The remaining nondramatic poetry of Mira deserves but brief mention. Adolfo de Castro has published two poems related to the canonization ceremonies of St. Francis Xavier in 1622,[69] which won a prize for Mira. A *silva* in which Mira describes an altar used in celebrating the canonization of San Isidro is published in an account by Lope de Vega of the ceremonies.[70] The *décimas* presented by Mira in the literary contest held during these festivities are published in the same account.[71] A rather uninspired fifty-six line *silva,* entitled *A Cristo en la cruz (To Christ on the Cross)* and attributed to Mira, was published in *Avisos para la muerte* (Madrid: Viuda de Alonso Martín, 1634).[72] José Simón Díaz has collected and published twelve more of Mira's poems[73] which he states had not previously been published by Cotarelo.

CHAPTER 3

Secular Theater: National History and Legend

S EVERAL years ago we wrestled with the difficult task of distinguishing between history and legend with respect to a theme treated by Mira.[1] We found that Spanish chronicle accounts themselves, ostensibly the repository of historical truth and accuracy, were strewn with legend, folklore, idealization, and epic exaggeration. Romanticized history, or the charming blend in historico-legendary themes, is in itself an art form of long standing. For the twelve plays treated in this chapter, Mira leans preponderantly toward the historical dimension, but the source of many details must be found either in legend or in Mira's own inventiveness. Five of the twelve *comedias* are powerful treatments of the theme of the fallen *privado*. The last four to be discussed are titles whose attribution has long been the subject of critical dispute. In our opinion, the plays dealing with Álvaro de Luna and with Bernardo de Cabrera definitely belong in Mira's canon. They are plays of great dramatic strength which have received critical acclaim through the years. Mira's stature as a dramatist becomes greatly enhanced by his convincing claim to these four excellent dramas.

I *Algunas hazañas de las muchas de don García Hurtado de Mendoza, Marqués de Cañete*
(Some of the Many Exploits of don García Hurtado de Mendoza, Marquis of Cañete)

One of the most extravagant of Golden Age collaborative efforts,[2] this play was written by nine different authors, whose contributions are as follows: Act I — Mira de Amescua, vv. 1-259; the Count of Basto (son of the Marquis of Belmonte), vv. 260-403; and Luis de Belmonte, vv. 404-1316; Act II — Juan Ruiz de Alarcón,

vv. 1–366; Luis Vélez de Guevara, vv. 367–748; and Fernando de Ludeña, vv. 749–901; Act III — Jacinto de Herrera, vv. 1–352; Diego de Villegas, vv. 353–582; Guillén de Castro, vv. 583–926; and again, Luis de Belmonte, vv. 927–1076.

As indicated by these figures, Mira's contribution was proportionately small, accounting for just under eight percent of the verses. Luis de Belmonte, who concludes both Act I and Act III, and who wrote both the prologue to the reader and the dedication to don Juan Andrés Hurtado de Mendoza, son and successor of the play's hero, had it published as a *suelta* (Madrid: Diego Flamenco, 1622). In addition, although, as Cotarelo has pointed out, "it does not have the literary value to augment the glory of any of [its authors],"[3] it was included in Hartzenbusch's 1852 edition of Alarcón's plays[4] and in the collected works of Guillén de Castro.[5]

Devoid of an integrated plot, the play contains a series of *tableaux* which reveal the supreme valor and magnanimity of García Hurtado de Mendoza, who historically led an expedition to avenge the death in 1554 of Pedro de Valdivia, conqueror of Chile. The Arauco Indians, led by their chieftain Caupolicán, are extremely romanticized, the better to reflect the almost god-like superiority of don García.

Although it may be interesting to find in the same play stylistic contrasts as striking as Alarcón's poetically straightforward satiric observations on Spanish customs and Vélez de Guevara's gongoristic syntax, one will enjoy this play, if at all, only as a literary curiosity. Mira's contribution is limited to the presentation of the Indian leaders as they exult over the death of Valdivia, their Spanish oppressor.

II El caballero sin nombre *(Knight No Name)*

Although this *comedia* was listed by both Medel[6] and Barrera,[7] it was apparently not known by Cotarelo,[8] whose brief observations are taken from Schaeffer's short summary[9] of the play's action. *El caballero sin nombre* was published only once, in the extremely rare *Parte XXXII* of *Doce comedias de diferentes autores* (Zaragoza: Diego Dormer, 1640).[10] Well written and well structured, it is, in our opinion, one of Mira's better *comedias*.

Its action, which dramatizes the genealogical founding of the Cabezas family, is set in the eleventh century after the fall of Zamora and the death of King Sancho at the treacherous hands of

Bellido Dolfos. In a castle two leagues from the Extremaduran frontier city of Trujillo, don Sancho is quarreling violently with his younger brother don Gonzalo over the customary supremacy of the first-born. Gonzalo's contention is that if birth has conferred the family property and fortune on Sancho, he, the second-born, has been invested with the family honor. When rebuked by his father, don Ramiro Altamirano, for fighting with his brother, to whom, by reason of his lesser age, he is "inferior in every respect," Gonzalo announces that he will go off to war and win with his own valor the recognition which he has been denied. Leaving behind a distraught family and an outraged fiancée, Gonzalo departs for Burgos, where the coronation of Alfonso VI is being prepared.

En route, Gonzalo leaves a picture of himself, which had been returned by his fiancée, on the skirt of the sleeping huntress, doña Blanca. Upon seeing the picture, Blanca falls hopelessly in love with its original, but her amorous hopes appear to be dashed following the revelation offered by her putative father Ricardo that she is, in effect, the illegitimate daughter of the deceased Emperor and his lover Garcinda, who is descended from English nobility. Following Garcinda's death in childbirth, the ailing emperor entrusted the care of the motherless infant Blanca to Alfonso, who was impeded from carrying out this charge by constant warfare against his covetous brother Sancho. Now that Alfonso is victorious, Ricardo plans to deliver Blanca to him in Burgos. The picture, therefore, infuriates Ricardo, who anticipates that Alfonso will want to arrange a noble marriage for his sister.

The scene shifts to Burgos as Act II opens with a dialogue between King Alfonso and don Diego Ordóñez, who historically challenged the city of Zamora to vindicate itself of charges of treachery in the death of King Sancho and who was victorious over the sons sent to combat him by Arias Gonzalo. Don Diego has just transmitted to Alfonso news of the widespread furor caused by the exile of the Cid (who never intervenes in the play's action), when Gonzalo erupts on the scene dueling with the captain of the guard, whom he leaves dead at Alfonso's feet. When questioned, Gonzalo justifies his act by claiming that the captain tried to hit him while attempting to bar his entry to the King's presence. Although his avowed goal of earning glory in the King's service seems unattainable after this offense, Gonzalo refuses to reveal his name, calling himself "el caballero sin nombre." Alfonso feels admiration for Gonzalo's valor, but his sense of responsibility dictates that he order him to be arrested and executed the following day. Here, as in the earlier family conflict, Mira has contrasted Gonzalo's obsession with honor with the more practical concerns of those who surround him.

Ricote, Gonzalo's lackey, overhears the news brought to Alfonso by a messenger of Baabdalí, Moorish king of Mérida and Badajoz. Suleimán, the youngest of Baabdalí's three sons, excluded from inheritance of any of his father's lands by Moorish laws of primo-geniture, has failed in a seditious attempt on his father's life. Should his flight take him to Alfonso's court, Baabdalí requests that he be returned to Badajoz in exchange for a guaranteed annual tribute. If Alfonso refuses, Baabdalí threatens to lay siege to Tru-jillo within a month. The message is dated June 15, 1073. When Alfonso honorably replies that, if Suleimán seeks refuge in his court, he will try to reconcile him with his father but that he will not surrender his life to a choleric and rigorous parent, Ricote's plot takes form.

Blanca has just arrived in Burgos and met her brother. Don Diego Ordóñez is so enraptured by her beauty that Alfonso prom-ises her to him in marriage. Ricote secures Gonzalo's liberty by passing him off as the Moorish infante Suleimán. Having achieved bodily liberty for his master, Ricote next ministers to the affairs of Gonzalo's heart. He tells Blanca that the picture she has seen in the forest is the image of the son of King García of Galicia, who has followed her to Burgos, and who hopes, pending her consent, for them to fly away together that very night. Gonzalo, a good sport throughout, goes along with both of the deceptions concocted by his daring and ingenious lackey and escapes from Burgos with Blanca.

In the opening lines of Act III we learn that the real Suleimán has arrived in Burgos. Word has also just reached Alfonso that, true to his threat, Baabdalí has laid siege to the castle of the Altamiranos. When Ricardo also arrives with news that Blanca has been abducted, Alfonso realizes that he has been deceived on two counts. He immediately departs for Extremadura to save the castle and Trujillo.

Gonzalo and Blanca, exhausted from their perilous journey, are found sleeping by the marauding Baabdalí and his two oldest sons, Benzoraique and Fatimán. Leaving Gonzalo tied to a tree, they ab-duct Blanca. Gonzalo is freed by Ricote and proceeds to kill Benzo-raique and Fatimán, and singlehandedly to wipe out the remainder

of the Moors, as Baabdalí flees. Following a quick reconciliation
with his father and brother, Gonzalo departs in pursuit of Baabdalí
as the forces of Alfonso arrive, having already freed Trujillo from
attack. Surprised to find the castle in the control of Christians,
Alfonso is greeted by Ramiro, who paints the heroics of Gonzalo in
such forceful terms that Alfonso, ignorant that Gonzalo is the condemned "caballero sin nombre," promises to reward him lavishly.
All ends well as Blanca, Gonzalo, and Ricote come before the king
bearing the heads of Baabdalí, Fatimán, and Benzoraique. Impressed with the valor of the unnamed knight, Alfonso is quick to
forgive and fulfill his promise of great rewards. Because Gonzalo
has presented him with the heads of his three enemies, Alfonso
authorizes him to use a shield with three crowned heads on a field
of blue and orders that he shall henceforth be named Altamirano y
Cabezas (heads). Alfonso accepts Gonzalo as his brother-in-law
and names him Count of Medellín and commander of his frontier
military forces. To the deserving Ricote goes a pension of a thousand *maravedís* as this delightful *comedia* comes to a close.

III   El conde Alarcos *(Count Alarcos)*

First published in *Parte V* of the *Escogidas* (Madrid: Pablo de
Val, 1653), this dramatization of a medieval legend was subsequently published in seven *sueltas* documented by Cotarelo.[11] Its
only modern edition is found in the 1951 doctoral dissertation of
A. T. Pickering.[12] From Williamsen's versification studies currently in progress, and from the fact that Ruth Lee Kennedy finds
in a play by Tirso borrowings from *El conde Alarcos,* a date at least
prior to late 1621 is indicated.[13] The basic literary source of the
tragic story of Count Alarcos is a ballad which probably dates from
the sixteenth century and which is signed by Pedro de Riaño.[14]
Among the several treatments of this popular theme which are
studied by Pickering, Wallach,[15] and Chamberlin,[16] the most important in Spanish, other than Mira's, are Guillén de Castro's *El
conde Alarcos,*[17] perhaps performed as early as 1602,[18] Lope de
Vega's *La fuerza lastimosa (The Pitiful Force),* published in 1609,[19]
El conde Alarcos of the Cuban poet José Jacinto Milanés, first performed in Havana in 1838,[20] and *El conde Alarcos* of Jacinto Grau,
written in 1907 and published nine years later.[21] Mira's version,
especially its first act, is heavily indebted thematically to Guillén de
Castro's play, and Lope's influence is also noted.

Mira's Infanta feels she has been spurned by Count Alarcos who, she learns, is the father of the newly-born daughter of doña Blanca. Concealing her true motive, she takes the infant Blancaflor to bring up in the palace. When Count Alarcos returns victorious from battle and asks the King's permission to marry Blanca, the Infanta threatens her rival with the death of her daughter if she marries the Count. Blanca reasons: "con hija y sin marido, no queda bueno mi honor" (vv. 701-2, "with a child and without a husband, my honor would not remain sound") and agrees to be the Count's bride.

Irate, the Infanta orders her servant Ricardo to serve to Blanca her daughter's blood in a washbasin and her heart on a plate. Blanca loses control of herself and attempts to take her own life when the Infanta cruelly states that the bloody fare set before her is her own daughter. In Act II, Blanca relates the Infanta's atrocity to the Count, who relays it to the King as he pleads for vengeance. When the King confronts his sister with the tale of her bloodthirsty act, she admits her guilt but lies and says that she was justified because the Count had enjoyed her amorous favors and then jilted her for Blanca. For this alleged offense, the King orders Alarcos to set Blanca loose at sea to die. The obedient vassal follows his monarch's orders, and, as Blanca screams her farewells to the Count, the King and Infanta arrive with the demand that the new marriage be effected immediately.

In Act III, in a *beatus ille* setting, the King comes upon the young, rusticized Diana (in reality, Blancaflor) and immediately pays court to her. Blanca, saved from death by a fisherman, appears in the midst of reciprocal tirades of hate directed at each other by the Count and his new wife, the Infanta. After saving the sleeping count from an attempt on his life by the Infanta, Blanca tells him of her own escape from death. The plot is clarified as the faithful Ricardo relates his substitution of a lamb's blood and heart for Blancaflor's. In a weak ending, the King is to wed Blancaflor and the Count and Blanca are reunited as the Infanta confesses that the Count never stained her honor.

Ticknor[22] and Wallach[23] concur in judging Mira's version to be the best of the legend's Golden Age manifestations. Cotarelo, although he considers Lope's treatment to be superior, admits that Mira's overshadowed Lope's and Guillén de Castro's in popularity.[24] Interestingly, Guillén de Castro, Lope, and Mira all superimposed a typically happy Golden Age ending on the tragic legend. As we have shown elsewhere, it fell to the lot of a Cuban poet of the

nineteenth century to dramatize for the first time the latent roman-
tic and tragic essence of the legend in treating the theme with
greater thematic fidelity than did his illustrious Golden Age inspirations and models.[25]

IV   La desgraciada Raquel *(The Unfortunate Rachel)*

La judía de Toledo (The Jewess of Toledo), published in 1667[26]
and attributed to Juan Bautista Diamante, was accepted as this
author's work until it was labeled by Ticknor, who possessed its
autograph manuscript,[27] as nothing other than a printed version
of Mira de Amescua's *La desgraciada Raquel.* Donald Alan
Murray has provided the only edition of *La desgraciada Raquel* in
his 1951 doctoral dissertation.[28] According to Cotarelo,[29] and Rennert,[30] the play was submitted to the ecclesiastical censors on April
1, 1625, and not approved until 1635. In two places, folios have
been torn out and replaced by others, presumably to meet censor-
ship requirements. Ticknor affirms that these added folios and the
marginal corrections which appear throughout the play are in the
hand of Mira de Amescua.[31] To our eye, unskilled as it is in graph-
ology, the emendations seem definitely to be written by quite another hand. Rennert[32] has also arrived at this conclusion. Even
apart from graphological considerations, however, biographical
data seem to preclude the possibility of Mira de Amescua's having
been his own corrector since there is no evidence that Mira continued to write for the stage subsequent to his retirement to Guadix
in 1632.

Ticknor does not claim to have made a complete collation of the
manuscript and the printing attributed to Diamante. However, the
results of our partial collation and of the complete ones of
Rennert[33] and Murray[34] show that, save for occasional very minor
differences and the passages contained in the added folios, the two
versions are identical. In spite of the obstinacy of Menéndez
Pelayo, who attempts to refute Ticknor's attribution to Mira without even seeing the manuscript version,[35] the evidence is conclusive:
the work attributed to Diamante is nothing more than a printed
version of Mira's *La desgraciada Raquel.*

This *comedia* is one of the important literary manifestations of
the legendary love affair of Alfonso VIII and the Jewess of Toledo,
whose sources and other literary treatments we have studied elsewhere.[36]

David, Raquel's father, comes to her as an emissary of the Jews of Toledo, who have been ordered into exile by King Alfonso VIII. At a meeting called to discuss their fate, the rabbi Rubén has suggested that Raquel, the most beautiful of the Jewish women, go before the King to plead for the revocation of his decree. As the King and the Jewess come face to face, the effect is undeniable; Alfonso confesses to himself that he has been conquered by her beauty.

As a result of their meeting, the decree is revoked. Alfonso acts not at all out of consideration for the Jews; his interest lies solely in obtaining the love of this beautiful woman. After acceding to the request of the Jews' emissary, Alfonso declares to her his passion. Raquel interrupts the King and there follows a long discussion which she completely dominates. The confusion she experienced on first seeing Alfonso would indicate an initial reciprocal attraction. Now, however, reason dominates her emotions; she asserts a personal *pundonor* and declares that she will not allow herself to be deceived by anyone, not even a king. With her instinctive passion and emotions subordinated to reason, and with the unsought victim now in her power, Raquel shows another stage in the development of her character, one which will last nearly to the end of the play and which will be exploited in subsequent treatments of the theme — her ambition: she speculates that, the conquest of Alfonso's will having been so easily accomplished, her personal ascendancy in his kingdom will naturally follow.

Raquel, installed in the King's villa, succeeds in having Alfonso transact all court business there. Alfonso goes one step further and invests her with all of his powers. The lovers receive a visit from an irate David, who curses his daughter for having dishonored her people by becoming a concubine of the King. He becomes violent and Alfonso orders him driven from the villa.

Alfonso departs for the hunt, having left the audiences to be heard by Raquel. She judges two petitions and makes decisions which, in both cases, are obviously wrong. Alvar Núñez reveals to Fernando Illán a conspiracy to kill Raquel, intending to enlist his aid. However, the loyal confidant rebukes the nobles for this vile treachery and storms off to inform Alfonso of the plot. David, having learned of the conspiracy, comes to warn Raquel — but too late! The nobles arrive; Alvar Núñez commands soldiers to take her into another room and kill her. The aging David tries to stop them, but his failing strength is of no avail. From within come the last words of Raquel, indication that her love for Alfonso was sin-

cere. Alfonso arrives to find only David, who is lamenting the
death of his daughter. The King swears vengeance — and here the
play ends, Alfonso's sin still unexpiated and his revenge not
satisfied.

Mira's treatment of the theme reveals no indication that Lope de
Vega's *Las paces de los reyes y Judía de Toledo (The Royal Reconciliation, and Jewess of Toledo)* served in any way as a source for
La desgraciada Raquel. The use of the name "Raquel" for the
Jewess, referred to prior to Lope as "Fermosa" and the placing of
the supposed love affair after the battle of Navas de Toloso (1212),
strongly indicate, however, that Mira did know Lope's epic treatment of the theme, the *Jerusalén conquistada (Jerusalem
Conquered),* published in 1609, in which the change of name and
the chronological placement of the love affair between the decisive
battle of Alfonso and his death two years later are seen for the first
time.

V   Las desgracias del rey don Alfonso el Casto
(The Misfortunes of King Alfonso the Chaste)

This play is known to have been published only in the rare *Flor
de las comedias de España de diferentes autores — Quinta parte*
which was printed twice, according to Cotarelo,[37] in 1615 and in
1616. For our analysis we have read both editions (Alcala: Viuda de
Luis Martínez Grande, 1615; Barcelona: Sebastián de Cormellas al
Call, 1616). Although the 1615 printing uses a shorter title,[38] in
content and pagination the two versions are otherwise identical.[39]

Las desgracias del rey don Alfonso el Casto is a conglomerate of
several actions which are related thematically, in one way or another, but do not achieve a coherent blend. As the action begins,
Alfonso is being crowned King of León (which historically he ruled
from 791 to 835). During the ceremonies his crown falls from his
head and the staff bearing his standards breaks. He timorously
interprets both events as omens of misfortune. Unbeknown to the
King, his sister Jimena has secretly married one of his chief nobles,
Count Sancho Diaz. The two have a twenty-year-old son, Bernardo,
who, unaware of his identity, has been brought up as a mountain
peasant by the noble Gonzalo. Suero, nephew of Count Sancho,
and son of Gonzalo, although the favored suitor of Jimena's lady
of honor, Elvira, has to suffer the arrogance of a rival, Ancelino.

Their rivalry gives rise to a situation which to modern readers almost seems a parody of the rigid code of honor but which actually is responsible for setting in motion much of the subsequent action involving all of the subplots. Over the deadly serious point of who gave the lie to whom, and an ensuing disrespectful fight in front of the King, Ancelino is imprisoned and Suero slinks off to the mountain home of his father, distraught because he considers himself dishonored by Ancelino and unworthy of Elvira until he avenges his enemy's affront. He even indulges in some pledges wholly medieval in flavor: he will resist all heat and cold while sleeping on the hard ground; he will not change his clothes, nor cut his hair until he obtains revenge.

Meanwhile, Ancelino, learning that the King has decided to give Elvira's hand in marriage to Suero, plots revenge on Alfonso. He escapes from prison through a window and incites Mauregato (historically King of Castile and Leon, d. 788), bastard son of Alfonso I, to rise in rebellion and become King of León. Before escaping, however, Ancelino leaves a note for Alfonso, in which he tells him of the son whom Jimena has borne to Count Sancho.

Alfonso, anxious to verify this report, is unable to make his sister reveal the identity of her husband, but he believes Ancelino's accusation when he notes the Count's explosive reaction to a false report that Jimena has been caught embracing a servant. Don Sancho is incarcerated in the tower as the first act ends.

Amidst scenes of Mauregato's relatively easy take-over, aided and abetted by some ten thousand Moors, the disconsolate Suero arrives at his father's home, only to be upbraided for not having slapped Ancelino in front of the King, even if he were to be beheaded for such a disrespectful act. Bernardo, leading up to his final heroics, offers to help Suero effect his vengeance. His first task is to go to the city and post several placards which carry Suero's challenge to Ancelino to meet him in a duel.

Mauregato, victorious, and at the high point of a monologue in which he asserts his invincible power, suddenly dies from a heart attack. Ancelino finds the corpse, comments: "Oh, wheel of fortune, how quickly you turn" (fol. 47r), and hypocritically offers his allegiance to Alfonso, who has just returned with forces now unnecessary in the face of Mauregato's death. Alfonso pardons Ancelino but honors Suero's request to seek personal vengeance in a duel.

The dénouement is now prepared for all but Bernardo. Mira provides for this last event by the announcement that Don Bueso, a French invader, has entered Oviedo. As Bernardo, because of his demonstrated valor with the Moor, leaves to defeat Bueso and his troops, Elvira saddens his rustic sweetheart Sancha by revealing to her that Bernardo is a nephew of the King. Sancha's feelings of unworthiness are instantly dispelled upon Bernardo's triumphal return by the Count's revelation that Sancha is the daughter of a noble mother and Aurelio, the King's uncle. When Suero returns, avenged of Ancelino's affront, the pairings are automatic.

This *comedia* is undoubtedly a youthful effort. Typical of Mira are several references to the inconstancy of fortune and to the precarious status of favorites. The thesis that noble blood will manifest itself even in those unaware that it courses in their veins is a traditional component of the stock theme of supposed peasants who populate rustic suburban surroundings under the varying surveillance of noble parents guilty either of promiscuity or of unsanctioned matrimony.

VI   La hija de Carlos Quinto *(The Daughter of Charles V)*

Cotarelo mentions only two *sueltas* of this play,[40] one which belonged to the collection of Agustín Durán and one which was located in the San Isidro Library in Madrid. Karl Selig's 1947 edition[41] and the rotograph facsimile from which it was made take on special importance when we consider the fate of the two *sueltas* cited by Cotarelo. The Durán copy, although it is supposed to have passed to the Biblioteca Nacional, is currently found neither there nor in the British Museum, ultimate repository of several other items in the Durán collection. In our own efforts to obtain a copy of this play, we learned that the San Isidro *suelta* has also been lost.[42]

La hija de Carlos Quinto begins with the decision of Carlos V, whose health has become undermined, to abdicate, leaving the Spanish throne to his son Philip II. It is not Philip, however, but rather his sister Juana, who occupies, with their father, the second of the two principal roles. In a series of scenes representing dramatic adaptations of historical *tableaux,* Juana is received with splendor in Portugal, where she is to marry the young Prince Juan. Early in the second act she has already been widowed eighteen days prior to giving birth to Sebastián, future King of Portugal. (Historically, the marriage took place on January 11, 1552, and the prince died on January 2, 1554.) Juana returns to Valladolid where there are plans to marry her next to the Duke of Segorbe, but doña Isabel de Borja, Juana's intended lady-in-waiting, has a vision, decides to enter a convent, and prevails upon Juana to retire with her from worldly concerns.

The historical Cazalla, canon in Salamanca, one of the first to propagate the ideas of the Protestant Reformation in Castile, has heard of two vacant bishoprics and appears before Juana to request one. She craftily claims that she has something better planned for him, only to give him a *coroza,* the tall, conical hat worn by victims of the Inquisition. The theme of the play is the religiosity and complete humility of Carlos and his daughter. Amidst the splendor of the abdication ceremonies in Brussels, a common soldier named Andrés de Cuacos disrupts the proceedings with a little song in which he asks for a coin from the Emperor. The poverty of the soldier contrasts so totally with the royal environment that Carlos decides to take him along as companion and chamber musician in his retirement at Yuste.

The play also contains an extremely long description of Juana's triumphal entry into Portugal (I, vv. 451–630) and an elaborate account of Madrid's history (II, vv. 1420–1566). The scene shifts frequently, and there is little development of dramatic action of any sort. As Cotarelo aptly observes,[43] this *comedia* provides an opportunity to reminisce on the days of glory and on the last chapter of the life of Spain's great Emperor, who was considered by his contemporaries greater for his final humility than for his celebrated deeds and immense power.

Selig dates the play 1613–16, in large part on the basis of the 1613 appearance of Góngora's *Soledad primera,* with which he finds parallels in Mira's imagery. He hypothesizes also that a book published in 1616 on the founding of the Descalzas de Santa Clara, the order entered in the play by doña Isabel de Borja, might even have been an inspiration or source for Mira.

VII   No hay dicha ni desdicha hasta la muerte
(There Is Neither Happiness nor Misfortune until Death)

First   published   in   *Parte XLV*   of   the   *Escogidas*   (Madrid:

Fernández de Buendía, 1679), where its title is *No hay dicha hasta
la muerte* and where it is attributed to "un ingenio desta corte" ("a
wit of this court"), this play was attributed to Mira and published
as a *suelta* with the correct title in 1748,[44] and again by Mesonero
Romanos in 1858.[45] In 1970, Williamsen published a critical edition[46] of *No hay dicha ni desdicha hasta la muerte* based on the
almost entirely autograph manuscript available in the Biblioteca
Nacional (Ms. R–76). Williamsen has elsewhere studied this
treatment of the theme of the fallen favorite as an illustration of
Mira's "creative" as opposed to Alarcón's "imitative" dramatization of the same historical background.[47]

Don Diego Porcelos[48] and his friend don Vela have come from
their native Castile to seek fortune in the court of León, where don
Ordoño is attempting to wrest the throne from his elder brother
García, who has inherited it from the recently deceased monarch.
The Castilian newcomers agree that each should serve one of the
contending princes so that whoever is on the winning side will be
able to help the other. Porcelos decides to serve Ordoño, leaving
Vela in García's service. Doña Violante, daughter of the King of
Navarre, arrives with the intention of marrying García just after his
defeat by Ordoño. Porcelos, who has previously served Violante as
a page in Navarre, with the help of her lady-in-waiting Leonor,
finally is able to persuade Violante to marry Ordoño.

In Act II, Porcelos asks King Ordoño to admit don Vela to his
service. Ordoño heaps new honors on his *privado* but has deaf ears
for his pleas on behalf of Vela. Ignorant of the amorous relationship which has developed between Porcelos and Leonor, Vela is
tricked by the servant Brianda into thinking that he is the object of
the lady-in-waiting's affection. As each friend acts magnanimously
in the other's behalf, an equivocal garden scene and a misunder-
stood note lead King Ordoño to suspect an illicit affair between his
wife and Porcelos. With his suspicions growing, Ordoño tests
Porcelos by offering him Leonor's hand. When Porcelos, out of
exaggerated loyalty for Vela, declines, the King concludes that he is
involved with the Queen. Ordoño later finds his *privado* asleep in
the garden and stabs him to death. Only after this impetuous act is
the truth revealed. Ordoño transfers all of Porcelos' possessions
and titles to Vela, to whom the Queen also gives Leonor's hand in
marriage; and the King repeats the moral of the play's title as the
curtain falls.

Anibal, in 1925, presented a convincing collation of several elements of this play which were thematically almost identical to corresponding elements in the companion plays *La próspera y la adversa fortuna de don Bernardo de Cabrera.*[49] It was Anibal's contention that *"No hay dicha* seems to be a sort of first draft for the two more finished plays. . . . There seems no doubt that *No hay dicha,* the signed autograph manuscript of which is dated July 20, 1628, preceded the *Próspera* and the *Adversa fortuna de don Bernardo,* which were printed in 1634."[50] Williamsen concurs with Anibal's evaluation of the quality of the two plays, but, basing his opinion on a versification study of Mira's theater which he is preparing and on internal evidence which would indicate a date prior to 1622 for the Bernardo de Cabrera plays, he disagrees with Anibal's conclusion, noting: "Anibal failed to realize that, far from proving the prior date of *No hay dicha,* the 'growth' that he saw demonstrated an opposite truth. Rather than technical improvement, we see here once more what happens when an author approaches too often a favorite, successful, but well-worn theme, with declining artistic effect."[51]

VIII   Obligar contra su sangre *(Obligations Against One's Blood)*

One of the better-known of Mira's plays because of its publication in the *Biblioteca de Autores Españoles,*[52] *Obligar contra su sangre* is otherwise known only from two early eighteenth-century *sueltas,* both attributed to Mira, and from a Biblioteca Nacional manuscript (Ms. 18.142), dated June 1636. We have elsewhere studied this play with relation to the Jewess of Toledo theme.[53]

In Burgos, the elderly don Lope de Estrada accuses Nuño de Castro of treachery and challenges him to a duel for the part he and others played in the assassination of Raquel, the Jewish paramour of King Alfonso VIII. Reluctant to duel with an adversary old enough to be his father, Nuño is nevertheless obliged to do so by the code of honor. He quickly kills don Lope. Meanwhile, Nuño's sister, doña Sancha, is entertaining her lover, don García, who is don Lope's son. Under the promise that he will not imitate the treachery and inconstancy exhibited by Aeneas with Dido, Don García is permitted to consummate his love with Sancha. Shortly thereafter, a distraught Nuño arrives unannounced. Afraid that he will discover and undo their plans, García hides and overhears

Nuño confess to the killing of his father. This news obliterates concern for preserving his secrecy as a lover and converts García into a wrathful avenger of his father's death.

The action progresses in true swashbuckling style. Nuño flees back to Burgos, where, by coincidence, he is granted asylum by Elvira, García's sister. García is sworn by his sister to the protection of the unknown gentleman. When García learns that the man to whom he has pledged his protection is none other than the object of his vengeance, his sense of honor is strained. It remains intact, however, as García not only permits Nuño to depart but gives him a sword to defend himself. Obliged only to respect the asylum granted by his sister in their home, García announces to Nuño that, once departed, his vengeance will be sought with renewed vigor.

Early in the third act, in an attempt to restore her own honor and to save her brother's life, Sancha pays Elvira a surprise visit and proposes a double marriage of herself to García and of Elvira to Nuño as a means for settling the family dispute. Thwarted by an adamant Elvira, who claims that honor could never permit either match, the undaunted Sancha first sends to Nuño and to García challenges, ostensibly from each other, to a duel. When they appear armed with swords, Sancha enters, wielding an anachronistic pistol (Alfonso VIII reigned from 1157 to 1214!) and threatens to kill García on the spot unless he marries her. When he concedes, she tells him he is now free to avenge the death of his father. Predictably, García not only refuses to kill his brother-in-law but also announces that he will marry Elvira to Nuño.

IX La próspera y adversa fortuna de don Álvaro de Luna

This two-part dramatization of the rise and fall of a historical *privado* is comprised of *La próspera fortuna de don Álvaro de Luna y adversa de Ruy López de Ávalos (The Prosperous Fortune of don Álvaro de Luna and Adverse of Ruy López de Ávalos)* and *La adversa fortuna de don Álvaro de Luna (The Adverse Fortune of don Álvaro de Luna)*.

These plays provide an essentially historical account of the ascendancy of don Álvaro de Luna and his subsequent fall from power as the controlling factor both of Castile and of its personable, cultured, but weak king, Juan II, culminating in Álvaro's beheading in the plaza of Valladolid on June 2, 1453. Both plays seem to have been inspired, at least in part, by three earlier plays written around 1604 by Damián Salustrio del Poyo and published in the *Parte III* of *Comedias de Lope de Vega y otros autores* (Barcelona, 1612): *La próspera fortuna de Ruy López de Ávalos, La adversa fortuna de Ruy López de Ávalos,* and *La privanza y caída de don Álvaro de Luna (The Favor and Fall of don Álvaro de Luna).* Historical sources employed seemed definitely to include *La crónica de Juan II (The Chronicle of Juan II)* and *Crónica de don Álvaro de Luna (Chronicle of don Álvaro de Luna).*

Much doubt has surrounded the paternity of these two plays, owing to the fact that they were first published in the perplexing *Segunda parte* of Tirso's *comedias* (Madrid, 1635), in whose *dedicatoria* Tirso himself states that only four of the twelve plays are his own.[54] Of the twelve plays, only three appear assuredly to be Tirso's: *Por el sótano y el torno (Through Basement and Hatch), Amor y celos hacen discretos (Love and Jealousy Make Men Wise),* and *Esto sí que es negociar (That's Business!).* An extensive body of critical comment has been generated in an effort to interpret Tirso's enigmatic statement. Some critics have tended to discount Tirso's words and to attribute to him all of the plays. Some of the titles, however, have been disputed, and others have finally and conclusively been removed from Tirso's canon.

In 1946, Santiago Montoto brought forth evidence that *La reina de los reyes (Queen of Kings),* one of the volume's remaining plays, was written in 1623 by Hipólito de Vergara.[55] As early as 1925, C. E. Anibal claimed *La adversa fortuna de don Álvaro de Luna* for Mira de Amescua, along with its companion piece, *La próspera fortuna...,* with the added suggestion that even *El condenado por desconfiado* might have been written by Mira.[56] His judgment on the Álvaro de Luna plays was shown to be sound when, in 1943, E. Juliá Martínez discovered Mira de Amescua's autograph manuscript of *La adversa fortuna de don Álvaro de Luna,* with an *aprobación* dated October 17, 1624.[57] In 1906, Cotarelo published both plays in his edition of Tirso's collected works,[58] and he made no mention of them in his monograph on Mira de Amescua. In 1960, two critical editions of *La adversa fortuna* appeared, one published in Mexico by Nellie E. Sánchez-Arce,[59] and the other in Florence, by Luigi de Filippo.[60] A modern edition of *La próspera fortuna* was provided by Sánchez-Arce in 1965.[61]

Scholars in general have accepted the attribution of both plays to

Mira, although Blanca de los Ríos had steadfastly maintained a Tirsian attribution, suggesting the possibility of collaboration with Quevedo,[62] rather than with Alarcón as had been suggested by Fernández-Guerra.[63] Another dissenting voice was raised in 1958 by McCrary,[64] who lends great weight to references made by Sánchez Arjona concerning the staging in Seville in 1616 of both Álvaro de Luna plays as works by Tirso. Another brief for Tirso was presented by Sandra L. Brown who argued somewhat unconvincingly in 1974 that available evidence did not justify categorical attribution to Mira of even *La adversa fortuna*.[65] Both plays have received close attention. Sister Mary Austin Cauvin studied them with special relation to their historical sources in 1957[66] and I. L. McClelland, in 1948, provided a provocative literary and psychological analysis of their content.[67] McClelland unhesitatingly assumes Tirsian authorship, which prompts one of her reviewers, having praised her masterly analyses, to comment: "She has, unwittingly, added greatly to Mira's stature as a dramatist."[68] Margaret Wilson considers *La próspera fortuna* "undoubtedly one of the best historical dramas of the period."[69] She assigns the play to Mira but suggests the presence of Tirso's collaborating hand in Act II.

1. *La próspera fortuna de don Álvaro de Luna y adversa de Ruy López de Ávalos*

The historical period covered runs from 1408, when the eighteen-year-old Álvaro arrived at court, to 1423, when he succeeded the fallen Ruy López de Ávalos as favorite of Juan II.

Ruy López, who has long served well and faithfully as *condestable* (highest officer of the crown and commander-in-chief of the armed forces) under King Enrique III, now serves additionally as tutor to the young Juan II, still six months away from his fifteenth birthday, until which time, by edict of his father, he is not entitled to rule. While being attended by Herrera, his loyal majordomo, and by García, his ambitious and treacherous secretary, Ruy receives a letter from the famed medieval historical astrologer Enrique de Villena (1384–1434) warning him that one of his two servants will be an example of loyalty while the other will be a traitor; one will cause his ruin, the other will restore his honor. He is also told that, very soon, one who will succeed him in his estates will appear in Ruy's house. A letter from Benedict XIII informs Juan that the Pope has sent his nephew, Álvaro de Luna, to serve in the Castilian court. When the young Álvaro enters, Ruy has a premonition that he has met his successor.

Elvira, lady-in-waiting of the Infanta of Castile, upon her first meeting with Álvaro, addresses him with words of foreboding:

> Luna sois, palacio os vea
> siempre con luz no eclipsada:
> felice ha sido la entrada,
> ansí la salida sea.

> Luna [Moon] you are, may the palace see you
> always without your light eclipsed:
> the entry has been happy,
> may the exit be the same.

(ed. Sánchez-Arce, vv. 367–70)

The first request for Alvaro's aid comes from the Infante of Aragón, who asks for support in his suit to win the Infanta's hand. Ruy's star begins to wane as he incurs the young monarch's displeasure over his failure to convince the Cortes to allow Juan to reign before his birthday. He comments to himself on the inexorable turns of fortune, always raising aloft new beneficiaries of its fickle rewards.

As was the case in the first act, a scene with Ruy and his two servants opens Act II. When he finds them fighting, he instinctively blames Herrera, in part because of his fiery Andalusian heritage, and orders him from his presence. Unaware of the vengeful wrath which he inspires in García upon declining to propose him for election to a military order, the ingenuous Ruy signs two blank sheets of paper, instructing García to use them to send news to his two sons.

Juan de Mena (1411–56), historically a favored poet and secretary in the court of Juan II, appears in Act II. He presents to Juan his *Laberinto de fortuna (Labyrinth of Fortune),* finished in 1444, and declares his intention to celebrate poetically the forthcoming coronation of the young monarch. The precocious king now intends, unbeknown to his tutor, to pursue nocturnal amorous adventures in the company of his malleable contemporary, don Álvaro. When Ruy scolds Álvaro for his part in the King's escapades, he again incurs Juan's displeasure. García, anxious to vent his wrath on Ruy, has sent, over his master's signature, an order to

Ruy's son Luis to turn over the city of Lorca to the Moorish king of Granada. The report of this alleged treachery causes the *privado* to be discredited and confined to his home.

The action of Act III resumes on the day following the coronation of Juan II, by which time the intrigues of the arrogant Infante have earned him imprisonment. During festivities to celebrate the coronation, Álvaro falls from his horse to the alarm of all. The young king tries to revive his favorite with the promise of new title after new title, prompting Álvaro's servant Pablillos to remark that, even if he were to revive, it would be politically and economically advantageous for Álvaro to feign unconsciousness as long as the honors kept flowing.

Still unaware of García's treachery, the indulgent Ruy rewards his secretary with his last possession, a jewel which belongs to his daughter María. Fearful that his guilt in the conspiracy will be revealed, García hastily departs when officials arrive to inspect Ruy's house. Meanwhile, the post has been intercepted and the King reads the letter mentioned by García, and another in which Ruy López has ostensibly written directly to the King of Granada, promising him the city of Lorca. Herrera somehow learns of the impending doom which threatens his master and once more proves his loyalty as he convinces Ruy to seek protection in the court of the King of Aragón. Herrera has sold his own home for ten thousand *escudos*. He gives six thousand to Ruy and reveals that he will employ the remainder for legal costs to vindicate his master in court. Ruy finally realizes that he has erred in judging his servants, and gratefully accepts Herrera's advice and aid.

As Álvaro intervenes with the King on behalf of the imprisoned Infante, who has declared his repentance and sworn submission and obedience to Juan, Pablillos arrives with a coffer confiscated from Ruy's home. Instead of the great riches which they anticipate finding, the coffer yields a scourge, a hair shirt, a shroud, and letters which reveal the penitent nature of the fallen *privado*. As Álvaro concludes that Ruy has been unjustly maligned by his treacherous secretary, Alfonso, King of Aragón, arrives to free his brother. Ruy López, about to leave for Aragón, prostrates himself at the feet of Alfonso, explains his fall from favor in the Castilian court, and asks to be admitted to the service of a new sovereign. Alfonso immediately proclaims Ruy governor of Naples. At this moment, Herrera triumphantly enters to read a court verdict which totally vindicates Ruy López and condemns García to be hanged and quartered as punishment for his treachery.

The Infante is granted both liberty and the hand of Juan's sister, the Infanta, whose dowry will include the castle-fortress of Trujillo. Doña Elvira will marry Álvaro on the morrow, and the Castilian king begs pardon for the faults of the play as he announces its sequel.

2. *La adversa fortuna de don Álvaro de Luna*

Sister Mary Cauvin is misleading when she states that the play's action begins relatively soon after the last scene of *La próspera fortuna*.[70] Actually, an opening expository statement by Hernando de Robles, royal treasurer, informs us that Álvaro is now a widower, having lost doña Elvira Portocarrera, to whom he was still not married at the conclusion of the first play. A prince, don Enrique, has just been born to the monarchs, and his baptism opens the play's action.

The position of *condestable* has apparently been vacant since the fall of Ruy López. The King, without formality, confers this title on Álvaro, even over the objections of his favorite that he is not deserving of such an honor because he has yet to defeat the Moors in battle. The *gracioso* Linterna (Lantern) wanders into court in the guise of an astrologer. Even after a scene in which the King derides astrological predictions, Linterna is asked by don Álvaro to reveal his horoscope. He outlines an impressive series of honors and triumphs but predicts that Álvaro will die on the scaffold. In spite of these forebodings. Álvaro is impressed with Linterna's wit and humor and invites him to enter his service. As we will see, Linterna is one of the few who will not betray Álvaro. We next learn that Álvaro is personally responsible for having obtained important posts for Hernando de Robles and for Bibero. MacCurdy has astutely pointed out that the guilt of playing God is Álvaro's tragic flaw. He is obsessed with creating *hechuras,* and his ultimate downfall is sealed by denials of the gratitude he expected from the beneficiaries of his favor.[71] Álvaro is often hopelessly ingenuous in not realizing that creditors, especially ones who constantly remind us of our debts, are not usually our most intimate friends. In addition to the favors granted to Robles and Bibero, Álvaro performs a great service in each of the first two acts for the infante of Aragón and the future queen of Castile, only to be repaid in each instance with ingratitude.

The King is served an ultimatum by his envious grandees. They see overweening ambition in Álvaro; they are offended at the great liberality shown him by the King; and they demand his exile from the palace and court. The pusillanimous King, unwilling to contest their demands, but still too spineless to announce the exile personally to his *privado,* commissions this task to doña Juana Pimentel, Álvaro's new fiancée. Álvaro stoically reads the document presented by the grandees and magnanimously declares his total submission. When he states that he will spend his exile in Ayllón, he receives his first disillusionment from the King, who has forgotten that he once gave that city to Álvaro. The period of exile shall not exceed three months, and Álvaro departs, leaving a muddled monarch and a distraught but profoundly devoted mistress.

Linterna welcomes Álvaro back in the opening lines of Act II. In the interim, the Queen has died. Álvaro's first act is to confront his *hechuras,* Robles and Bibero. He had recognized that the document calling for his exile was written in Robles' hand, and he has discovered that the conspirators had held two meetings in Bibero's home. When the King arrives to greet Álvaro, he is infuriated to note the hypocritical presence of the treacherous Robles, whom he orders imprisoned. On his *privado,* he confers new honors, naming him Duke of Escalona and of Riaza.

In this act, Álvaro, in his first military exploit as *condestable,* recaptures for Juan II from the troublesome Infante of Aragón, the castle-fortress of Trujillo, given as a dowry to the Infanta in the closing lines of *La próspera fortuna.* He also takes it upon himself to arrange a second marriage for Juan, to Isabel of Portugal. After officially committing his sovereign to this union, he discovers that Juan aspires to marriage to the beautiful Resiunda, a Frenchwoman whose portrait he has obtained. A portrait-switching carried out while Juan sleeps informs the King of a conflict in plans for his marital future. In a test of wills, and of the King's dependency on Álvaro, Juan agrees to discard his own plans and to marry Isabel. The always patriotic Álvaro, who has impressed upon Juan that kings marry not for love but for reasons of state, nevertheless has personal reward in mind as he anticipates that Isabel will be beholden to him for his part in her ascension to the

Castilian throne. For this "service," Juan appoints Álvaro *Maestre* (Grand Master) of the famed Order of Santiago. For his military victory, he is named Duke of Trujillo. Aware of the envy caused by such continual rewards, Álvaro unsuccessfully begs Juan to stop the flow of gifts. Unaffected, Juan names him Duke of Verlanza and, as the act comes to a close, Álvaro trips in attempting to kneel and kiss the King's feet. In this abject position, he ends the act with a foreshadowing of his impending doom: "My tripping / was caused by the weight of these honors. / Stop, good fortune, stop; / Fortune, I want no more; / you have me at the feet of the King" (ed. de Filippo, vv. 1976–80).

Act III opens with an expository dialogue in which we are informed of the double wedding which has just been celebrated. Bibero suggests that Álvaro's marriage to doña Juana marks the apogee of his good fortune, and even the Infante of Aragón has appeared to witness Juan's marriage to Isabel of Portugal. The scheming Bibero finally declares himself openly and, speaking as royal auditor, relays to the King the dissatisfaction of the nobles over the proportion of his properties which Juan has given to Álvaro. The Infante and Queen Isabel next besiege Juan with complaints about the excessive power entrusted to Álvaro. Although the King recognizes vile ingratitude in each of these beneficiaries of Álvaro's favor, he receives a document much more difficult to discount, a call to exile or imprison don Álvaro, signed by the most powerful and influential nobles of the realm. As Álvaro confronts in turn the Infante, the Queen, and Bibero, he is pathetically unable to grasp the fact that they can repay his generous aid with ingratitude and cruelty. The musician Moralicos sings lyrics which underscore the themes which have brought about Álvaro's downfall: the fickle turns of fortune, the mutability of all things, and the precariousness of the lives of all *privados*. When armed soldiers come to arrest her husband, doña Juana brandishes a sword to prevent their entry, urging Álvaro to flee. She is disarmed, and Álvaro surrenders when he is assured in writing that the King has guaranteed his personal safety. The Infante and the Queen both gloat over the arrest of their greatest benefactor, and the King hopes against hope that he will not be forced to punish his *privado* severely; he is later numbed to learn that they condemn him to be beheaded. When the King shows his inability to sign the death decree, the Infante holds the document and the malefic Queen moves his hand to compose the words "Yo el Rey" ("I the King"), which seal Álvaro's fate.

On the way to hear his sentence, Álvaro concludes a philosophic comment on fortune by acknowledging that if he has, during his life, scaled the uppermost heights of good fortune, he now is the most unfortunate of all men. Doña Juana, in a last, desperate effort, persuades the King to spare Álvaro's life, but as they arrive at the scaffold, they see that the act has been committed. When Moralicos begs for alms to bury Álvaro's body, the King cynically refuses, concluding that if he did not give life to his *privado,* his burial is of no importance.

Praise for this play has been generous. MacCurdy states that "it is one of the finest tragedies of the Golden Age, and, to my mind, the best tragedy written in Spain on the theme of the fallen favorite."[72] Cotarelo[73] and Ruth Lee Kennedy[74] are convincing in their arguments for dating it close to the death of another historical *privado,* Rodrigo Calderón, who was executed in 1621. McClelland has noted parallelism between the Ruy López — don Álvaro tragedies and that of Wolsey in Shakespeare's *Henry VIII*[75] and throughout her study underscores the high artistic merit of the companion plays.

<h3 style="text-align:center">X La próspera y adversa fortuna de
don Bernardo de Cabrera
(The Prosperous and Adverse Fortune of
don Bernardo de Cabrera)</h3>

This is another two-part dramatization of one of Mira's favorite themes, the contrast of two friends whose political careers ride Fortune's wheel. The two plays, *La próspera fortuna de don Bernardo de Cabrera* and *La adversa fortuna de don Bernardo de Cabrera* are an organic unit which constitutes one of the best dramatic treatments of the theme of the fallen favorite. Their first known appearance is in the apochryphal *Doce comedias de Lope de Vega Carpio — Parte XXIX* (Huesca: por Pedro Blusón, 1634), a bound volume of *sueltas.* Although both plays are here attributed to Lope, *La adversa fortuna de don Bernardo de Cabrera* is listed twice by Medel,[76] once attributed to Lope and once to Mira. Medel's entry for *La próspera fortuna de don Bernardo de Cabrera* is defective and of little help.[77] Barrera unhesitatingly attributes *La adversa fortuna* to Lope but lists *La próspera fortuna* as a doubtful attribution to either Lope or Mira.[78]

In 1925, Anibal argued convincingly that the use in both plays of the name Lisardo, a suggested pseudonym for Mira, was sufficient proof to resolve the doubtful attributions in Mira's favor.[79] His arguments were reinforced by a thematic comparison of both *La próspera* and *La adversa fortuna* with an undisputed Mira play which treats the same theme, *No hay dicha ni desdicha hasta la muerte.* Cotarelo, who in 1917 had published *La adversa fortuna* in the new Academy edition of Lope's plays,[80] was not convinced by Anibal, as evidenced in the preliminary remarks to his 1930 edition of *La próspera fortuna* in the same collection[81] and in his monograph on Mira.[82] The comparison with *No hay dicha ni desdicha hasta la muerte* causes Anibal to date the Bernardo de Cabrera plays 1628-34.[83] Williamsen, as we have indicated on page 49, disagrees with the chronological order suggested by Anibal and, on the basis of versification and internal evidence, argues that they were written prior to 1622.[84]

In our opinion, there can be no doubt that both plays are the work of a single author. *La adversa fortuna,* which is announced in the concluding lines of its companion-piece, is a smoothly effected continuation of the action of the first play, and the two constitute a clear orchestration of the contrasting fortunes of two friends, one fortunate, one unfortunate, one who alternately rises as the other falls from capricious favor. Internal evidence strongly suggests Mira's hand. The plays' obsessive mention of fortune, favorites, inconstancy, etc., is Mira's most indisputable characteristic. The rightful return to his canon of this pair of dramatic efforts should go a long way in effecting an upward reevaluation of Mira's stature among fellow Golden Age dramatists.

1. *La próspera fortuna de don Bernardo de Cabrera*

Don Bernardo de Cabrera and don Lope de Luna meet in Zaragoza, to which they both have traveled in the hope of finding favor in the Aragonese court of King Pedro IV. Although both are courageous and brilliant soldiers who descend from illustrious fathers, their initial statements contrast them in terms of the ill or good fortune which they customarily experience. Don Lope always receives wounds in battle, his efforts are always doomed to failure, he never gambles without losing, and he is unsuccessful in love. Don Bernardo's experiences have always been exactly the opposite in all of these pursuits. Having met with a common purpose, the two pledge eternal friendship.

Their first encounter is with the lackeys Lázaro and Roberto, who are searching for employment. The more loquacious is Lázaro, who guarantees their ability to serve as pilots for novices navigating in court and who picks don Lope as his master. When the King appears to give audience, both Lope and Bernardo outline for him their impressive and very similar credentials. Lope has the tremendous misfortune, however, to state his case to a totally inattentive King, who has just been spurned by Leonor, lady-in-waiting to the Infanta. Victim of the King's temporary but complete distraction, Lope does not receive the position he had hoped for. He is amazed, however, to note that don Bernardo's almost identical presentation is awarded with a court position.

The new arrivals are inspected with interest by the Infanta Violante, Leonor, and the elderly and uncomely Dorotea. The first two immediately fall for Bernardo, while Dorotea has designs on Lope, whose father she had known when she served in the court of the previous queen. The scheming Leonor, unreceptive to the King's amorous attentions, attempts to convince Bernardo that he is detested by the Infanta and to convince the Infanta that it is she, Leonor, whom Bernardo loves. She goes so far as to dress in male disguise and pose as Violante's lover, while Dorotea tricks Lope into a balcony interview in the palace garden by feigning in a note to be the beautiful Infanta.

Don Lope's misfortune is compounded by seemingly trivial circumstances. On his second attempt at an audience with the King, the monarch drops his petition before reading it as the two are interrupted by Leonor. Early in Act II, upon their return from a triumphal suppression of rebels in Sardinia, don Bernardo extols the heroic efforts of don Lope and gives proportionately shorter accounts of the exploits of other soldiers. Having had a sleepless night, the King dozes during Bernardo's account, missing only what is said about don Lope. Generous rewards are accorded to all but the incredulous Lope who, as always, blames his ill fortune. When don Bernardo and the Count of Ribagorza arrive to intervene personally on behalf of Lope, the King suspects that they have come to defend a secretary whom he has just apprehended composing a *billet doux* of his own to Leonor. He forbids the two ever to mention the name of the man whose suit they have come to press. As Act II comes to a close, news arrives of another rebellion, this time in Corsica. Don Bernardo, now Admiral in addition to his many court offices, leaves with the unfortunate Lope to quell the disturbance.

When, upon his return, don Bernardo extols the vital part which Lope has played in the victory, without forgetting the King's admonition about mentioning his name, his effort backfires. Both the King and the Infanta believe that Bernardo is describing his own exploits and that he is inhibited by extreme modesty from naming himself. Lope is again ignored, and Bernardo has new honors heaped on him as the Infanta goads her brother on and on for the purpose of elevating Bernardo sufficiently to make feasible his marriage to her.

Through the scheming of Leonor and the deception of Dorotea, don Bernardo comes to believe that the Infanta loves Lope. The depth and sincerity of Bernardo's friendship is manifested when the King announces his intention of marrying Bernardo to the Infanta. Out of respect for don Lope, Bernardo is prepared to retire from his positions of eminence to avoid further cruelty to his friend. At this point, two scenes, neither entirely dramatically convincing, set in motion the quick dénouement. For some unexplained reason, Lázaro tells Dorotea that his master has seen through her subterfuge and loves her. This causes Dorotea openly to confess her trick, disillusioning Lope completely. In the last scene, Lisardo, not included in the cast of characters, makes his first appearance. He reads from the chronicles of Aragón a prose account of the illustrious services and unrewarded merits of don Lope de Luna. Finally, the King realizes that don Lope de Luna was the unnamed hero of Bernardo's account. Both he and Violante, unaware that they have frequently seen don Lope, express interest in becoming acquainted with this illustrious hero. The King announces the marriage on the following day of Bernardo and the Infanta as the play ends with Lisardo's invitation to *La adversa fortuna*.

2. *La adversa fortuna de don Bernardo de Cabrera*

This is a masterful treatment of the theme of the fallen *privado*. Its action is set in Aragón during the reign of King Pedro IV (b. 1319; d. 1387) and involves complete reversals of fortune for the two friends: don Bernardo de Cabrera descends precipitously from the pinnacle of *privanza* to his death (the historical Bernardo was executed in 1364), and don Lope de Luna rises from indigence to supplant Bernardo as *privado*. The unfortunate Bernardo invariably has premonitions of impending doom and, in this sense, reflects some of the grandeur of Classical tragedy.

Suddenly the victim of circumstance, Bernardo runs afoul of the Infanta, doña Violante, in the first act. Bernardo and Lope come separately to the palace garden on St. John's Eve, both hoping to see the Infanta. Violante expects Bernardo, but Lope is again the victim of a trick perpetrated by the elderly widow Dorotea who, undaunted by the discovery of her deceit in the first play, has issued another invitation in the name of the Infanta, to whom she knows Lope is powerfully attracted. Before Bernardo's arrival, don Lope is angered to have his visit interrupted by music and impetuously kills the musician Leonido. Bernardo and Roberto find the body and conscientiously remove it to prepare for its burial. Just as Lope returns, Violante appears on her balcony. Taking her caller to be Bernardo, she bids him enter and discovers that he is not her fiancé only when the light brought by her servant Leonor (still deeply in love with Bernardo) illuminates the couple in an intimate embrace. Openly furious, but secretly intrigued by the gallant stranger, who refuses to reveal his name, Violante knows only that she has seen this man in the company of Bernardo. Violante is also angry with Bernardo because she thinks he has forgotten their tryst, and she suspects his relationship with Leonor. She decides impetuously that she will refuse to give Bernardo her hand in marriage and shocks the King by telling him to cancel the wedding plans just as Pedro has decided to honor the long-neglected warrior, don Lope de Luna. As don Lope appears in court to be honored, Violante discovers that he is the man in whose embrace she found herself on St. John's Eve and ponders the possibility of replacing Bernardo with Lope.

Here, as throughout the play, the imagery of lightness and darkness is impressive. The image of the sun is used uniformly to symbolize Bernardo's courtly, political, and military brilliance in contrast with don Lope's surname, Luna (Moon). Predictions of the downfall of both men are expressed poetically as the eclipse of light produced by these celestial bodies. Don Lope is honored with an appointment as chamberlain to the King shortly before Bernardo's appearance on the scene. Bernardo, when informed of the honors bestowed upon Lope, sees therein a prediction of his fall from favor, and at the conclusion of a passage laden with references to the inexorable inconstancy of fortune and to the moon's ascendancy, he decides to withdraw from his political positions and retire to his home. As Act I ends, the servants, whose patterns of good and ill fortune seem to foreshadow the imminent reversal, switch masters. As don Bernardo announces his retirement, Roberto asks to leave his service, intending to ride the ascending fortune of don Lope. Lázaro, unaccustomed to anything but ill fortune, becomes Bernardo's servant.

As Act II opens, Pedro refuses to permit Bernardo to enter a religious order and persuades him to return to his position as *privado,* over Bernardo's warnings that this second appointment to royal favor could increase the envy normally directed toward favorites. At this moment, Bernardo's final downfall is set in motion. First, Leonor, offended by Bernardo's preference for the Infanta, falsely informs her brother, the Count of Trastamara, that the *privado* has broken a promise to marry her. She further increases Violante's growing disdain for Bernardo by claiming that he has paid her nocturnal visits. Next, when the Prince calls for Leonido, his favorite musician, only to be apprised of his murder, allegedly at the hands of Bernardo, another enmity arises. Finally, King Pedro overhears, out of context, portions of a letter being composed by Bernardo and thinks he detects treachery. Pedro convenes the nobles, substitutes don Lope for Bernardo in the positions of Majordomo and Admiral, and decrees house arrest for his rapidly falling *privado.*

Amidst demands from royal auditors that he give a close accounting of his confiscated wealth, Bernardo decides to write to the King of Navarre to request his assistance. Lope, still a totally loyal friend, interrupts a visit with Bernardo to prepare for a hunt in which the King is to participate. As Lope departs, Bernardo receives a visit from a peasant to whom he had once been generous. Aware of the disfavor into which his former benefactor has fallen and anxious to aid him in recovering his lofty position, the peasant makes Bernardo privy to news of a plot to ambush and kill the King during the hunt. Once again, however, circumstances conspire against the loyal Bernardo, who breaks his house arrest and rushes off to save the life of his king. The conspirators decide to call off the assassination attempt, of which the King is warned by a note received during the hunt, and Bernardo and Lázaro are apprehended and accused of attempting the heinous crime of regicide.

Bernardo is condemned to die for all of the crimes which have unjustly been imputed to him. Early in Act II, King Pedro had instructed Bernardo to have his father and son journey from Barcelona to serve him at court. As they arrive bouyant with pride in Bernardo's success and fame, they encounter the royal executioner carrying Bernardo's head. Immediately following Bernardo's death, proof of his innocence of all charges floods upon the disillusioned King, now distraught for having acted so rashly. He confers a hero's burial on Bernardo, restores all of his confiscated estates to his son, marries the Infanta to Lope, and relates himself to the house of Trastamara through marriage to Leonor. In the name of Lisardo, the King closes the play, requesting the audience's pardon for its many faults.

In many ways the fall of Bernardo is the more pathetic in that it is caused by circumstances rather than an obvious tragic flaw in his character. As noted by Cotarelo,[85] the Bernardo de Cabrera plays were reworked by Rojas Zorrilla into a single *comedia* (Biblioteca Nacional Ms. 15.568) titled *También tiene el sol menguante (The Sun Also Wanes)*.

CHAPTER 4

Secular Theater:
Classical and Foreign History
and Legend

UNDER the above rubric we have four of Mira's *comedias* which dramatize themes from Classical mythology and eight which deal with topics related to a variety of foreign countries, including Italy, France, Hungary, and the Netherlands, as well as the far-flung Roman Empire. At times the distinction has been difficult between plays which merely have a foreign setting and those which in some real sense dramatize a specific period or event of the country in question. Some of the titles treated here, but for a foreign historical context of dubious significance, would otherwise have been assigned to the category of plays of intrigue and novelesque interest. In composite, the plays treated in this chapter appear to form the least distinguished category of Mira's dramaturgy.

I   Classical History and Legend

1. Hero y Leandro (Hero and Leander)

This *comedia,* which existed in manuscript only (Biblioteca Nacional, Ms. 15.264) until it was first transcribed for an M. A. thesis in 1951[1] and then published by Moya del Baño in 1966,[2] has the distinction of being the only extant Spanish dramatic rendering of the famous mythological tragedy of Hero and Leander.[3] A direct allusion to Mira's play which appears in Calderón's *La dama duende*[4] (presented at the time of the baptism of Prince Baltasar Carlos, celebrated probably on November 4, 1629), indicates a date of composition in the late 1620's.

In adapting the Classical myth to Spain's seventeenth-century stage, Mira includes the indispensable *gracioso,* employs such con-

65

ventional motifs as jealousy and feigned insanity, and adds two other lovers to form a traditional intrigue. The love of Hero and Leander resists conventional onslaughts, but on the night that Leander is to cross the Hellespont to see Hero, the sea is raging during a horrible storm and no boats are available. Since Hero is to be waiting with a beacon light in the tower the intrepid Leander dives into the dangerously turbulent waters and, in a passage which contains a *glosa* of six lines of Garcilaso's sonnet, "Pasando el mar Leandro el animoso"[5] ("The courageous Leander crossing the sea"), arrives at his destination, only to die in exhaustion as he leaves the water. At dawn, when Hero is able to perceive his body, she hurls herself from the tower to die in the inert arms of her tragic lover.

As Cotarelo notes, the versification and general style of the play are good, but the development of the action is confusing. It contains, in addition to the glossed verses of Garcilaso, six lines of song which are identical to verses in the poem which Góngora devotes to Hero and Leander,[6] and a scene in which Leander recites a correlative passage[7] reminiscent of Segismundo's first monologue in Calderón's *La vida es sueño (Life Is a Dream)*.

2. *El hombre de mayor fama (The Man of Greatest Fame)*

This play, which traces several of the famed twelve labors of Hercules, two of his major amorous exploits, his death, and subsequent elevation to immortality and marriage to a goddess, has come to us only in two *sueltas*. The first appeared in *Doce comedias de Lope de Vega — Parte XXIX* (Huesca: Pedro Blusón, 1634). In spite of the title of the volume, the *suelta* is attributed to Mira. The second, which we have used for our analysis, is an undated Seville printing[8] which appears to be from the beginning of the eighteenth century. This must be one of Mira's earliest and most precipitously written *comedias*. Several scenes and characterizations are extremely naïve, characters are referred to by different names, and Mira's Hercules is a boisterous braggart and philanderer who represents little more than a ludicrous parody of his mythical prototype.

Having just left Jason after the Greeks' destruction of Troy, Hercules slays a lion and the cattle thief Cacus, both of whom had been victimizing a group of shepherds. The slaying of the lion was the first of the twelve labors and is here followed by the traditional skinning of the beast and the use of its impenetrable hide as a cloak for Hercules, the jaws covering his head. Mira skips Hercules' first marriage to Megara and weds him to Deianira, after having him impress her by killing a seemingly invincible boar (labor No. 3) and easily defeating her two pretenders, Aquileo and Anteo.

As Act II begins, the newlyweds are in Thebes, home of Hercules. The centaur Nessus volunteers to take them, one at a time, across a raging river. When he makes the first crossing with Deianira, he treacherously attempts to abduct her. He is thwarted by an arrow fired by Hercules' mighty bow, but before his death he urges Deianira to take some of his blood and to annoint with it a shirt which, when worn by Hercules, will restore his love to her if it ever begins to stray.

Juno, wife of Jupiter, jealous because Hercules had been born to her husband's lover Alcmene, constantly plots against her stepson and Eristeo, his envious uncle, invokes the aid of three goddesses, Juno, Pallas, and Venus, to avenge him on his nephew. Against such adversaries Hercules remains unscathed but ultimately falls victim to the treachery of Nessus. According to legend, Deianira sent to Hercules a garment stained with the centaur's blood. Adapting to conventions of Golden Age theater, her dramatic avatar dresses in male disguise and brings the shirt to Italy. As Hercules dons it for a ceremony of animal sacrifice, we learn that Nessus has lied to Deianira; his infected blood burns and devours Hercules' flesh, but not fast enough to deter the dying protagonist from reciting one last, boastful catalogue of his fabulous exploits. Hercules hurls himself to death in an offstage fire, and is closely followed by a distraught and repentant Deianira. Hercules' demise is short-lived, however, as Jupiter appears in the heavens and elevates him to join the immortals and to wed Hebe, goddess of eternal youth.

3. *La manzana de la discordia y robo de Elena*
   ### *(The Apple of Discord and Abduction of Helen)*

This collaborative effort by Mira and Guillén de Castro compresses into three acts the Trojan War and important preliminary events starting as far back as Paris' upbringing as a shepherd. Although this title is included in the 1735 Medel list,[9] the only pre-Medel version of which we know is a Biblioteca Nacional manuscript (Ms. 15.645), which appears to be an actor's copy from the late seventeenth century. The play's only known printed version is found in the collected works of Guillén de Castro.[10] Stylistic and thematic elements in Guillén de Castro's contribution lead Juliá to propose 1623 as an approximate date of composition.[11] Although Cotarelo does not recount the play's action, he erroneously claims that the playwrights "have faithfully followed the twist given to the legend in the Homeric poems."[12] Actually, several aspects of the plot, including the competition for the apple of discord, are not found in Homer's poems but rather are derived directly from later elaborations of the legend.

In a charming opening scene, rustic shepherds and musicians are preparing to select, according to tradition, a king to preside over their celebration of the New Year. When Delio is chosen, Paris feels unjustly slighted and petulantly appropriates the crown for himself. Although Paris is aware of his humble upbringing, he has had from birth a gold ring with mysterious letters engraved on it, and he feels stirring in him qualities which belie his current social status. The goddesses Juno, Pallas, and Venus entrust to Paris the decision as to which should receive the apple inscribed "for the fairest." Deaf to Juno's promises of wealth and to Pallas' of power, Paris selects Venus, who promises him the beautiful Helen, wife of the Greek chieftain Menelaus. Paris thereby incurs the wrath of Juno and Pallas, who vengefully predict the fall of Troy and Paris' death.

Venus reveals to Paris the story of his royal birth to Hecuba and King Priam, and of his father's order to have him killed, an order which the compassionate Polinesto could not carry out. She urges Paris to depart for Troy to reveal his identity. In Troy, after defeating his brother, the redoubtable Hector, in a wrestling match, Paris is sent to Greece as Ambassador, replacing Antenor, who has been ineffectual in his attempts to redress the infamy of Telamon, abductor of Priam's sister. Paris proposes a vengeful rather than a corrective solution: with the pledged collaboration of Venus, he will pay the Greeks in kind by abducting Helen. His plot is lauded by all but the wise Cassandra, who foretells doom for Troy as the first act ends.

Act II dramatizes Paris' easy conquest of the fickle Helen while in the Temple of Venus. Having decided to flee to Troy together, the new lovers pretend that Helen is being forcefully abducted in order to preserve her reputation. Act III faithfully follows the legend: Achilles kills Hector and in turn is killed by Paris. The playwright in charge of this act took for granted the audience's acquaintance with the ultimate fall of Troy and includes just one fleeting reference to the famous wooden horse. Cassandra's most dire predictions come true and the vengeful goddesses are appeased as the destruction of Troy is complete. Menelaus' love for Helen sways him to accept the deceitful account of her abduction, and as the curtain falls he is planning to carry her triumphantly back to Greece.

Cotarelo[13] thinks it probable that the first half of the play is Mira's. Juliá,[14] basing his conclusion on uniformity of style in general and on a passage which recalls lines in Mira's contribution to *Algunas hazañas de las muchas de don García Hurtado de Mendoza, Marqués de Cañete,* feels safe only in assigning Act I to Mira and Act II to Guillén de Castro. The fact that the last mention of the amorous subplot involving Irene is made late in the second act might serve to corroborate Juliá's theory.

4. *Polifemo y Circe (Polyphemus and Circe)*

This collaborative effort, to which Mira contributed the first act, Montalván the second, and Juan Yáñez and Calderón the third, was first published, according to Fajardo, in *Parte II* of *Varios autores,* of which no copies are known to exist. In 1850, Hartzenbusch published it among the collected works of Calderón,[15] for which edition he used two manuscripts provided by Durán. A largely autograph Biblioteca Nacional manuscript (Ms. R-83), which was apparently unknown to Hartzenbusch, carries an April 1630 date, indicating that this collaboration may have been one of Mira's last dramatic compositions. Calderón, who signed the third act, later based his *El mayor encanto amor (The Greatest Enchantment — Love)* on *Polifemo y Circe.*[16]

Dramatic structure and character development were not the prime concerns of the authors of this account of Ulysses' Sicilian sojourn, from shipwreck to sneak departure. Woven into the framework of his attempt to resist the dangerous wiles and magical powers of Circe is the legend of Polyphemus, Galatea, and Acis. Mira's contribution covers the action from the time of the arrival of the shipwrecked Greeks, recently victorious at Troy, until Circe's magic and amorous charms are successful in overriding the entreaties of Ulysses' warrior companions that he depart the soft comfort of the palace for the honorable exercise of arms. In the interim, after an unsuccessful attempt to have Ulysses drink poison, Circe receives a visit from the maiden Galatea who is desperate to escape the tenacious pursuit of the giant cyclops, Polyphemus. Acis, one of Ulysses' loyal followers, falls in love with Galatea immediately and evokes a reciprocal reaction in her. With the *gracioso* Chitón (interjection: "Hush!"), Acis departs to accompany her back to her native valley, the three having been rendered invisible for the day by Circe to preclude trouble en route from Polyphemus. Here Mira's act ends as Ulysses' men are unsuccessful in extricating their master from Circe's court. The opening scenes of Mira's act contain extremely baroque imagery, due in large part, one would surmise, to a desire to emulate Calderón.

Montalván and Calderón handle the remaining action: the deaths of Galatea and Acis at the hands of Polyphemus; Ulysses' infatuation with Irene, who reminds him of his wife Penelope; Circe's jealousy; the strategem whereby Ulysses obtains entry to the cave of the cyclops, blinds him with a torch, and engineers the escape of his men dressed in sheep skins; and the final departure of the Greeks.

II   Foreign History and Legend

1. Los carboneros de Francia (The Charcoal Burners of France)

First published in *Parte XXXIX* of the *Escogidas* (Madrid: Fernández de Buendía, 1673), this play also appears in several other editions, primarily *sueltas,* and in two seventeenth-century manuscripts which bear the titles *La Reina Sevilla, Infanta vengadora (Queen Sevilla, Infanta Avenger)* and *La Reina Sevilla y carboneros de Francia.*[17]

The play deals with the legend of Charlemagne's old age according to which he married Sevilla, daughter of the Emperor of Constantinople. As the action opens, the marriage has already taken place in Marseilles and Ganalon's son, the Count of Maganza, has been sent as an ambassador to bring Sevilla to Paris. In the town of Mirabel, just short of their destination, Maganza's treacherous nature conceives evil designs on the beautiful Sevilla while she sleeps. Before he is able to carry out his intention, however, three *carboneros* come to pay effusive homage to their new queen and to urge her to correct many of the ills which beset the country. After their departure, the Count is again thwarted by the arrival of a fourth *carbonero,* the *gracioso* of the play, Zumaque,[18] who in Sancho Panza-like fashion transposes the name of the king from Carlo Magno to Caldo Magro ("thin broth").

By this time, Charlemagne is approaching Mirabel to meet the Count and Sevilla. Just before his arrival, the Count attempts to kiss Sevilla's hand and is slapped for his efforts. Deeply offended, he plots vengeance. Deceitfully convincing his liege that Sevilla has been engaged in an illicit affair with a servant, the Count succeeds in persuading Charlemagne to send her back to Constantinople in the care of the loyal Florante, in spite of her protestations that she is pregnant with a child conceived at the time of their marriage in Marseilles. Fifteen years pass and Sevilla and Florante are thought to have been shipwrecked and killed between Marseilles and Constantinople. Her father, Emperor Ricardo, has neglected to avenge himself on Charlemagne only because constant war with Persia has kept him occupied.

While hunting, the Count and Charlemagne encounter the same group of *carboneros* who had greeted Sevilla in the first act. The group is now augmented, however, by Sevilla herself and her robust and proud son Luis. We learn that Sevilla, now using the pseudonym Diana, and Florante were hidden in a cave to avert her forced departure and that they have lived as *carboneros* in the mountains ever since.

When news arrives that the vengeance-minded Greeks have arrived in Marseilles, Diana's surprising resemblance to the supposedly deceased Sevilla suggests the stratagem that they pass her off as Ricardo's daughter who, repudiated by Charlemagne, has lived in the mountains all those years. Diana is taken to Paris to implement the great deception.

In charming scenes which involve some highly ironic self-impersonation, Sevilla switches easily from regal to rustic lexicon. Ricardo does not believe that Diana is his daughter, however, and commissions Luis to kill the Count, initial cause of all the trouble. Falling at Charlemagne's feet, the Count confesses all, anagnorisis is convincingly accomplished, King and Queen are reunited, strained international relations are transformed into joyful celebration, and to the valiant young Luis is awarded the hand of Blancaflor, niece of Charlemagne.

The stock themes of rustic hideaways and the undeniable force of noble blood are here combined with excellent poetry and some delightful peasants to produce an engaging play, one which has enjoyed great popularity through the years, both on the stage and in printed form.

2. La confusión de Hungría (The Confusion of Hungary)

This is another of Mira's plays which was published in the famous *Escogidas* (*Parte XXXV* — Madrid: Lucas Antonio de Bedmar, 1670). One of Mira's liveliest efforts, its action and dialogue are constantly moving and interesting, but its overall quality is impaired by the blatant improbability on which its plot is constructed.

Ausonio, crown prince of Thrace, has become enamored of Fenisa, Infanta of Hungary, after seeing her portrait. He commissions Count Vertilo to deliver to Fenisa a letter in which he outlines his intent to request her hand in marriage. By coincidence, Vertilo has also been smitten by Fenisa. With his servant Ricardo, he conceives the ingenious but unlikely scheme of attempting to wed Fenisa himself under the assumed identity of Ausonio, whom Fenisa has never seen. With irony reminiscent of Rojas Zorrilla's comic creation don Lucas del Cigarral and his go-between don Pedro,[19] the trusting Ausonio secures a promise from the treacherous Vertilo that he will deal with Fenisa as if he were arranging his own wedding. Amidst the complications of another amorous subplot involving the Hungarian king, Duke Floriseo, who is an insufferable fop, and his sister Leonor, Vertilo succeeds in passing himself off as Ausonio. When, in order to avert disruption of his scheme, he sends a false notice of Fenisa's death to Thrace, the complications increase. A distraught Ausonio declares a state of mourning in Thrace and departs immediately for Hungary to pay homage to his allegedly deceased fiancée. Upon his arrival and request to see Fenisa's grave, Ausonio is jailed as a demented impostor. After an exaggeratedly contrived and confusing garden scene, which provides one of the most subtle examples of Mira's *voces del cielo* technique,[20] Vertilo is tricked into a confession of his treachery.

At this point, Ausonio's father, King Trebacio of Thrace, arrives victorious from war with Poland. He immediately identifies his son, remits punishment of Vertilo to Ausonio who in turn remits it to Fenisa. Exultant in her own happiness, and aware of Leonor's love for Vertilo, she magnanimously pardons him on the condition that he wed Leonor. Ricardo ends this delightful play of unlikely intrigue with a boast which would be difficult to implement:

| Si esta comedia no es buena, | If this play isn't good, |
| ¡puede haber más confusión! | there can be more confusion! |

(p. 316)

3. *El ejemplo mayor de la desdicha*
(The Greatest Example of Misfortune)

The autograph manuscript of this play, approved by its censor, Lope de Vega, in 1625, is in the Biblioteca Nacional (Ms. R–112). It was first published under the title *El capitán Belisario* in *Parte XXV* of *Comedias de diferentes autores* (Zaragoza, 1632), where it is attributed to Juan Pérez de Montalván. It was also attributed to Lope de Vega in one of his now lost *Partes,* and again in *Parte VI* of the *Escogidas* (Zaragoza: herederos de Pedro Lanaja, 1653). Several more appearances in volumes of *comedias,* as well as in *sueltas* attest to the high level of popularity enjoyed by this excellent play;[21] it was edited in 1928 by Valbuena Prat.[22] It is interesting to note that the play was attributed also to Matos Fragoso in 1697 and that, until Valbuena's edition, it had never in printed form been assigned to its rightful author.

Mira's source could have been Procopio's *Historia secreta,* published two years prior to the composition of the play, but certainty as to a specific source is difficult since the tragic events of the life of Belisarius had been, for centuries, so widely known. Already a commonplace example of the inconstancy of fortune, this ancient story coincided perfectly with one of Mira's most obsessive themes.

The heroic Captain Belisario returns to the accolades of Emperor and populace following his conquest of eastern lands. In the midst of his triumphal entry, the exiled general Leoncio plans to stab the hero to death in the disguise of a beggar. He discards his scheme, however, and confesses his evil intention when his intended victim pledges to obtain from the Emperor the pardon of Leoncio, whom the feigned beggar claims to have served in the war. The assassination has been ordered by Teodora, wife of the Emperor, who once considered herself rejected in love by Belisario. Although Leoncio is unwilling to reveal the identity of the person from whom he received his orders, he is magnanimously pardoned and honored by Belisario. The only hint given by Leoncio is that Belisario's enemy is a woman. This narrows possibilities to the Empress and her niece, Antonia Patricia, who is fervently loved by Belisario. He erroneously theorizes, for reasons he cannot fathom, that Antonia Patricia is his mortal foe.

Teodora, anxious to marry her cousin Filipo to Antonia Patricia,
tries to bend her niece's will by threatening to have Belisario killed
if she so much as looks at him. Antonia's obedience convinces Belisario of the accuracy of his theory. Upon learning that Leoncio has
failed in his assignment to kill Belisario, Teodora commissions the
same deed to Narses, to whom she promises Italy as a reward. In
the meantime, however, the Emperor has asked that Belisario decide to whom should be entrusted the government of Italy. Three
aspirants have submitted *memoriales,* outlining their merits: Leoncio, Filipo, and Narses. Leaving the selection to chance, Belisario
shuffles the *memoriales* and picks the one submitted by Narses. He
endorses Narses' selection on the *memorial* and goes to bed.
Narses' treachery is transformed into gratitude as he steals in to kill
Belisario, luckily stopping first to read of his selection as governor
of Italy. Anxious now, as was Leoncio, to protect the life of the
exemplary Belisario, Narses appends a message of his own: "Good
deeds saved your life" — "Watch out for a woman" (I,
vv. 893, 895).

In Act II, the extravagant praise and favors heaped on Belisario,
just returned after making short shrift of African rebels, exacer-
bates Teodora's ire. She now commissions Filipo to kill Belisario,
unaware of the fact that this new plot is overheard by her two past
henchmen, Leoncio and Narses, who pledge to defend their benefactor. In a garden scene, Belisario saves Filipo's life when he is at-
tacked by Leoncio and Narses. In gratitude, Filipo desists from his
intent to assassinate.

The Emperor finally deciphers Teodora's involvement in the attempts on Belisario's life and exiles her to her parents' home in
Antioch while heaping still more rewards on the victorious Belisario, who is named heir to the Empire. Once again the magnanimity of Belisario shines through as he obtains from the Emperor a
cancellation of Teodora's exile. Both of the first two acts sound the
note of extreme good fortune for Belisario. True, however, to the
concerns always associated with the inconstancy of fortune, Belisario ends Act II with reference to Fortune's wheel:

El postrer paso	The last step
de la fortuna di agora.	of fortune I have just taken.
No hay más que subir.	One can rise no more.

(ed. Valbuena Prat, vv. 1881–83)

¿Quién subió a lugar tan alto?	Who ever rose to such heights?
Fortuna, tente; fortuna,	Fortune, stop; Fortune,
pon en esta rueda un clavo.	put a nail in this wheel.

(vv. 1891-93)

In Act III, the ungrateful Teodora undertakes a last vengeful attack on Belisario as she intercepts a written declaration of his love for Antonia and arranges for the Emperor to find it in her possession. Jumping to the conclusion that Belisario has deceitfully been involved with the Empress, Justiniano orders Belisario's eyes removed. The deed is performed before Antonia has a chance to reveal to the Emperor that the incriminating note was intended for her and stolen by Teodora. The distraught Emperor rants that Teodora will be repudiated and that Antonia will take her place as Empress. Antonia's sobering refusal of this proposition emphasizes that Rome has had many Caesars but that there has been only one Belisario. One of Mira's greatest plays, *El ejemplo mayor de la desdicha* was the inspiration for Rotrou's tragedy, *Bélisaire*.

4. *Las lises de Francia (The Lilies of France)*

Printed in *Parte XLVI* of the *Escogidas* (Madrid: Roque Rico, 1678), *Las lises de Francia* was edited by Carol L. Krumm in 1946.[23] This *comedia,* which represents one of the more novel of many literary attempts to explain the probable origin of the French *fleurs de lys,* dramatizes a mixture of history and popular legends.

King Clodobeo, just returned to Paris after his victory over the seditious Sagrio, is counseled to wed Crotilda, niece of Grundibaldo, King of Burgundy. Clodobeo is not a Christian, and he anticipates possible difficulty with Crotilda, who is portrayed as one of the epoch's few Catholics. As he fears, Crotilda is initially opposed to the marriage, until told in a dream by the spirit of her father that Clodobeo will eventually become a Christian.

Woven into the play's action is the intervention of Amalasunta, who arrives in male disguise to avenge the slain Sagrio, only to fall in love with Clodobeo, her intended victim. Unsuccessful in her attempt to win Clodobeo by bearing false witness against Crotilda, she finally marries Teodato, who consistently has spurned the love of Clodomira. Act II contains a scene in which Teodato, unable to rid himself of Clodomira, binds and abandons her in a bramble patch. One by one, each of the three key figures approaches and hears her seemingly disembodied lamentations, each feeling that the words are laden with divine warnings and recommendations. Anibal claims that the *voces del cielo* device is here worked out with greater care than in any of Mira's other *comedias.* [24]

The theme of Act III is the defeat of the Gothic forces led in war against Clodobeo by the vengeful Amalasunta and her ally Alarico. Having been apprised of the unfavorable numerical odds in the impending battle, Clodobeo has promised to become a Christian if victorious. An angel appears and gives him three lilies as a sign that God is on his side. Clodobeo proceeds to win the battle and to kill Alarico in hand-to-hand combat. The enemy flees to Vienna in disorder, pursued by Clodobeo. The Goths enter the city and close the gates just as their pursuers arrive. Crotilda takes St. Martin's sword and prays that God will make the walls crumble, which prayer is granted. It is reported that all of the French are now baptized. Converted to Christianity, Clodobeo of course weds Crotilda.

Cotarelo aptly labels this one of Mira's weakest plays and suggests that its poor quality explains the fact that it cannot boast a second printing. [25]

5. *Lo que le toca al valor, y el Príncipe de Orange (Pertaining to Valor, and the Prince of Orange).*

This play, dealing with the assassination of William the Silent, Prince of Orange (1533–84), was printed in each of three volumes of the famous *Escogidas,* each time under a different title and each time attributed to a different author. [26] We have used the title and printing attributed to Mira, *Parte XXXIV* (Madrid: Fernández de Buendía, 1670).

The historical Prince of Orange tried unsuccessfully to shake Holland loose from the yoke of Spain's control. As portrayed in Mira's play, the Prince is arrogant, cruel, lascivious, and, most importantly for the central theme, anti-Catholic. What more could be expected, we are asked, of the son of a Calvinist father and a Huguenot mother?

While the Kings of Navarre and Denmark are being entertained by the Prince, Baltasar Gerardo and his companion Leoncio arrive from France. Baltasar has managed to procure a strong letter of recommendation from the Duke of Alençon, respected friend of the Prince. His purpose in coming to Holland, however, as an agent of Alexander Farnese, Duke of Parma, is to assassinate the Prince and thus rid the world of a hated scourge of Catholicism.

The love intrigue centers around Isabel, lady-in-waiting of the Prince's wife, Blanca. When still in her native France, Isabel shared a strong love with Baltasar, whom she has not seen for years. Her beauty, however, kindles fires of lust in the Prince and in Leoncio. Baltasar first attempts to poison the Prince during a party, but Leoncio treacherously reveals the plot to Lafín, the intended victim's secretary, in the hope of a double reward: Isabel, and a favored court position. Lafín, alerted to the danger with the party already in progress, barely stops the Prince from toasting with the poisoned drink.

Later, Leoncio, left alone in the Prince's office following an interrogation, is mistaken by Baltasar for his intended victim and slain. The Prince returns and, in the darkened room, duels with the unrecognized Baltasar who engineers an ingenious escape by moaning "I'm dead," pretending to fall where Leoncio's body lies, and then stealthily slipping out. Circumstances now have conspired to indicate the guilt of Leoncio and to absolve Baltasar.

The Prince's mind does not remain at ease, however, and in Act III he dispatches Baltasar to Antwerp to deliver a letter which contains instructions to put its bearer to death. Princess Blanca, well aware of her husband's lecherous designs on Isabel, plans to marry her lady-in-waiting to Baltasar that very night. When the shameless Prince opens the door to Isabel's chambers and finds himself face to face with Baltasar, the presence of his disobedient messenger convinces him that Baltasar is the assassin. The irate and unchastened Prince prohibits the wedding. When he again visits Isabel after arranging for his wife to be away and reordering Baltasar's departure for Antwerp, the Prince finds, to his dismay, that Baltasar has again disobeyed orders. Now in possession of a pistol, Baltasar kills the Prince with a single shot, allowing his victim just enough time to acknowledge that death is the proper reward for one who has been so arrogantly rebellious against God. The widowed Princess wants Baltasar to be killed but accedes to Lafín's suggestion that he be tortured instead to make him reveal the names of his accomplices. Disillusioned with Isabel, the Princess suggests for her the same treatment. Isabel ends the play by stating that this *comedia* has seen the death of the Prince but that "the death and emprisonment of Baltasar / remain for a second part / for which such a piteous tragedy / awaits a more learned pen." No great loss to world literature, the sequel apparently never materialized.

6. *Nardo Antonio, bandolero (Nardo Antonio, Brigand)*

The only seventeenth-century version of this play was extracted from a now unknown volume. Its folios are numbered 235–54, and it is attributed to Lope de Vega. Rennert, however, discovered a list of titles which formed the 1628 repertory of the *autor de comedias* Jerónimo Almella, in which the play is attributed to Mira.[27] Although Cotarelo published *Nardo Antonio* in the new Academy edition of Lope's plays,[28] he concludes his preliminary remarks by stating: "Without any scruple, we would assign this play to Mira de Amescua, although the gift is of no great value for the fame of this poet."[29] He bases his statement on the Almella date, the occurrence in the play of "truculent and ferocious scenes," more characteristic of Mira than Lope, and the treatment of brigandage in the Viceroyalty of Naples just a few years prior to Mira's own presence there in the court of the Count of Lemos. Morley and Bruerton, on the basis of versification, conclude that the play is not Lope's.[30]

The setting is Naples, where the Spanish Count of Miranda has just arrived to assume the duties of Viceroy. Nardo Antonio, a valiant Italian soldier of humble birth, has been promised the hand of the beautiful Leonarda by her father Ricardo. Subsequent to the promise, however, Ricardo decides to give his daughter, who deeply loves Nardo, to the wealthy Gerardo instead. When the Viceroy announces that Leonarda will marry Gerardo that day and that Ricardo was justified in breaking his word because of the great disparity in social status between Leonarda and Nardo, the stage has been set for the play's remaining action.

The intrepid Nardo plans to abduct Leonarda before her marriage to Gerardo and then to instigate a reign of terror in and around Naples. He leaves Batistela as a spy to work in the service of the Viceroy, and he issues one firm instruction, which will be repeated emphatically throughout the play: no Spanish soldiers are to be harmed. Cotarelo feels that Nardo's exaggerated reverence for everything Spanish is a patriotic note sounded by Mira, intended to indicate that "the rebelliousness of the brigands was not directed against Spanish domination, but rather against private property or personal enemies."[31]

Moments before his planned marriage to Leonarda, Gerardo is chided by his servant for having himself broken a promise to marry the beautiful Celia. Haughtily, Gerardo replies that Celia is no more than a peasant. He proclaims condescendingly: "In the city I will have my honor, / and in the country, my desires." The abduction scene is short: Ricardo is killed, Gerardo escapes, and Leonarda willingly flees with Nardo. The Viceroy announces a reward of 10,000 ducats for Nardo's head. The thought of such wealth overrides Batistela's loyalty to Nardo. In the meantime, Celia's father falls into the hands of Nardo, who learns that Gerardo has broken his promise to marry Celia, now four months pregnant, with whom he still lives when anxious to satisfy his physical desires. Nardo forces Gerardo to marry Celia and then, urged on by the literally bloodthirsty Leonarda, kills him. In one of the most sanguinary scenes in Golden Age drama, Leonarda falls upon the slain Gerardo, whom she has held responsible for the death of her father, and drinks his blood.

Nardo now hopes to marry Leonarda in honor, with the Viceroy as his best man, but Batistela's treachery is prepared. He lures Nardo into a house filled with soldiers. When he signals them to appear, he himself is stabbed and dies. The force of numbers proves too much even for Nardo, who attempts to leap to safety from a window and breaks his leg. The Viceroy will sponsor the marriage of Leonarda and her brigand in the palace, and then Nardo will be killed. The widowed Leonarda will then enter a convent and the reward will go to the Spanish captain who worked with Batistela. Devoid of artistic merit, this play stands primarily as a literary souvenir of Mira's years in Naples.

7. *El primer conde de Flandes (The First Count of Flanders)*

The only known printing of this play is found in *Parte XXIX* of the *Escogidas* (Madrid: Fernández de Buendía, 1668), where it is attributed to Fernando de Zárate. According to Cotarelo,[32] a Biblioteca Nacional manuscript (Ms. 16.688), copied from another dated November 24, 1616, which attributes it to Mira, renders impossible the attribution to Zárate, who did not begin to publish his *comedias* until after 1644.

The complicated plot is typical of Mira's tendency to fuse a historical subject with conventional love intrigues. Ludovico, Emperor of the Holy Roman Empire, has just been treacherously assassinated. Balduino, a gallant noble from Flanders, overtakes the three fleeing assassins and brings their heads back to the battlefield where the Emperor's body lies before Carlos, King of France and Ludovico, King of Germany. Each of these two brothers, uncles of the deceased Emperor and grandchildren of Charlemagne, assumes that he should succeed to the imperial throne. The elderly rivals seem on the verge of deciding the issue through internecine warfare when the prudence of their children, Ludovico and Margarita of France, and Rodulfo and Matilde of Germany, convinces them that the decision should be left to Pope León. They cross their hands on the chest of the deceased Emperor and pledge to abide by the Papal choice. The solemnity of their pledge is sealed as their hands are grasped by the corpse's own hand. Carlos sends as his emissary to the Pope his son, Prince Ludovico, who is in love with his cousin Matilde; Rodulfo, who loves Margarita, is sent to represent King Ludovico.

Balduino is appointed Admiral of France and becomes deeply involved in the love intrigue. Lamberto, governor of Paris, has aroused jealousy in his current paramour Alfreda, by courting Matilde. Both Matilde and Margarita, however, have shown clear interest in the Flemish hero, Balduino. The more enterprising of the two is Margarita, who sends him anonymous notes summoning him to nocturnal meetings at which she refuses to reveal her identity. Although Balduino hopes that the mystery woman is Margarita, her coldness in public keeps him uncertain. When Margarita's father announces that she is to marry Prince Carlos of Germany, she decides that she must make a decisive move.

At this moment, the princes Ludovico and Rodulfo arrive from Rome with the news that Carlos has been elected Emperor. King Ludovico is furious over his defeat and reviles Rodulfo, whose illegitimate birth he now reveals, for what he feels must have been a weak representation before the Pope. Rodulfo begins to show his evil nature by proposing war to overturn Carlos' election. During a masked ball held that night in honor of Carlos' victory, Margarita, disguised as a page, escapes with Balduino after Carlos conveniently orders his Admiral to journey to Flanders to spread the election results. The court is astounded by a report that Margarita has been abducted by Balduino, and Prince Ludovico leaves in pursuit.

When Balduino and Margarita stop to rest, a priest passes on the way to administer the Holy Sacraments to a sick man. Unhesitatingly, Balduino offers his mount to the priest and guides him on the remainder of his journey. By the time he returns to their resting spot, Margarita has been found by her brother and taken to Paris. The voice of Christ then announces that Flanders will be given to Balduino as a reward for service rendered to the priest. Balduino witnesses the arrival of the warring German forces and immediately departs for Paris to warn Carlos of this threat.

King Ludovico receives conflicting counsel from his children: Rodulfo urges him to wrest the Emperor's throne from Carlos, while Matilde urges him to respect the oath made over the body of the deceased Emperor. When the persistent Rodulfo again proposes going against the wisdom of the Pope, Ludovico accuses him of being a heretic, whereupon the ground opens and swallows Rodulfo.

In Paris, Carlos orders Margarita killed, to be joined in death by Balduino, who has just returned to warn his sovereign of impending military attack. Before the King's orders can be carried out, however, a contrite King Ludovico enters, confesses his evil intentions, and pleads forgiveness for Margarita and Balduino. His international difficulties settled, Carlos quickly resolves the domestic situation by marrying Margarita to Balduino, whom he also names Count of Flanders. Carlos announces his abdication in favor of his son Ludovico, who will marry Matilde. Lamberto timidly asks to marry Alfreda as the long and tedious play comes to an end. Cotarelo judges this *comedia* very harshly, labeling it "a true chaos in that its events are presented with neither logic, antecedents, or prior explanations."[33]

8. *La rueda de la fortuna (The Wheel of Fortune)*

This youthful effort, first published in 1615,[34] was performed as early as 1604, in Toledo, as Lope de Vega attests in a letter dated August 4 of that year: "The company of Morales is performing here ... *La rueda de la fortuna,* a play in which a king beats his wife, and many cry over this scene, as if it were possible."[35] Lope again mentions Morales' staging of *La rueda de la fortuna* and adds its attribution to Mira, in his own play, *Virtud, pobreza y mujer (Virtue, Poverty, and Woman),*[36] which was not written, according to Morley and Bruerton, until "1612–15 (probably 1615)."[37] One of the five plays published by Mesonero Romanos, in 1858,[38] *La rueda de la fortuna* was edited critically in the 1972 dissertation of Edward W. Hopper.[39]

An extravagant absence of verisimilitude characterizes this loosely episodic play which, nonetheless, is interesting in that it represents an unmistakable, although technically inept, interpretation of a theme which Mira was later to handle masterfully: the inconstancy of fortune. The title, of course, directly states the theme, and references to the wheel of fortune abound throughout, culminating in the play's last lines:

Y la historia prodigiosa	And the prodigious story
Aquí tiene fin, Senado,	Here ends, Senate,
No *La rueda de la fortuna*	Not *The Wheel of Fortune*
Porque siempre está rodando.	Because it rolls on always.

(BAE, XLV, 22)

Although Mira in no way achieves here an artistically happy rendering of the theme, a timid step in this direction is evident in the prosperous and adverse turns taken in the military careers of generals Filipo and Leoncio, both of whom are highly loyal and virtuous. Each returns to Constantinople from battle as the action opens: Filipo has been victorious, while Leoncio has been defeated by immense hordes of Persians. Leoncio returns with a hostage, the beautiful Mitilene, whom he has found in the tent of the Persian commander. Filipo is elevated to the position of *privanza,* and the former favorite, Leoncio, is ridiculed and sent off with a distaff hung on his neck to symbolize a lack of manliness.

The presence of Mitilene awakens prurient desires in Emperor Mauricio, Prince Teodosio, and even in Filipo. Abusing his authority, the Emperor orders everyone away while he unsuccessfully makes a play for the captive. Mauricio even drags the Empress by the hair and orders her imprisoned for attempting to thwart his lascivious intentions. The Prince next abducts Mitilene, ties her to a tree, and threatens her with death unless she submits. The banished Leoncio, who has witnessed this scene while in hiding, frightens the Prince away with ominous words. Filipo happens along just at that moment, is tempted to take advantage of the bound woman, but sublimates his lust and frees her.

The plot thickens with the appearance of the elderly Heracliano and his ward Heraclio who, in fact, is the son of Mauricio and the Empress. A vision of danger caused the Empress to hand over her son upon birth to be reared in safety by Heracliano. She substituted the son of a Scythian and of a Phonecian slave, a fact which explains, although weakly, the abhorrence which the Emperor and Teodosio feel for each other, and the lack of filial love which causes Teodosio to slap the Empress on stage.[40]

Chronology is respected no more than verisimilitude in this play. Although the three emperors mentioned in its action are from the sixth and seventh centuries, the Pope sends to Mauricio a plea for help which is dated May, 1303! The Emperor's refusal of help, compounded by overt dislike for the Pope, calls forth another subplot. Mutinous soldiers, angered by Mauricio's non-support of the Papacy, unite to elect a new emperor. Leoncio is nominated, but he declines. While further nominations proliferate, an eagle deposits on stage a sheathed sword which carries the caption: "Take it and rule for just one day." Each in turn, the ambitious soldiers fail in their attempts to draw the sword from its sheath. The peasant Focas arrives and, to the bewilderment of all, unsheathes it with no difficulty. At the head of the soldiers, he then sets out with them to kill Mauricio. Aware of the uprising, Mauricio sends his wife and the Infanta to the mountains for safety. Just prior to her departure, the Empress reveals to him the secret of Heraclio, who has enlisted as a soldier just before the mutiny. Heraclio learns from Mitilene that she is of royal Persian blood, a fact which seems to deny him any right to her love, until, when he encounters his dying father, he learns the truth of his own royal birth.

In the meantime, the rampaging soldiers have captured the Empress, the Infanta, and Mitilene. Filipo, known to be honorable, is told that the life of the woman he picks will be spared. Loyalty dictates that he name the Empress. They then allow him one more choice. Torn again between love for Mitilene and loyalty to the Infanta, who loves him, Filipo saves the latter. At this moment, Cósroes, commander of the Persians, arrives to rescue his sister Mitilene, either by fighting anyone who will accept his challenge, or by ransoming her with untold Persian riches. Pursued by soldiers, Heraclio dashes on stage. Having just killed Focas, his identity is revealed to all. He is proclaimed Emperor and will marry Mitilene. Filipo and the Infanta will also wed.

According to Cotarelo,[41] this strange play is responsible for the lack of esteem in which Mira is held by those who have read but few of his works. It is of interest primarily as Mira's earliest known dra-

matic treatment of the theme of the inconstancy of fortune. Mesonero Romanos pointed out in 1858[42] that *La rueda de la fortuna*
was the direct inspiration of Calderón's *En esta vida todo es verdad
y todo es mentira (In This Life Everything Is Truth and Everything
Is False)* and Corneille's *Héraclius.* In separate articles, Ruth Lee
Kennedy has demonstrated the influence exerted by *La rueda de la
fortuna* on two of Tirso's plays, *La república al revés (The Inside-
Out Republic),*[43] and *La vida y muerte de Herodes (The Life and
Death of Herod).*[44]

CHAPTER 5

Secular Theater:
Plays of Intrigue
and Novelesque Interest

E IGHT of the fifteen plays treated in this chapter have Italian settings (Naples, Palermo, Ferrara, Mantua, Sicily); one deals with a historical Asturian king; one is not geographically identified, although several of its characters are of Portuguese origin; and the remaining five are set in Madrid. Yet, in these *comedias,* geography, history, and national origin are only incidental to the pure inventiveness with which Mira weaves his plots of intrigue and novelesque interest. His heavy didacticism recedes in these plays and is replaced by a more buoyant atmosphere of adventure, of women in male disguise, and, with one notable exception, of the ingenious and bloodless resolution of problems. It is in the plays of this category that Mira's *costumbrista* vein is most evident.

I   *La adúltera virtuosa (The Virtuous Adulteress)*

La adúltura virtuosa is one of two Mira titles which exist in a single known *suelta* in Munich's Bayerische Staatsbibliothek. In Naples, the marriage of Mauricio, Duke of Milan, and Juana de Aragón is being delayed by the late arrival of the King of Naples, who is to serve as *padrino.* Upon arrival, the King is struck by Juana's charms and plots to win her favors. This love triangle is further complicated by the arrival in Italy of Don Felipe de Cardona, who·was Juana's fiancé until the pressure of self-interest caused her father to promise her hand to Mauricio, son of their Italian benefactor. Felipe has come to Italy in pursuit of Mauricio, who, in addition to having stolen his fiancée, is guilty of treacherously killing Felipe's brother.

The smitten King, inspired by the Biblical story of David and Uriah, first schemes to send Mauricio to defend his coasts from a feigned attack by the Turks and then commissions Felipe with his murder. Felipe's commitment to the code of honor prevents compliance, however. To the already encumbered plot is now added the element which provides the play's title. The Queen, angered by the now openly scandalous behavior of the King, upbraids the Count and the Baron, her husband's two underlings, for their part as go-betweens. Undaunted by her authority, the two threaten to accuse her of adultery. In a ponderous third act, after Juana, in male disguise, is first taken for the alleged lover, Mauricio defeats the Queen's accusers, who confess their treachery and are summarily consigned to the fire which had been prepared to punish her alleged guilt.

Although Felipe has spared Mauricio only to be able to fight him in a manner befitting men of honor, he magnanimously pardons his brother's assassin. Mauricio and Juana will live happily together and the King and Queen are reunited; but the weak and philandering monarch has undergone no visible growth. Felipe has been successful neither in his search for love nor in his search for vengeance; nevertheless, the strength required for his several impressively magnanimous acts qualifies him as the outstanding character in this uneven, and probably youthful effort.

II   Amor, ingenio y mujer *(Love, Wit, and Woman)*

Although at least three seventeenth-century printings exist, two of which are attributed to Mira, and the other to Calderón,[1] some scholars who have commented on *Amor, ingenio y mujer* give evidence of not having read the play with care. In 1860, Barrera, in his eagerness to give double titles,[2] indicated that *Amor, ingenio y mujer* is an alternate title for Mira's *La tercera de sí misma (Go-between for Herself:*[3] see pp. 105–106). Anibal, in 1925, spoke of "*La tercera de si misma* (a title also sometimes assigned to Mira's *Amor, ingenio y mujer*)."[4] Although the plays are completely different, the confusion of Barrera and Anibal is likely explained by the fact that the exact words which make up the title *Amor, ingenio y mujer* are used five times in *La tercera de sí misma.*[5] Cotarelo was the first to note the erroneous tendency to confuse the two titles.[6] *Amor, ingenio y mujer* was edited in 1946 by Joanne Irene Limber.[7]

In Valencia, on January 22, 1624, *Amor, ingenio y mujer* was announced as one of the "comedias nuevas" in the repertoire of the *autor de comedias* Roque de Figueroa.[8]

With the Salic Law in effect in Sicily, its king has managed to disguise his daughter Matilde in male attire and pass her off as "prince Carlos." A typical love intrigue, rich in dramatic irony occasioned by the feigned sex of the protagonist, paves the way for the ultimate repeal of the Salic Law. After feigning love for the Duchess as part of her cover-up, Matilde subsequently falls in love with Enrique, nephew of the King of Aragón, who has come to Sicily to pay court to the Duchess. She has also aroused jealousy in another of the Duchess' suitors, the Marquis.

Because of the obstacle represented for their political aspirations by the Salic Law, both the Duchess and the Marquis (he is the son of the sister of the King and would inherit the throne if there were no prince) are persuaded by Matilde and the King to campaign for its repeal. Their success allows a happy dénouement in which Matilde marries Enrique and the Duchess is paired with the Marquis.

III   Los caballeros nuevos *(The New Knights)*

A single manuscript version of this *comedia,* which passed from the Durán library to the Biblioteca Nacional (Ms. 15.284), is dated March 7, 1608. An obvious error is found in the *comedia's* full title, *Caballeros nuevos y carboneros de Tracia (New Knights and Charcoal Burners of Thrace),* for the action passes in *Francia* and not in *Tracia.* This play is not to be confused, however, with Mira's *Los carboneros de Francia,* whose plot is different.

The King of France loves Ricarda, his niece. Duke Reymundo is a rival of the King, but Ricarda is in love with Roberto, a nobleman who, out of respect for his sovereign, receives her attentions coolly. When Roberto advises the King to keep close surveillance over his niece, he himself is assigned this task and is threatened by Ricarda with a proposed accusation that he has tried to force himself upon her, unless he responds to her love. He remains firm in spite of Ricarda's suicide threat as Act I ends.

Subsequently, Duke Reymundo craftily gains entry to Ricarda's chamber, only to be found there by Roberto, who magnanimously permits him to escape. Meanwhile, the King has become lost while hunting and, without revealing his identity, has been taken in by hospitable charcoal burners. In gratitude, he invites his rustic hosts to court, where they discover his identity and are richly rewarded for their kindness. Ultimately, Roberto's nobility of character is responsible for effecting the King's pardon of Ricarda's inconstancy and for the marriage of monarch and niece.

This play is not of high quality and is only doubtfully attributed to Mira. Williamsen's awaited versification study may well remove this title from Mira's canon.

IV   La casa del tahur *(The House of the Gambler)*

La casa del tahur existed only in the largely autograph Biblioteca Nacional Ms. R–118, dated December 20, 1616, until it was edited critically in John C. Fameli's 1970 dissertation[9] and in a 1973 published version by Vern Williamsen.[10] An alternate title found in the manuscript is a popular proverb which expresses well one of the play's principal themes: "En la casa del tahur poco dura la alegría" ("Happiness is brief in the house of the gambler"). Two *aprobaciones* are found in the manuscript, one dated November 15, 1619, which authorizes its presentation in Zaragoza, and the other, dated December 3, 1621, authorizing presentation in Madrid. In view of the fact that the play denounces gambling, one of the favorite vices of Philip III, Cotarelo postulates that perhaps it could not be played in Madrid until after Philip's demise.[11]

Marcelo Gentil, a wealthy Genoese, as a remedy for his son Alejandro's proclivities toward gambling and philandering, has married him to the virtuous Isabela. A short eight days after the wedding, Alejandro is invited to gamble at the home of a beautiful Sevillian named Angela by his friends Diego and Luis, who themselves have been introduced to the girl by her *novio* Carlos. The girl's mother, similarly named Angela, has instructed her daughter well on the extraction of wealth from their guests. Alejandro loses everything, including a diamond chain which had been given to him by his bride. Isabela comforts her distraught husband by giving him her last jewels, including a rose of diamonds which Alejandro instructs his servant Roque to deliver to Angela as a token of his esteem. The honorable Roque disobeys and returns the precious piece of jewelry to Isabela. When Alejandro subsequently sends an elegantly embroidered dress of his wife's to Angela, Roque again neglects to deliver as instructed and returns it to Isabela.

The loyalty of Alejandro's wife is pushed to the breaking point when, irate because she has no money left with which to obtain food and drink, he threatens her with a dagger and orders her to provide for their needs however she is able. When Isabela confides this degradation to Marcelo, the wise father sets about immediately to teach his son a lesson. With firm enjoinders that she not reveal its source, Marcelo showers wealth on Isabela. He then visits the home of the two Angelas and impetuously proposes marriage to the mother, on the condition that she will not dishonor him by hosting any more gambling in her home.

The two situations engineered by Marcelo lead inexorably to the redemption of his son, although Marcelo himself is tricked into actually marrying the elder Angela in a proxy wedding. Her daughter marries Carlos, and, when Marcelo explains the strategy by which he aroused his son's jealousy, a thoroughly chastened Alejandro and his loyal Isabela are happily reconciled.

An interesting literary note is found in the last act. The shrewd mother feigns deafness almost to the end of the play and pretends to read while actually eavesdropping on conversations. She is discovered to be both a liar and illiterate, however, when, after claiming in v. 2385 to be reading a book by Fray Luis de Granada, it is discovered by Roque in v. 2425 that the book in question is actually *Don Quixote*.

V Cuatro milagros de amor *(Four Miracles of Love)*

Cotarelo mentions two known *suelta* copies of *Cuatro milagros de amor* and a Biblioteca Nacional manuscript (Ms. 15.252) produced from one of them.[12] In our opinion, this is Mira's most successful venture into the areas of social satire and *costumbrismo*, and it must be classified as one of his best plays. References in the play to celebrations of the birth of Prince Baltasar Carlos prove that it was written in or after 1629, making it one of the last plays written by Mira prior to his literary retirement in Guadix.

The beautiful doña Lucrecia and the wealthy but homely doña Ana open the play by sharing notes on their suitors. Each has two, and each of the four men has a particularly irksome defect. Ana is being courted by don Juan and by don Fernando. The former is uncouth and an untidy dresser, and the latter is insufferable because of the artificiality and pseudo-Gongoristic tendencies of his speech.

Doña Lucrecia's suitors, don Sancho and Captain Alvarado, the former of excellent lineage and the latter a recently returned *nouveau riche* from America, are virtually pure manifestations of cowardice and avarice. These traits, however, have simply been reported to Lucrecia and Ana, neither of whom has yet had contact with either of her suitors. In order to check on whether or not the men may be simply victims of calumny, the ladies hatch a plot and implement it immediately.

Each pretends to be the other as the four suitors arrive. Since Ana has been reputed to be ugly, Fernando and Juan are pleasantly surprised by the portent of beauty they encounter. The outcome of these visits, Ana remarks, is that she will henceforth not have to worry about being followed by these two suitors, while Lucrecia notes that she will have two more pestering her.

The scene next shifts to the street, where Lucrecia's two suitors are quarreling. Captain Alvarado wishes to resolve their rivalry by the sword, but Sancho timorously declines. Both have seen Lucrecia strolling along the Prado and now wish to meet her personally. When they call at Lucrecia's house, they are greeted by Ana, pretending to be Lucrecia. As the two callers stifle surprise over the appearance of their hostess, Aldonza and another servant, the play's *gracioso*, Gómez, state that a servant named Mari-Ramírez has been borrowing Lucrecia's headdresses and other finery and wearing them to the Prado, where she has been mistaken for Lucrecia. All consideration of social status is disregarded as both men fall instantly in love with the alleged servant.

Early in Act II, the brash Captain Alvarado meets Alberto, Lucrecia's uncle and guardian and requests in marriage the servant who wears headdresses. There being no Mari-Ramírez, Alberto interprets this as a petition to marry Aldonza. The Captain's request is granted, and the ceremony, to be held in Ana's house, is set for that very evening. News of a wedding in Ana's house strikes despair in Sancho and Juan and convinces the conceited Fernando that he himself is to be the bridegroom. At the appointed hour of the ceremony, Sancho and Juan arrive masked, although the latter's facial disguise is ludicrously insufficient to cover the identity symbolized by his dirty clothes and winter stockings and shoes. Fernando jauntily arrives, ostensibly for his own wedding, only to have his opening comments rejected summarily by the feigned Ana, who then launches into a witty parody of Fernando's speech, espe-

cially his use of hyperbaton. In a scene reminiscent of the dénouement of Alarcón's *La verdad sospechosa (Suspicious Truth)*,[13]
when Alberto instructs the groom to take the bride's hand,
Aldonza is ignored as both Captain Alvarado and Fernando grasp
Lucrecia's hand, the former taking her for Mari-Ramírez, the latter
for Ana. Lucrecia rashly promises the Captain that she will be his
when he is no longer avaricious, and she makes a similar promise to
Fernando, contingent upon his "becoming discreet and speaking
the Spanish language in a manner unadorned with metaphors and
harangues" (p. 23).

By this time, each of the four pretenders has had ample opportunity to see the negative results produced by his personal defect.
Don Sancho is the first upon whom the effect of love's miracles is
detected. In disguise during nocturnal visits, Sancho serves Lucrecia and wins her love with great displays of valor but is unsuccessful by day in convincing her that he is her masked hero. The transformation from Sancho's pusillanimous former self to the bravery
of her unknown love seems difficult to believe, and Lucrecia dis-
misses him. In nocturnal guise, Sancho gives her half of a ring
which will be used later to confirm his identity.

The miraculous trend seen first in Sancho has spread. Reports
arrive that, in the celebrations of the prince's birth, Juan has been
declared the most gallant competitor in an eight-day tournament
and that Captain Alvarado has showered gifts on Lucrecia's servants. When Fernando arrives and recites a good sonnet, totally
devoid of artificiality, the fourth miracle has been wrought. The
real Ana is now impressed with this reformed poet and procures
Fernando's written promise to marry her.

When Alberto announces that he has arranged for Lucrecia to
marry Sancho, the opposition of the losers is couched in surprising
terms. Juan wants to resolve the issue by the use of his sword; the
Captain prefers reason to swordfighting, and Fernando agrees with
the Captain. Each claims the miracle of his own transformation to
be the greatest, but Sancho is the most convincing:

Para que el cobarde pecho	For the cowardly breast
tenga el ánimo atrevido	to be imbued with daring
con valor, milagro ha sido	and valor, it has been a miracle
que en sólo el alma se ha hecho.	effected in the soul.

Lucrecia concedes that Sancho's transformation was the most miraculous but states her desire to wait longer to discover the true identity of her masked lover. Sancho finally produces his half of the ring and wins Lucrecia. Ana will wed Fernando and give her cousin Clara to Juan. Sancho offers his sister to the Captain, who chooses not to marry on those terms.

This undeservedly forgotten play merits publication; its availability would certainly enhance Mira's reputation. Striking plot similarities between this play and *La ventura de la fea* (*The Good Fortune of the Ugly Girl*—see pp. 107–108) justify Anibal's conclusion concerning the source of *Cuatro milagros de amor*: "Mira has unquestionably taken the elementary plot material of *La ventura de la fea,* and, after an interval of at least thirteen years, with different stress and a stronger tendency to the comedy of manners, has worked it over into the more matured and surprisingly well disguised *Cuatro milagros de amor.*"[14]

VI   Examinarse de rey *(Examination in Kingliness)*

This play, which exists under the above title in Ms. 14.953 of the Biblioteca Nacional, was printed as a *suelta* entitled *Más vale fingir que amar (It's Better To Feign Than to Love).*[15] The manuscript, obviously an actor's copy, has several marked-out passages and frequent marginal indications of "sí" and "no." Cotarelo[16] reports that José Sánchez Arjona made a short edition of the manuscript in Seville in 1887, from which he excised all of the marked-out passages, and to which he gave the composite title *Más vale fingir que amar, o Examinarse de rey.*

The plot presents a variation on the stock theme of the offspring born out of wedlock and reared in rustic surroundings. In this case, Federico, King of Naples, and his bastard brother Manfredo have each entrusted an illegitimate son to the same woman. Both children, to complicate matters, are named Carlos, after their grandfather. The only person who knew the identity of each child was their guardian, who died suddenly without communicating this information to her husband.

Several years have passed. Manfredo has died, and the King, anxious to wed his niece and only legitimate heir to his son, journeys to the village in which Carlos resides only to find two young men who pass for sons of the peasant who has raised them from infancy. He decides to return to the court with both of them, hoping to discover there which is his son. The King decides to name after himself the youth who most appeals to him. He notes that both wish to marry the heiress Margarita, but whereas the young Federico's motives appear to be grounded in sincere love, those of Carlos seem to be more pragmatically related to Margarita's claim to the throne. Finally, Margarita learns that Carlos is actually in love with one of her ladies-in-waiting.

This manifestation of less than noble aspirations, when viewed in the context of other proofs which show Federico to be of noble qualities and Carlos to be hypocritical and egotistical, enable the peasant guardian to confirm the thesis that royal blood has manifested the superiority of its correlates. Federico is declared to be the King's son — an unsurprising ending to a mediocre play.

VII   La Fénix de Salamanca *(The Phoenix of Salamanca)*

First published in *Parte III* of the *Escogidas* (Madrid: Melchor Sánchez, 1653), *La Fénix de Salamanca* was written, as is determined by internal evidence, prior to the fall of 1610.[17] It is available in the *Biblioteca de Autores Españoles*[18] and in Valbuena Prat's *Clásicos Castellanos* edition.[19] Cotarelo[20] considers this to be Mira's oldest and best *comedia* of intrigue.

The action takes place in Madrid. Doña Mencía, a young and beautiful widow, has come disguised as a courtier[21] in search of her erstwhile suitor, Garcerán, who suddenly suspended his university studies in Salamanca and left her with no explanation. Garcerán, we learn late in the first act, the second son of a noble Valencian family, originally had married a young lady from Huesca. After passing through an economically discouraging period, Garcerán was convinced that he should undertake an academic career in Salamanca. He departed without his wife and soon met Mencía, widely known as the Phoenix (in the sense of "marvel," "prodigy") of Salamanca. Finally, his conscience got the best of him, and, anxious no longer to deceive Mencía, he returned to Valencia, whereupon his wife died. The newly widowed and now eligible Garcerán would have returned to Salamanca had not he been erroneously informed by a friend that Mencía was about to marry. The disconsolate gallant has therefore arrived in Madrid to enlist as a soldier for battle either in Flanders or in Italy.

The convergence in Madrid of widow and widower, each there for different reasons, is soon tied in to the subplot which involves the beautiful Alejandra, who shares mutual love with Count Horacio; but Don Juan, her brother, supports the marital suit of her elderly uncle, the Captain don Beltrán, and has delayed official announcement of their marriage only while awaiting a papal dispensation.

Mencía, in male disguise and under the pseudonym of don Carlos, is met and befriended by Alejandra as Garcerán simultaneously arrives in Madrid only to be recruited by Horacio to protect his retreat with Alejandra when they fear being discovered along the Prado by Juan and Beltrán. Mencía, truly Tirsian in the feminine beauty and the virile strength which characterize her transvestism, is equally at home wielding a sword and in donning seductive feminine attire to charm don Juan in the hope of convincing him to permit his sister to marry Count Horacio rather than her stodgy old uncle. In the midst of the unresolved dual intrigue, a refusal of the requested dispensation arrives from Rome. Beltrán magnanimously blesses the union of Alejandra and Horacio, and Mencía, finally recognized by her none-too-perceptive former suitor, will marry Garcerán.

The play suffers from ailments common to the genre and the epoch: overabundance of intrigue, improbable gullibility of the characters and the overly contrived relation of the plots. Mira was aware, as we see in Carlos' own words ("She thought I was single / ...for married students / are not found very often," I, vv. 997-1000), that the circumstances surrounding the presence of his *galán* in the academic halls of Salamanca were somewhat unlikely, and the fate of the all-important dispensation is perhaps prematurely forecast when Juan reveals that Horacio, Beltrán's rival, is nephew to the Cardinal (II, vv. 2486-88). Nevertheless, there is freshness in several *costumbrista* scenes, and the play is, overall, most entertaining.

VIII El galán secreto *(The Secret Suitor)*

Published as Mira's under this title in *Parte XXXIV* of the *Escogidas* (Madrid: Fernández de Buendía, 1670), *El galán secreto* appeared again eleven years later in the *Tercera parte* of Moreto's plays (Madrid: Antonio de Zafra, 1681), under the title *El secreto entre dos amigos (The Secret Between Two Friends).* Although Medel lists both titles, attributing *El galán secreto* to Mira[22] and *El secreto entre dos amigos* to Moreto,[23] Barrera noted in 1860 that the two plays were identical.[24] Fernández-Guerra seems to be unaware of the prior printed attribution to Mira[25] and he includes *El secreto entre dos amigos* in his 1856 edition of Moreto's *comedias.*[26] Cotarelo excised this play from Moreto's canon in 1927[27] and declared in 1931[28] that the plays are identical except for a minor modification in the last four lines.

Highlighted in this play of intrigue are the laudable magnanimity and sense of honesty exhibited by its protagonist César, poor but of noble lineage, who has come from Florence to serve in the court of the Duke of Ferrara. Frequently the victim of misleading circumstantial evidence, and unjustly maligned by false friends who covet the favor he enjoys at court, César steadfastly and ethically serves the Duke while courting his sister. In many ways César parallels Mira's royal *privados,* and his ascendancy is here distinguished from theirs only by the reduced splendor and magnificence of a ducal context.

César's loyalty and goodness are extreme, extending even to the confession of a guilt which is not his in order to save a would-be assassin of the Duke. Rather than a tragic fall, however, the not uncommon end accorded to many of Mira's virtuous *privados,* César is here rewarded with vindication from false testimony, increased favor, and the hand of the Duke's sister. The play's emphasis on magnanimity and on alternatives to the rigid code of honor, motifs usually associated with Moreto but more common in Mira's theater than is generally assumed, perhaps contributes to the erroneous attribution.

IX   Galán, valiente y discreto *(Gallant, Valiant, and Discreet)*

By all estimates, *Galán, valiente y discreto* is one of Mira's finest plays. A partial autograph manuscript and other manuscript copies may be found in the Biblioteca Nacional. The only known seventeenth-century printing is included in *Parte XXIX* of *Comedias de varios autores* (Valencia: Silvestre Esparsa, 1636), but several were forthcoming in the following century. In the nineteenth century it appeared in the collections of Ortega (Madrid, 1830), of Ochoa, *Tesoro del teatro español* (Paris, 1838), and in Mesonero

Romanos' 1858 edition for the *Biblioteca de Autores Españoles*. Ochoa's inclusion is accompanied by a backhanded compliment; he unequivocally calls it Mira's best play while labeling Mira a very second-rate dramatist. Edward Nagy's 1969 edition[29] is based on the text provided by Mesonero Romanos.[30] William Forbes, who published a critical edition in 1973,[31] convincingly postulates a date of composition early in 1632.[32]

For political reasons, Serafina, Duchess of Mantua, is obliged to marry even though she states that love and marriage hold no appeal for her. Her major concern, nonetheless, is to select wisely from among the four claimants to her hand. Since she and her suitors have never seen each other, she conceives a plan to determine whether they are sincere in their love or are guided solely by the incentive of marrying for prestige and power. She and her cousin Porcia will pretend to be each other. Before meeting the suitors, Serafina establishes the three criteria on which they will be judged: gallantry, valor, and discretion, which correspond to the play's title. Each of the acts is devoted primarily to the evaluation of all four men in one category.

The group of suitors is comprised of three Italian noblemen, the dukes of Ferrara, Parma, and Urbino, and a Spaniard, the dashing don Fadrique, poor, but of noble ancestry. Through the good services of his servant Flores who, under the pseudonym Roque, feigns madness to obtain admission as a jester in the ducal palace, don Fadrique learns before the competition actually starts that Porcia and Serafina have switched roles. Privy to the secret, Fadrique's advantage is immense. As Cotarelo wisely notes,[33] Serafina's stratagem is quite puerile and improbable; it in no way holds promise of helping to discover ignoble motives, but it does make possible an entertaining and technically well-executed plot.

At a dance featured in the first act, Fadrique is declared the most gallant. Subsequently he also proves to be the most discreet in a contest to test mental acuity and articulate expression. To support the case for his winning entry, he recites a sonnet on the theme of the irrevocable passage of time, acknowledging (vv. 1579–80) that it is the work of a great Spanish poet. It is, in fact, the beautiful sonnet "Flores que fueron pompa y alegría" ("Flowers that were pomp and joy") which Calderón, in 1629, included in *El príncipe constante (The Constant Prince)*.[34] As Act II ends, Serafina prays that Fadrique will distinguish himself for valor as he already has for gallantry and discretion.

Victorious in a joust in the third act, Fadrique wins the hand of Serafina, who then reveals her identity and claims that her husband is the one who has proven himself to be "galán, valiente y discreto." Although the ending impresses us as weak, one cannot but concur in the praise generally accorded this play for its well-executed plot. Thematic parallels have been noted in Alarcón's *El examen de maridos*[35] *(Exam for Marriage),* but inconclusive knowledge of the chronology of these two plays leaves us uncertain as to which inspired which. Mabel Harlan[36] argues that Mira's play was one of the inspirations for Moreto's masterpiece, *El desdén con el desdén (Disdain Conquered by Disdain).* While less certain that *Galán, valiente y discreto* inspired *El desdén con el desdén,* Ruth Lee Kennedy[37] has found that Mira's play was certainly an inspiration for the subplot of Moreto's *Hacer remedio el dolor (Making Grief a Remedy).* In Barbara Matulka's study of the feminist theme in Golden Age theater,[38] *Galán, valiente y discreto* is the only Mira title discussed.

X *Lo que es no casarse a gusto*
(What It's Like Not To Be Happily Married)

The only known copy of *Lo que es no casarse a gusto,* found in a bound volume of *sueltas* in the British Museum,[39] is perhaps the copy formerly possessed by Durán. The play's action, which takes place in Asturias during the reign of King Fruela (757–58), is Calderonian in nature, and its quality is uneven.

Enrique, *privado* of the despotic King Fruela, has just married Elvira. Actually, Enrique and doña Mayor had been in love and planned to marry, as was the case with Elvira and Mayor's brother, Álvar Ramírez. While on a hunting trip, however, Enrique accidentally killed Álvar with an errant shot fired at a wild boar. Although Mayor admits that her brother's death was accidental, a strong sense of honor compels her to seek Enrique's arrest and exile. Secretly, however, and unaware of Enrique's sudden marriage to Elvira, she confesses that she is anxious to regain his love, since she does not know how to hate him. Enrique, who has seen in Mayor's overt expressions of vengeance the impossibility of continuing their relationship, has acceded to his monarch's request that he marry Elvira to atone for the loss of her fiancé.

What no one but Elvira knows, however, is that Prince Bimarano, Fruela's brother, who has secretly loved Elvira, is furious because of her marriage and intent upon getting Enrique out of the way. As Act II ends, Fruela sends Enrique on an ambassadorial mission to France to seek Charlemagne's aid for the reconquest of territories dominated by the Moors. Enrique is taken prisoner by the Moors but finally escapes and returns home after a year's captivity. During his absence, Mayor has accused Elvira and the Prince of treachery in Enrique's capture, a complicity which the Prince confesses. Upon Enrique's return, his wife's pregnancy can be explained only by an adulterous relationship with the Prince. To restore his blemished honor, Enrique stabs his wife to death. He prepares to exact a like vengeance on the Prince, but Fruela, who has had inklings since the first act of his brother's treachery, both against Enrique and against the crown, himself takes Bimarano's life. Once again Fruela orders Enrique's marriage, this time to Mayor, in compensation for having impeded their union in the past. Mayor concludes the play with a line quite different from the play's title: "Pues ya me caso a mi gusto" ("Now I marry happily").

XI   Lo que puede una sospecha *(What Suspicion Can Do)*

Improbability and a pseudo-Calderonian, baroque element predominate in the inferior play *Lo que puede una sospecha,* which was published, for the first and only time, in *Parte IV* of the *Escogidas.* Jealousy is not among the themes handled best by Mira; this is quite a liability in a play whose plot deals almost exclusively with that motif. Briefly stated, the intrigue centers around the havoc almost wreaked in two happy and promising romances by don Alonso Atayde, an arrogant and insincere philanderer. Don Carlos of Portugal and his sister doña Inés are lovers respectively of doña Isabel and don Iñigo. Further, Inés and Isabel have just become acquainted and pledge their joint efforts to support Carlos' pretensions. A confused nocturnal scene beneath Isabel's window, replete with the conventions of unrecognized voices and mistaken identities, almost results in the award of Isabel's hand to the deceitful Alonso. The aftermath of this scene also threatens the anticipated union of Isabel and Iñigo, and rampant jealousy finally erupts in multiple challenges to duel.

While delivering Carlos' challenge to Iñigo, the servant Cardillo tells us that once his mother sent him to his teacher with a note that carried instructions to beat him upon delivery. That experience, he tells us, has led him to read everything he is supposed to deliver. When he meets Alonso, who asks him to transmit to Carlos a challenge to duel on the banks of the river, the servant sees a way to resolve the very complicated intrigue. He alters Carlos' written message to make the time and place of the challenge correspond to those of the challenge issued by Alonso. As Cardillo had hoped, Iñigo and Alonso keep the nocturnal meeting which he arranged. Iñigo kills his friend Alonso while thinking he has slain Carlos, and the two original couples are reunited.

The hollowness of the attempt at baroque imagery, the loose plot structure, and certain extravagant departures from verisimilitude are of such magnitude that one is hard pressed to find many redeeming aspects of this play. There is one passage, however, of considerable interest for the documentary nature of its comment on the contemporary theater. Cardillo, in the first act, recites interesting lines which relate the spectators to the action, and which corroborate the essentially democratic nature of Spain's seventeenth-century theater-going audience:

mosqueteros, ballesteros,	*mosqueteros,* crossbowmen,
homes-buenos, y fidalgos,	good men and *hidalgos,*
escuderos, ricos hombres,	lackeys, rich men,
que de todo hay en el patio,	(for there's some of everything in the theater)
querrán saber el suceso,	will want to know what happened,
pero si lo callamos	but if we refuse to talk
aviendo dicho algo dél	after having made mention of it
abrá silvo de contado.	there will be whistles for sure.
	(fols. 212r, v)

XII No hay burlas con las mujeres, o casarse y vengarse
(Women Cannot Be Tricked, or Revenge Through Marriage)

Printed only once, in *Parte V* of the *Escogidas* (Madrid: Pablo de Val, 1653), and edited only in the 1950 M. A. thesis of John Lihani,[40] this cape-and-sword play could well serve as a model for the excesses of which Mira is to some degree usually guilty in his handling of complicated plots. Simply stated, *No hay burlas con las mujeres, o casarse y vengarse* is a love intrigue featuring two *damas*

and four *galanes,* but Mira's inventiveness adds several new twists
to the conventional variants. A reference to Philip IV indicates a
date of composition subsequent to March, 1621, when Philip
ascended the Spanish throne.

Don Jacinto opens the play by revealing to Lope, who has been
his military companion in Flanders, that he suspects trouble because a certain don García has been serenading his sister Arminda
at night. The death of the father of Arminda and Jacinto was the
reason for his return from Flanders, and he now undertakes the
care of his sister with the overzealousness typical of fraternal
guardians.

Lope, who thought he shared a strong mutual love with
Arminda, feels betrayed and prepares to return to his native
Segovia. A note from Arminda proposes that they meet that night
in the Casa de Campo and flee together to Segovia. Don Lope
keeps the appointment, but solely for the purpose of avenging himself on his allegedly deceitful lover. He slaps Arminda and departs,
just as García, who has coincidentally been summoned for a duel to
the same spot by Jacinto, witnesses the aggression and offers to
help the damsel in distress. Arminda quickly covers her face as her
brother bursts upon the two and wounds García seriously. García
departs on horseback never to be heard from again, and Jacinto
takes the masked woman home, intending to entrust her to his
sister's care.

The love intrigue is rounded out by the arrival from Zaragoza of
Jacinto's cousin, don Diego de Mendoza, with his fiancée, Laura
de Moncada, and her father don Pedro. They will all live in the
home of Jacinto and Arminda until the wedding. Laura, who has
been observed by a fretful Diego to be melancholic throughout the
journey, reveals in an aside that her heart had been won in Zaragoza by a man to whom she has spoken only twice. She never
learned his name, and he, since she was veiled both times, is ignorant of her identity. Laura's melancholy dissipates the moment she
recognizes in her host the stranger whom she met in Zaragoza.

At first jealous of the veiled woman brought home by Jacinto,
Laura finally believes his explanation, and the two plot to undo the
plans for her impending marriage to Diego. The play's title is enun-
ciated for the first time by Arminda, who ominously states that
Lope should realize that women cannot be tricked. Already ill-
disposed toward Lope, who has returned once more to solicit her

forgiveness, the flames of Arminda's vengeful ire are fanned to white heat as Moscón unexplainedly vilifies his master by piling one terribly damaging lie upon another, accusing him of lecherous and deceitful behavior in the most explicit terms.

As Laura waits for Jacinto to keep a nocturnal appointment in the garden, the wandering don Lope appears. While momentarily with Laura, he is seen from a window by Diego and Pedro, each of whom descends with sword in hand to kill the *galán* and extirpate the sin of this deceitful woman. Before they arrive, Lope enters the house in search of Arminda and is replaced by Jacinto, jealous in his turn after finding Laura with another man. Pedro and Diego attack Jacinto, and, as he defends himself valiantly, a pistol shot rings out. Certain that circumstances will no longer permit Diego to carry out his wedding plans, Pedro offers Laura's hand to Jacinto, whose jealousy causes him to reject the offer. Arminda then arrives to inform everyone that she has just killed don Lope. When she unravels the mysteries surrounding García, Lope, and her own role as the *tapada,* the play is ready for final marital arrangements. Jacinto happily accepts Laura's hand, and Diego readily will marry Arminda, for whom he had had a penchant in years past.

Cotarelo[41] is justifiably bothered by the brutality of the dénouement. We are also bewildered by the grossness of language, the prevarication, and the extreme disloyalty of the servant Moscón. Mira at times is obviously more interested in momentary shock value than he is in verisimilitude of dramatic structure and plot development.

XIII   No hay reinar como vivir *(There's No Reigning Like Living)*

Printed only once, in *Parte XIII* of the *Escogidas* (Madrid: Mateo Fernández, 1660), this ingenious *comedia* was edited critically in the 1949 M. A. thesis of Ralph E. Angelo.[42]

The throne of Sicily, upon the death of King Manfredo, was given to Recaredo, younger half-brother of Conrado, illegitimate son of the deceased king. Upon Recaredo's death, Conrado had been named regent until his niece Margarita attained the age of twenty-three and a half. Margarita is about to become of age to rule, and Conrado does not wish to lose his power. Anxious to eliminate her, he administers a test to his sons to discover which of the two will be the better accomplice. Carlos, the younger, reveals that he would be incapable of any form of treason, while Otavio is perfectly amenable to his father's proposed regicide. The plan includes Otavio's playing up to Margarita's lady-in-waiting, Serafina, whose aid in administering a death potion will be secured if she can be led to believe that she will become queen. Serafina convinces Conrado and Otavio that it would suffice to give Margarita a potion which would induce insanity. Loyal to her queen, she then reveals the conspiracy to Margarita and substitutes water for the poison. Margarita, who several times uses the title of the *comedia* to indicate that living is more important than reigning, plans to save her life by feigning the insanity the conspirators want to induce.

At this point, an emissary arrives from Federico, ruler of Naples and heir to the Roman Empire, to pay his respects to the Queen. He announces himself as the Marquis of Pescara (a historical figure mentioned in Mira's *La hija de Carlos Quinto:* the Marquis of Pescara was Charles V's most outstanding general in the victory over the French at Pavia in 1525). In reality, Federico himself has come, using the pseudonym to conceal his identity. In an attempt to detain the emissary, Margarita feigns anger, accuses him of being an imposter, and orders him arrested. Federico, captivated by the Queen's extreme beauty, although bewildered by her conduct, willingly submits to detention in order to find out more about Margarita. After his servant Camilo has revealed Federico's true identity to Margarita, there ensue several scenes in which she seeks an opportunity to tell Federico of her sad plight, but she is always too closely guarded by the conspirators.

The rest of the play is devoted to sporadic but continuing proof of the loyalty of Carlos and the feigned promise of marriage extended to Otavio by Margarita in the hope that this will protect her life. When news reaches Naples that Federico is being held prisoner, Neapolitan ships and troops besiege Sicily. When this military intervention leaves her with no reason to fear her seditious relatives any longer, Margarita ends her feigned insanity, first decreeing death for the two conspirators, but then softening their punishment to exile. She rewards the loyalty of Carlos and Serafina by arranging their marriage and gives her own hand to Federico.

By all standards, this seems to be one of Mira's better plays. His treatment of feigned insanity, as pointed out by Cotarelo,[43] is similar in some respects to Lope's *El cuerdo loco (The Sane Madman)* and *La boba para los otros y discreta para sí (The Fool for Others and Discreet for Herself)*. *No hay reinar como vivir* represents the oddity of using only three verse forms, *redondillas, romance,* and *décimas.* Because of the lack of *quintillas,* Angelo considers it to be one of Mira's late plays. In 1621, Philip IV ascended to the throne and Rodrigo Calderón, a fallen royal favorite, was executed. Lingering suspicions that Rodrigo Calderón may have poisoned Margarita, mother of the new king, prompted Angelo to wonder if Mira might have named his heroine Margarita with that contemporary happening in mind. As dates he proposes 1616–25 (probably 1621–22).

XIV   El palacio confuso *(The Confused Palace)*

This undistinguished treatment of the Menaechmi theme has long been alternately and timidly attributed both to Lope de Vega and to Mira. *El palacio confuso* was first mentioned and, at that time attributed to Mira, in a list of *comedias,* dated June 4, 1628, which formed the repertory of the *autor* Jerónimo Almella perhaps as early as 1624.[44] Under Lope's name it was printed in *Parte XXVIII* of *Comedias de varios autores* (1634) and again in Lope's *Parte XXIV* (Madrid, 1640). It appeared as Mira's in *Parte XXVIII* of the *Escogidas* (Madrid: Fernández de Buendía, 1667). Although Cotarelo published the play in the new series of the Royal Academy edition of Lope's plays[45] (Madrid, 1930), he stated at that time[46] and in his later study of Mira[47] that the play should be taken from Lope's canon and added to Mira's. The 1939 edition of Charles Henry Stevens[48] definitely attributes the play to Lope (although the reasons advanced are not convincing) and dates it 1619–24.[49] Morley and Bruerton concluded in 1940 that their findings on the play's versification "all prove that Lope was not the author."[50] In 1943, Raúl Moglia attempted to refute the attribution to Lope,[51] arguing that the protagonist, Carlos, is not a typical Lopean character and that the play's style in general is too baroque to be Lope's.

The action of this treatment of the Classical theme takes place in Palermo, where rumor has it that when twin sons were born to Eduardo, King of Sicily, the Queen told him of only one and secretly entrusted the other's upbringing to a peasant. When an astrological omen led the King to believe that the remaining son would be an unjust and tyrannical ruler, he set the child adrift to

die in the ocean. Upon the death of the apparently childless
Eduardo, his niece Matilde has inherited the Sicilian throne.

As the action opens, Matilde, followng Sicilian custom, is expected to choose her consort. Although ancient Sicilian statutes
specify that the king may be chosen from any level of society, Duke
Federico, Matilde's cousin, is the expected choice. As the noble
aspirants gather, they are joined by Carlos, a brash soldier who insists on his right to be a candidate for Matilde's hand and who recounts in a boastful, self-adulatory panegyric his own impressive
feats of valor. His self-assurance sways Matilde, and Carlos is
chosen. As the irate nobles protest, the commoners flock to the
support of Carlos and a precarious polarization develops. The
nobles back down and swear allegiance to Carlos. Perhaps partly to
rid himself of competition, and certainly out of inherent tyranny
(recall the astrological prediction), Carlos exiles all the nobles from
court.

In this dismaying situation, at a time when Matilde is convinced
that her impetuous feelings for a young soldier have started the
ruination of the kingdom, the Count of Pompei proposes a solution. He has brought from one of his villages a young peasant
named Enrico, who is physically indistinguishable from Carlos,
except, as we later learn, for a mole on Enrico's right hand. The
ingenuous plan is to dress Enrico in duplicate kingly attire and have
him countermand every bad order issued by Carlos. The whole second act is devoted to such doings as Enrico invalidates the decree of
exile, names the erstwhile exiles to important governmental positions, and disbands a popular army formed by Carlos. Enrico explains that the conflicting regal edicts are the function of a memory
disorder which impels him to leave complete responsibility for
governing in the hands of Matilde.

With the arrival at the court of Lisardo, "father" of Enrico, the
tangled plot begins to unravel. Anxious for the success of Enrico,
Lisardo falsely identifies Carlos as his son. Matilde allows this
deceit temporarily to stand, to the bewilderment of Carlos. For un-
fathomable reasons, Matilde has come to love Carlos and to conclude that he will be a fine husband and king if his superficial arrogance and cruelty can be overcome. Early in the third act her
efforts to humble Carlos yield dividends; now, convinced that this
latest blow to his ego has eliminated his objectionable traits, she re-

veals that Carlos is the real king. Lisardo, however, has waited patiently and now plays his trump card: Enrico is the son of the deceased King Eduardo, as the mole on his right hand and documents will prove. The Count assumes then that Carlos is the other son, whom Eduardo tried to drown, but who was saved and reared by fishermen. A birthmark in the form of a cross confirms Carlos' natural right to occupy the throne. It has truly been a confused palace, in which there is enough mention of the inconstancy of Fortune and her wheel to label the play as Mira's. Moreover, if Anibal's theory on Mira's use of the pseudonym Lisardo is correct,[52] further corroboration may be found in the use of that name for Enrico's peasant guardian.

XV   La tercera de sí misma *(Go-Between for Herself)*

Until Cotarelo offered clarification in 1930,[53] much confusing misinformation had been published regarding this play. In 1852, Mesonero Romanos praised the naturalness of a dialogue which he claims to be from *La tercera de sí misma* but which actually is from *La Fénix de Salamanca.*[54] In addition to this careless mistake, other scholars have erroneously taken *La tercera de sí misma* to be an alternate title for Mira's *Amor, ingenio y mujer* (See pp. 86–87). Both plays were listed as separate entries by Medel,[55] and aside from the coincidental use in *La tercera de sí misma* of the exact words which form the title *Amor, ingenio y mujer,* the *comedias* have in common only the stock convention of a woman in male disguise and an Italian setting.

In the Biblioteca Nacional, there is a manuscript copy (Ms. 17.149) signed by Juan Calderón and dated August 7, 1626. *La tercera de sí misma* was published in *Parte VIII* of the *Escogidas* (Madrid: García de la Iglesia, 1657), and it was edited critically in 1968 by George Ann Huck,[56] who postulates a date of composition shortly after 1616, when the memory of Italy was fresh in Mira's mind.[57] Huck rejects Schack's implication that Mira, in *La tercera de sí misma,* was imitating Tirso de Molina's *La celosa de sí misma.*[58]

Lucrecia, Duchess of Amalfi, has come to Mantua in male attire using the pseudonym Carlos in the hope of establishing a relationship with the Duke, who stole her heart when she saw him at a tournament in Naples. Claiming that she is being pursued by armed attackers, she forces a meeting with the Duke. When she learns that he is awaiting the arrival of Porcia, Countess of Flor, his betrothed whom he has never seen, the scheming Duchess concocts a story which will affect the play's action until its final scene. She passes herself (Carlos) off as a loyal subject of the Duchess of Amalfi who for a time served in the court of Flor and upon whom the libidinous Porcia forced her affections. Infuriated by this alleged looseness of his betrothed, the Duke sends a message to Fisberto, who is en route from Flor to Mantua with Porcia. It contains instructions to return Porcia, whom he now abhors, to her native province.

Prior to receipt of the message, however, Fisberto has conceived lustful designs on his master's fiancée, whose favors he hopes to enjoy by pretending to be the Duke. Although Porcia is taken in by this deception, she finds Fisberto repulsive and resists his advances. When the messenger arrives and hears Porcia address Fisberto as duke, the traitor claims that she has gone crazy. He sends word to his master that he will take Porcia back to Flor, but he instead entrusts her to the rustic household of Lisardo, still hoping to overcome her resistance.

The Count, younger brother of the Duke, has journeyed to Mantua to attend the wedding and is present when "Carlos" displays an equestrian hunting picture of the Duchess of Amalfi. The brothers have opposite reactions; the Duke is unimpressed, and finds her too masculine in appearance and interests, but the Count is instantly enamored. While hunting, the Duke meets Porcia in rustic costume. Anxious not to frighten this woman whom he takes for a peasant, the Duke tells her that he is Fisberto. When Lucrecia hears that the Duke is courting a peasant girl, she bribes Lisardo to take her into his household as a daughter named Laura. Unsuccessful in attracting the Duke's attention to herself in rustic female attire, the persistent Lucrecia appears resplendent in the third act — as herself. When she fails again to win the Duke's affection, she rewards her loving Count with her hand. As identities become revealed, the Duke is disillusioned to learn that his beautiful peasant is, in effect, the allegedly immoral Porcia. It is only when the identity of Carlos is explained that the intrigue dissipates. The Duke and Porcia will marry, and Fisberto is magnanimously forgiven. Lucrecia, as "Carlos," as "Laura," and as herself, although unsuccessful in the attainment of her primary goal, has almost single-handedly sustained the intrigue in her attempt to be the "go-between for herself" in this smoothly developed and interesting play.

XVI *La ventura de la fea (The Good Fortune of the Ugly Girl)*

Restori in 1903[59] and Buchanan in 1905[60] felt that Lope alluded to this play in an *auto* dated 1612 and noted that in the *Entremés del doctor Carlino (Interlude of Dr. Carlino)* it is mentioned again and attributed to Mira. Menéndez Pelayo, in his edition of the *auto* in question, *Del pan y del palo (Of Bread and of Wood)*, also indicated that the passage in question referred to the *comedia,* which he considered to be Lope's:

De señora de una aldea,	A village woman
con el Rey casada está:	is married to the King:
por ella no se dirá:	they won't say about her:
"La ventura de la fea."	"The good fortune of the ugly girl."

(*BAE,* CLVII, 231a)[61]

The assumption that this is a reference to *La ventura de la fea* seems to us unwarranted. The title, which happens to scan as an octosyllabic verse, is, as Anibal noted in 1925,[62] also the first half of a common proverb, one of whose principal variants is "La ventura de la fea, la bonita la desea" ("The good fortune of the ugly girl is desired by the pretty one"), and its presence in *Del pan y del palo,* in our opinion, should not seriously be considered a reference to Mira's *comedia.* Although it is attributed to Lope in both of its known versions — a *suelta* in the British Museum and a manuscript copy, dated 1805, in Madrid's Biblioteca Municipal — Morley and Bruerton concluded emphatically in 1940: "The play, as it stands, is not Lope's."[63] In 1925, Anibal pursued the study of Mira's possible use of the pseudonym Lisardo which Buchanan had initiated in 1905.[64] The use of the pseudonym in this play, probable references to Mira's stay in Naples, the close relationship of one passage to another in *El amparo de los hombres,* and plot elements strikingly similar to *Cuatro milagros de amor,* all lend support[65] to Anibal's claim that *La ventura de la fea* should be included in Mira's canon. In a subsequent article,[66] Anibal further strengthens his case by demonstrating that a *redondilla* from *La ventura de la fea* is almost identical to four verses of a *quintilla* from *El esclavo del demonio.*

The British Museum *suelta,* which we have used for our analysis, is lacking in signatures A 2-7, which originally must have included virtually all of the expository material of Act I and the first part of

Act II. Although we have not been able to compare the printed version with the 1805 manuscript, Morley and Bruerton report that the
latter is comprised by only 2,264 verses, which could indicate that
the mutilated *suelta* served as its model.

Alberto has two daughters, Angela, who is beautiful, and Francisca, who is homely. Francisca loves don Juan de Sotomayor, a
wealthy *indiano,* just returned from Mexico, but he and Carlos are
ardent rivals for the hand of Angela. Diego and Claudio are friends
respectively of Carlos and Juan. When, following the lost section
of the *comedia,* Francisca announces that her sister is to wed that
evening, Carlos and Juan each fears that he has lost to his rival.
Apparently, however, Angela is under the impression that the
bridegroom is to be Carlos, an aspiring poet who has been reviled
for not studying law by his father, Captain Valdivia. Carlos,
Diego, Juan, and Claudio, all masked, have already assembled to
witness the mysterious marriage that evening when Captain
Valdivia arrives. Angela assumes that he has come only to serve as
padrino for Carlos, but as Valdivia derides his own son, claiming
even that he is illegitimate, it becomes apparent that the father, who
has mistakenly received a *billet doux* which Angela intended for
Carlos, himself expects to become her husband. When Angela
haughtily refuses this match, Valdivia transfers his interest to Francisca to whom he offers a dowry of 14,000 ducats and the sole
inheritance of his estate in exchange for her hand in marriage.

Following a garden balcony scene in Act III which is designed to
show that Juan and Carlos are still ardently in love with Angela,
word arrives that Valdivia has died. As Claudio, Diego, Juan, and
Carlos appear in order before Alberto, the hidden Angela assumes
that they have come to ask for her hand in marriage, only to learn
that each of the four, pretending ignorance of Francisca's marriage, greedily solicits the hand of the wealthy widow. This is a
wicked blow to Angela's ego, and she corroborates the proberb
which provides the play's title as she bewails the decision of the previous evening by which the benefits she rejected were transferred to
Francisca. Jealousy prompts Angela to try to discourage by letter
all four pretenders from marrying Francisca. When Francisca
favors Juan, Carlos decides to marry Angela. Francisca, in
Lisardo's name, delivers the final curtain speech. This *comedia* will
serve years later as the inspiration for a play of much greater
quality, *Cuatro milagros de amor.*

CHAPTER 6

Religious Theater:
Comedias

U NDER the general rubric of religious theater, Mira wrote both *autos* and full-length *comedias*. The former will be studied separately in our next chapter, and we have classified the *comedias* as Biblical, devotional, or hagiographic. It appears abundantly evident that the least successful of these categories is the one devoted to dramatizing well-known Biblical themes and stories. The faithful rendition of these sources obviously imposed limitations on Mira's dramatic inventiveness. Valbuena Prat has judiciously noted that the two best plays in this category are *El arpa de David (The Harp of David)* and *El rico avariento (The Avaricious Rich Man)*.[1] Of particular interest is the fact that four of the five titles in this category seem clearly to reflect Mira's penchant for dramatizing the inconstancy and reversals of fortune, especially as they pertain to a royal favorite.

Two of the hagiographic plays are generally conceded to rank extremely high in Mira's dramatic production. Although its structure and organization leave much to be desired, the strength and majestic sweep of *El esclavo del demonio (The Devil's Slave)* have prompted Valbuena Prat unequivocally to label it as Mira's best play.[2] *La mesonera del cielo (The Innkeeper of Heaven)* must, by any standard, be considered Mira's second-best hagiographic effort.

The settings of the thirteen plays studied in this chapter, although predominantly Spanish and Portuguese, range from Biblical scenarios to contemporary Algerian prisons. While maintaining strict theological and doctrinal accuracy, Mira has constantly incorporated *comedia* techniques and conventions in order to inject as much relevance as possible for his contemporary audience.

I *Biblical Plays*

1. *El arpa de David (The Harp of David)*

Until edited masterfully by Anibal in 1925,[3] this dramatization of
the Biblical account of David's rise from shepherd to psalmist king
(Samuel, I and II) existed only in two Biblioteca Nacional manuscripts (Mss. 15.516 and 16.326). Although *El arpa de David* is
attributed to Mira by both manuscripts and in the catalogues of
Medel[4] and García de la Huerta,[5] Cotarelo[6] leans toward a Lopean
attribution because of the presence of a character named Lisardo,
an alleged pseudonym of Lope. Anibal devotes an extensive part of
his edition to a discussion of the occurrence of the name "Lisardo"
in several Golden Age literary works,[7] and his convincing argument
that Mira used it as his pseudonym serves as an important corner-
stone in Anibal's reclaiming for Mira several titles of recognized
merit.

References to the play in *La ventura de la fea*,[8] written probably
in the period 1610–16, in Cervantes' *Viaje del Parnaso (Voyage to
Parnasus)*,[9] whose prologue is dated June 14, 1613, and in Lope de
Vega's *Laurel de Apolo (Apollo's Laurel)*,[10] written between 1628
and 1630, support Mira's authorship and permit Anibal to set a
probable date of composition "within the two or three years immediately preceding July 14, 1613."[11]

The play opens with a display of King Saul's melancholic hypo-
chondria. His son Jonathan suggests that a certain shepherd, famous for his singing, be brought to attempt to relieve the King's
indisposition. David's song works the miraculous cure, and both
Jonathan and his sister Michal feel an instantaneous attraction for
the boy. His duty performed, David returns to his flock.

The remaining action faithfully dramatizes its Biblical source:
for heroically slaying the giant Goliath, David receives Michal's
hand in marriage and becomes the object of the vengeance of Saul,
made jealous by the populace's cheers of acclamation, "Saul has
conquered a thousand, and David has conquered ten thousand"
(see Samuel I, 18:7). Saved by Jonathan's friendship, David
ascends the throne upon receiving word that both Saul and Jonathan have died. He soon enters into an adulterous relationship with
Bathsheba and arranges for Uriah to meet his death at the
battlefront.

Pangs of conscience momentarily assail David following Uriah's departure, but, when news of his warrior's death arrives, he shamelessly decides to marry Bathsheba. When the Prophet Nathan predicts God's punishment for the King's crime, David proves himself truly contrite in a passage (vv. 3225–306) which is a rendering in *romance* form of Psalm 50. Nathan assures him that God's forgiveness has been granted, and David sets to the task of composing and singing songs of praise. In the last scene, he foretells Christ's death on the cross (v. 3377), a device found in several *autos* which use the Old Testament as their background. Lisardo closes the action with the apparently unkept promise of a second part.

2. *El clavo de Jael (Jael's Nail)*

In spite of the fact that Barrera lists this title among Mira's *sueltas,*[12] *El clavo de Jael* seems to exist only in an undated, mid-seventeenth-century manuscript in the Biblioteca Nacional (Ms. 15.331). With minor obeisance to the *comedia's* standard requirement of a love intrigue, Mira has faithfully dramatized the Biblical story found in Judges IV, according to which the beautiful Jael becomes the heroine of the oppressed tribe of Benjamin.

Distraught and weary after having been denied her share of the family inheritance by three brothers, Jael is taken in and generously provided for by the wealthy farmer Fineo, whose almost immediate marriage proposal is rejected until the time that he can share Jael's strong religious beliefs. Following scenes which display the military supremacy of the Canaanites, the voice of God reveals that Sisera, their military captain, will die at the hands of a woman. Even Sisera himself recounts a dream in which he meets his death through a nail driven into his temple by a celestial woman. When Ruben and the Prophetess Deborah visit Jael and request provisions to feed the soldiers of Israel, Fineo, in order to please his beloved Jael, complies and delivers them personally to the troops.

The forces of Sisera are suffering a complete rout as the last act begins. When Sisera falls from his chariot, Deborah has the opportunity to kill him but permits him to flee. Fineo's servant Simanco observes that as the fleeing Sisera approaches, Jael recognizes him and warmly offers him the hospitality of her tent for the night. From his hiding place, Simanco interprets this scene as one of blatant infidelity and departs to inform his master. He immediately encounters Fineo, who has returned from the victory of Israel.

Simanco embellishes his account by reporting that Jael's cheeks reddened when she saw her visitor and by repeating her actual words, that she was able to take him to her tent only because her husband was away. Fineo draws his sword, and, as he hovers in the doorway with thoughts of vengeance, he sees Jael take a nail from the wall and hammer it through the temple of Sisera, pinning him to the floor.

The followers of Israel come to celebrate Jael's heroism and the victory over the Canaanites. The triumphant Jael gives her own hand to Fineo and her maid Tamar's to Simanco as the curtain falls. Cotarelo[13] aptly notes the static quality of this play. Because Mira strictly adhered to the Biblical story, with the exception of the happy incorporation of Fineo and the two servants, not even the fact that much of its poetry is excellent could provide a framework for dramatic success.

3. El más feliz cautiverio, y los sueños de Josef
(The Happiest Captivity, and the Dreams of Joseph)

Barrera attributes to Mira a *suelta* titled *Los sueños de Faraón y más feliz cautiverio*.[14] Cotarelo, having mentioned the Barrera attribution, goes on to note that the play is considered to be anonymous by Mesonero and that it is not even mentioned by Medel or García de la Huerta. He concludes that the *comedia* is currently unknown.[15] However, the following entry in the study published by Ada Coe of *comedias* announced in Madrid's newspapers from 1661–1819 sheds some light on this matter:

MAS (EL) FELIZ CAUTIVERIO, Príncipe, 14–24 febrero 1784 (*Mem. Lit.*); Cruz, 15–21 enero 1787 (*Diario*). *El más feliz cautiverio y los sueños de Josef* (*Gaceta,* 1792); 9 febrero 1792 (*Diario*). *El más feliz cautiverio y sueños de Faraón,* Cruz, 29 marzo 1814 (*Diario*). *Los sueños de Josef vendido a los Ismaelitos y más feliz cautiverio,* Cruz, 25 dic. 1799 (*Diario*). *Los sueños de Josef,* drama sacro, Caños, 17, 19–21 marzo 1808 (*Diario*). *Faraón o José en Egipto,* Cruz, 25 dic. 1816 (*Diario*). *Los sueños de Josef* en *Máiquez,* 619, 762, 808.[16]

Miss Coe concludes by asking if all of these titles might not be variants for the same play. Paz y Melia documents the existence of Biblioteca Nacional Ms. 15.034, written in the late eighteenth century with a license for printing dated 1791 and entitled *El más feliz cautiverio y los sueños de José*.[17] We have read the printing for which this license was obviously granted (Madrid: Librería de Quiroga, 1792) and are led by thematic elements typical of Mira to include it in his canon. One inclines to see Mira's hand in the choice of another Biblical *privado* and in the recurrent motifs of envy and fortune. Rather pedestrian language would seem to indicate a youthful effort. The *comedia's* action does little more than recount the story of Joseph (Genesis 37–45) and would be appropriately entitled by each of the variants found in Coe's entry.

The haughty self-assurance of Joseph, favorite son of Jacob, is a thorn in the side of his half-brothers: Reuben, Simeon, Levi, Judah, and Isacar. When Joseph comes before them in the field and recounts two dreams which foretell that his brothers will one day obey and worship him, they fall upon him and leave him to die in a cistern. As two merchants approach, however, the brothers become fearful of fratricide and sell Joseph into slavery for thirty pieces of silver.

The scene now shifts to the Egyptian court, where the slave Joseph, already known for his ability to interpret dreams, rises mercurially to fame and power by foretelling from Pharaoh's dream the seven years of abundance to be followed by seven years of famine. Joseph is acclaimed savior of Egypt and named by Pharaoh to the status of *privado*. The famine has already struck as Act II opens. When word arrives that full Egyptian granaries are supplying relief to neighboring countries, Jacob's sons prepare for their voyage, leaving behind only Benjamin upon the orders of a father who will run no risk of losing his second favorite son. When Joseph receives the visit of his brothers who, not recognizing their benefactor, prostrate themselves at his feet, he sees that his dreams have come true. Noting his younger brother's absence, Joseph first threatens to imprison all of them until Benjamin is brought to him, but he finally relents and keeps only Simeon as a hostage. A sumptuous banquet is served for all the brothers when they return with Benjamin. As they prepare to depart again, Joseph orders placed in their luggage a precious goblet. In Act III, Pharaoh is attempting to retain Joseph in Egypt by marrying him to Asenet as the captured brothers are brought back, the goblet having been found in Benjamin's luggage. When Joseph remarks that the alleged thief will have to remain in Egypt as his slave, each of Joseph's vendors volunteers to stay in Benjamin's place, knowing that another such loss would be fatal to Jacob. Warmed by this filial love, and unable to restrain himself longer, Joseph reveals his identity to his brothers. With five years of famine still to come, Jacob is brought to Egypt to be reunited with Joseph, who marries Asenet.

4. *Los prodigios de la vara, y Capitán de Israel* *(The Prodigies of the Rod, and Captain of Israel)*

Printed only in *Parte XXXVII* of the *Escogidas* (Madrid: Melchor Alegre, 1671), this dramatization of the Biblical account (Exodus 2-14) of the ascendancy enjoyed by Moses over Pharaoh's court, his escape from death, and his return to lead the Hebrews from their Egyptian captivity is largely couched in terms of Mira's favorite theme, the fallen favorite.

An opening expository dialogue between the envious courtesans Nacor and Eliacer focuses on the stunning victory just achieved over Ethiopia by Moses, commander of Egypt's military forces. When the war with Ethiopia was going badly, an oracle told Pharaoh that victory would be his if he named a Hebrew commander of his forces. Eliacer also recalls omens of national disaster growing out of Moses' great ascendancy. When the triumphant military commander enters and delivers a long account of his victory, Pharaoh confers upon him the great distinction of his personal friendship; but in spite of this generosity, he does not know how to interpret the magnitude of Moses' loyalty and ponders: "o es inmensa lealtad, o traición suma" ("it's either immense loyalty, or supreme treachery", p. 160). This suspicion feeds on complaints concerning the excessive royal favors heaped upon a Hebrew, complaints which are filtered through to Pharaoh by Nacor and Eliacer, who counsel Moses' death. Pharaoh resolutely resists renouncing his friendship with Moses.

Criticism develops also on the side of the Hebrews. Datán reveals that many fellow Hebrews consider Moses responsible for the prolongation of their captivity, prompting Aaron to propose a typical comment on *privanza* which could have been lifted verbatim from any of Mira's treatments of the fallen favorite:

Ha, privanza, privanza,	Oh, court favor, court favor,
objeto de envidiosos y enemigos.	object of the envious and of enemies.
Si el que pide no alcanza	If he who requests doesn't receive
enemigos se vuelven los amigos.	friends turn into enemies.
Triste del más privado,	Sad is the greatest favorite

pues del pequeño al grande es envidiado.	since the least to the greatest is envied.

(pp.162-63)

Pharaoh, suspecting a motive of envy, has resisted still more demands for the deposition of Moses. He has even become enamored of Aaron's sister María, and enlists the services of Masar, a turncoat Hebrew who is the play's *gracioso,* to attempt to win her favor. Finally, however, Pharaoh hears what he takes to be proof of the accusations leveled against Moses and of the feared presage that a Hebrew will overthrow the Egyptian government. Pharaoh confronts Moses, accuses him of disloyalty, and, too impatient to await the official executioner, he commissions Masar to kill Moses. By divine intervention, Masar is blinded and Pharaoh rendered mute until Moses has heeded the words of a heavenly voice to flee from Egypt to serve God in more important endeavors. He flees to Midian, and there marries Zipporah.

An angel appears to Moses while he is laboring in the fields. The miracle of the bush which burns but which is not consumed by fire convinces Moses that he is in the presence of God. Interestingly, the Biblical affirmation of God's divinity, "Yo soy el que soy" ("I AM THAT I AM," Exodus 2:14), is similar to the formula used by Golden Age nobles to affirm their honor.[18] The Lord names Moses leader of Israel and instructs him to return and demand from Pharaoh the freedom of the Hebrews. In the event that the Egyptians are not cooperative, God imbues Moses' shepherd's staff with miracle-working properties, including the power to separate the waters of the Red Sea.

In Act III, Masar is being pursued by Pharaoh, dagger in hand, because of the failure of his intercession with María. The resistance offered by María together with the ire and distrust caused by the actions and departure of Moses have brought about a severe repression against the already downtrodden Hebrews. Upon his return to Egypt, Moses identifies Aaron in a garden scene only after a conventional series of cloak-and-sword suspicions and threats takes place. Pharaoh has deaf ears for Moses' request to free the Hebrews, and, irked by his own latest failure with María, his edicts are more oppressive than ever. He draws a dagger to kill Moses, but smoke and fire erupt to deter him. When water is brought to quench his thirst, it is transformed into blood. Leprosy, locusts, pestilence, and plague run rampant in Egypt, afflicting all but the Hebrews. Still not convinced of Moses' divine mission, Pharaoh orders the Egyptian forces, now led by Nacor, his new *privado,* to follow the fleeing Hebrews between the parted waters of the Red Sea. Moses touches the waters with his staff and the pursuers are all killed except for Masar, who limps repentant into Moses' camp as the curtain falls.

A sequel, of which nothing is known, is announced in the play's last lines. Although it lacks dramatic unity, *Los prodigios de la vara* is successful in portraying faithfully several moments of the Biblical account of Moses' life. It is perhaps most interesting as another testimony of Mira's tendency to infuse in his religious theater the language and the conventions of the *comedia* and to show his preference for subjects which permit development of the theme of the royal favorite who is tumbled from the pinnacle of success by envy, circumstance, and the inconstancy of fortune.

5. *El rico avariento (The Avaricious Rich Man)*

Cast in a religious context, this play is still another study of Mira's favorite theme, the contrast of prosperous and adverse fortune. *El rico avariento* was first published in 1655.[19] Two years later it appeared in *Parte IX* of the *Escogidas* (Madrid: Gregorio Rodríguez, 1657) under a different title: *La vida y muerte de San Lázaro (The Life and Death of St. Lazarus);*[20] with Act III reworked, it also exists in a 1688 manuscript (Biblioteca Nacional Ms. 16.805). It was edited under the longer title in the 1951 M.A. thesis of Robert Jeffers Bininger.[21]

As noted by Anibal, economy and distribution of plan are "qualities especially marked in Mira's *El rico avariento,* or *La vida y muerte de San Lázaro,* and in his *Capitán Belisario,* in both of which the plan of procedure, with its logical progression of episodes, is so clearly marked out that it almost becomes a fault through allowing the structure to be too clearly seen."[22] In its simplicity of structure, this is one of Mira's most striking efforts. Competition among three suitors for the hand of the beautiful and virtuous Abigail is a light veneer to this dramatic amplification of the parable of the rich man and Lazarus (Luke 16:19–31).

The reversal of worldly fortune could not be greater for the two male leads. Nabal, as the action begins, is destitute. Lazarus, Abigail's second suitor, a striking contrast to Nabal both economically and spiritually, twice in the first act uses white lies in an attempt to remedy Nabal's poverty. He first hands to Nabal a purse containing money which he falsely claims to have found while leaving church. His instructions are for Nabal to keep the contents if he is unable to discover their rightful owner. Later, Lazarus feigns having neglected repayment to Nabal's father of a debt of 1500 *escudos,* which he now delivers to Nabal. Although Nabal frequently has sworn that, with money, he would be more magnanimous and liberal than Lazarus, this sudden boon produces the opposite result. Rather than expressing gratitude, Nabal inveighs against Lazarus for having neglected for so long the payment of this debt.

A guardian angel and the Devil intervene at the close of each act. In the first, they outline the rest of the action. The angel, in order to test Nabal's promises, asks God to grant him great wealth. The Devil announces that if Nabal becomes rich, Lazarus will be dragged down into abject misery. In Act II, Nabal's fortune is multiplied as his purchases of livestock and lands prove to be extravagantly bountiful, while news arrives of a pestilence which has totally destroyed Lazarus' flocks. As news of contrasting fortune mounts, Lazarus' attitude remains one of gratitude to God, while Nabal becomes more avaricious. Great treasure is found on land purchased by Nabal, while Lazarus' crops are devastated by locusts. In the first act, Lazarus was Abigail's obvious choice over Nabal and the vain Joseph. Now, however, when Nabal, buttressed by his immense wealth, requests her hand in marriage, she submissively announces that she will, in all things, follow the wishes of her father, who is quick to grant Nabal's request. As Nabal refuses to give food to the starving Lazarus and rebukes his wife for attempting to be kind to him, the guardian angel and the Devil arrive dressed as beggars to assay the situation. The Devil is pleased to be rebuffed by Nabal, but dismayed when the pious Lazarus, bereft of all worldly riches but his health, offers to carry him on his shoulders to the hospital if that will help in any way. As the second act ends, the Devil announces that he will bring Lazarus to his knees by having him contract leprosy, while the angel is confident that Lazarus will surpass Job in his patient acceptance of any adversity.

In the last act the avarice of the odious Nabal reaches its acme. The wheel of fortune having made its customary half rotation,

Lazarus easily justifies the trust placed in him by the guardian angel, while Nabal fulfills the most dire predictions of how he would mishandle his immense wealth. In an ending no better than Mira's typical efforts, Nabal has his death by apoplexy announced to him while asleep. Both he and Lazarus die unceremoniously, Lazarus to be borne to Limbo on the shoulders of angels and Nabal to be dragged by demons into eternal fire. In an ending reminiscent of an *auto sacramental,* the Devil and the angel close the action. The Devil sounds the moral: that damnation identical to Nabal's awaits men whose spirits are controlled by avarice and gluttony. The angel, in Lazarus' name, invites the spectators to the celestial tables and concludes with the only known use of Mira's own name in one of his plays, as he emphasizes the author's typical didactic thrust:

Y aquí acaba la comedia	And here ends the play
de Nabal, cuyo prodigio	about Nabal, whose mystery
escribió Mira de Mescua	Mira de Amescua wrote
para escarmiento de muchos.	as a lesson for many.
Perdonad las faltas nuestras.	Please pardon our mistakes.

(ed. Bininger, vv. 3008–12)

In Act I, Nabal includes in the lamentation of his ill fortune seven *redondillas* (octosyllabic quatrains with rhyme *abba*) which are easily recognizable as antecedents of Segismundo's famous monologue in Calderón's *La vida es sueño.*[23] The same passage is the first of three in this play studied by Gregg to elucidate Mira's use of the life-river equation which is so beautifully poeticized in Jorge Manrique's famous *Coplas.*[24]

II   *Devotional Plays*

1.   *El amparo de los hombres (The Protector of Men)*

The only known published copy of this play is the *suelta* owned by the Bayerische Staatsbibliothek in Munich. It was edited as an M.A. thesis in 1951 by Wilfred Wilenius.[25] As demonstrated by José María Bella,[26] a pious legend of the thirteenth century, known in Spain during the early seventeenth century, seems to have served as Mira's principal source. Cotarelo is of the opinion that this *suelta* was printed at the same time and place as the other found only in Munich, *La adúltera virtuosa*. He suggests that they were both published by the same printer in Seville in the second half of the seventeenth century.[27]

Federico, Italian soldier from the city of Apulia in the province of Naples, has just distinguished himself for valor in the battle of Pavia (historically, 1525). His reward has been limited to strong letters of recommendation designed to help him obtain favor and a position in Spain. Unfortunately, this boon is not translatable into tangible benefits as he and his starved servant, Marín, arrive in Genoa. Coincidentally, they come in contact with the wealthy profligate Carlos, who, impressed with Federico's valor, takes him into his service.

While the two men are on the way to a meeting with Carlos' fiancée, the beautiful Julia, Carlos notices that the light which illuminates a statue of the Virgin has gone out. Since the Virgin Mary is the special object of Carlos' devotion, he goes to procure a new light and appoints Federico to receive from Julia a picture of herself. Federico is instantly taken by Julia's beauty. As he muses that he would give anything to have her, the alert Devil appears and lays out the conditions for the traditional Faustian transaction: wealth, power, fame, and the lady . . . in return for Federico's soul.

As Act II begins, the Wheel of Fortune, cited directly several times in this play, has already reversed the socioeconomic status of Federico and Carlos. Having lost his fortune through careless and extravagant spending, Carlos has retained nothing more than an image of the Virgin. In his campaign to win Julia for himself, Federico easily enlists the full support of her father Horacio, who had long been annoyed by Carlos' profligacy and who is, until the play's dénouement, governed exclusively by self-interest. Julia, however, cannot be tempted; her love for Carlos remains unshaken.

Federico appeals to the Devil, who admits that Carlos cannot be killed because, in spite of his sinful ways, he has retained a strong devotion to the Virgin. Federico, leagued deceitfully with the Devil, tries to undermine Carlos' devotion. During a meeting held in the wilderness, the Devil succeeds in having Carlos renounce God, but he is unable to wrench from him a renunciation of the Virgin. Noting that the day is ending without an expression of his devotion, Carlos leaves a distraught Federico and a defeated Devil and gallops off to the hermitage of the Virgen de la Candelaria where, by coincidence, Julia and her father are also paying a nocturnal visit.

Father and daughter hear the approaching hoofbeats and hide. Kneeling, Carlos begs forgiveness of the Virgin and the Christ child. As in the thirteenth-century source, Christ is at first stern and does not want to obey his Mother's plea that He pardon Carlos. When the Virgin kneels before her Son to beg His clemency, Christ accedes and pardons Carlos, calling her, as Carlos has before: "Protector of men." Witness to his miraculous pardon, Horacio turns his fortune over to Carlos and welcomes him as his son-in-law. A servant arrives with the news that Federico has entered the Order of St. Francis. Good having resoundingly triumphed over evil, the action terminates.

Cotarelo has commented: "The plot of this *comedia* is somewhat similar to that of *El esclavo del demonio,* and could almost be called a first-draft outline of this famous work."[28] There are obvious similarities in the intervention of the Devil and the pact he makes successfully with one character but fails to make with another, but since the first known edition of *El esclavo* was published in 1612, the precedence suggested by Cotarelo must be denied if Anibal and Bella are correct in assuming, on the basis of knowledge of Italy expressed in the play, that it was written following Mira's return from Naples in 1616.[29]

2. *Lo que puede el oír misa (What Hearing Mass Can Do)*

This play has the distinction of appearing in the first volume of the famous *Escogidas* (Madrid: Domingo García y Morrás, 1652). It also exists in manuscript and in another printing, both from the eighteenth century.[30] Pickering, who has provided the only modern edition in his 1947 M.A. thesis,[31] uses the low percentage of *quintillas* to hypothesize a date of composition rather late in Mira's career.

Here we find blended the folkloric tradition of divine intervention on behalf of one who unfailingly attends Mass every day and a slightly romanticized version of the ill-fated historical marriage of the Infante, García Fernández, son of the famous tenth-century Fernán González, first Count of Castile. The intrigue involves the enthusiastically reciprocal love of the Infanta Violante and of the protagonist, Sancho Osorio, which is threatened by a rival in Fortún, *privado* of the Infante. Fortún's sister, Blanca, shares a mutual love with the Infante.

The theme expressed in the title is evident in a different context in each of the three acts. When Fortún, in Act I, challenges Sancho to a duel at an hour when predictably Sancho will feel obliged to attend the only Mass of the day, thus counting on a victory by default and the consequent embarrassment of his rival, an angel takes Sancho's place and wounds Fortún. In Act II, folklore provides the source for Fortún's plot to eliminate his competition. He uses his influence to cause the Infante to send Sancho to a nearby castle with a message designed to have its bearer killed upon arrival. A stop on the way to hear Mass saves Sancho's life as the impatient Fortún hastens to the castle to gloat over the success of his scheme only to meet with the fate intended for his rival.

The third act is devoted largely to the impetuous marriage of the Infante (in exile because of his part in the death of Fortún) to Argentina, a French woman on a pilgrimage with her father to Santiago de Compostela, and the bloody revenge taken on her and the French lover with whom she has run off between the ceremony and the consummation of their marriage. Not surprisingly in a tenth-century setting, a Moorish attack is announced. It is, however, time to hear Mass — and again, an angel replaces Sancho on the battlefield and is instrumental in routing the foe. As he descends from the hermitage where Mass had been celebrated, Sancho first interprets the accolades he receives to be ironic jibes for having missed the battle, but when the Count offers to him Violante's hand in marriage, he realizes that God has once again defended his honor. Upon learning that the Infante has fought valiantly in disguise because of his exile and the violent displeasure of his father over his unapproved and capricious marriage, the Count pardons his son and the play ends, implying in its last lines that it is a dramatized version of Castilian history.

Typical of Mira is the episodic nature of the play. An interesting anachronism is found in a reference made by the *gracioso* Mirabel to syphilis (v. 2636), unknown in Europe until late in the fifteenth century. Also typical of Mira is the failure to resolve all of the subplots in the dénouement.

An episode in the *Crónica general* refers to the miraculous power derived from attending Mass; and Vélez de Guevara's *La devoción de la misa (Devotion to Mass)* contains thematic parallels to Mira's play.[32] In the eighteenth century the theme is again treated in Antonio de Zamora's *Por oír misa y dar cebada nunca se perdió jornada (A Day Was Never Lost Hearing Mass or Feeding Barley).*

III   Hagiographic Plays

1.   El animal profeta (The Prophetic Animal)

In three seventeenth-century manuscripts, one of them dated 1631, this play is attributed to Mira. It was presented by the company of Juan de Morales on June 24, 1630.[33] All of its known published versions, however, starting with a now unknown volume seen by Juan Isidro Yáñez Fajardo,[34] including several *sueltas,* and extending to Menéndez Pelayo's Academy edition of Lope's plays,[35] are attributed not to Mira but to Lope de Vega. Cotarelo admits that the early manuscripts represent strong support for attribution to Mira, but he unhesitatingly accepts Menéndez Pelayo's judgment based on the play's internal evidence and catalogues it among Mira's apocryphal works. Beristain de Souza provides the exotic information that the play was translated into Nahuatl.[36] *El animal profeta* was edited critically twice in 1973, in the doctoral dissertations of Shirley Tock[37] and Bonnie Wilds,[38] both of whom favor attribution to Mira. This hagiographic play deals with the legend of Saint Julian the Hospitaller, venerated as the patron of hospitality and safe travel as early as the twelfth century, whose life inspired literary treatments in the *Decameron* as well as by La Fontaine and Flaubert.

While hunting in Albania, where he lives with his parents, Julian is told by a mysterious voice that he will kill his mother and father. When a deer, wounded fatally by Julian, reiterates the prophecy, Julian abruptly departs, leaving distraught and bewildered parents and a furious sweetheart. In distant Ferrara, where he expects to evade the prophecy, he has saved the life of the Duke and been awarded for his heroism the hand of Laurencia, who has also been the object of the attentions of Federico, the Duke's brother. Federico's persistent interest in Laurencia and mysterious words uttered in her sleep by the innocent bride arouse jealousy in Julian. During his brief absence, his elderly parents arrive, having discovered his new home after long and diligent searching. Exhausted, they lie down to sleep in Julian's bed. The suspicious husband returns to check on his wife and, upon discovering two people in bed in the darkened room, kills them. The remainder of the action consists of a journey to Rome to seek clemency from the Pope and a penitent pilgrimage to Jerusalem, France, and Spain. Accompanied by his loyal wife, Julian finally settles in Calabria, where he ministers to the poor and infirm. Satan vies with the Child Jesus for Julian's soul which, of course, is ultimately saved and ascends heaven-bound.

The verse "ser esclavo del demonio" ("to be a slave of the Devil"; ed. Tock, v. 2789) may be more than incidentally reminiscent of Mira's masterpiece. Wilds convincingly notes: "The intense dramatic and religious force . . . first projected in . . . *El esclavo del demonio* is more smoothly developed later in *El animal profeta.*"[39]

2. *El esclavo del demonio (The Devil's Slave)*

Although many scholars have not agreed that *El esclavo del demonio* is Mira's best play, none can dispute the fact that it is currently his best known. Ángel Valbuena Prat considers Mira to be a dramatist who has "succeeded brilliantly in a single work, *El esclavo del demonio,*"[40] while Ruth Lee Kennedy characterizes the work generally accepted as Mira's masterpiece as "a formless, chaotic mass."[41] *El esclavo del demonio* served as a model for certain scenes of Calderón's *El mágico prodigioso*[42] *(The Prodigious Magician)* and *La devoción de la cruz (Devotion to the Cross)* and was adapted by Matos, Cáncer, and Moreto for their collaborative effort, *Caer para levantar (Falling in Order to Arise).*[43]

Published first in the *Tercera parte de las comedias de Lope de Vega y otros autores* (Barcelona: Sebastián de Cormellas, 1612) and again the following year in another edition of the same volume (Madrid: Miguel Serrano de Vargas, 1613), it has also appeared in a volume dated 1654[44] and in several *sueltas*. It was first edited critically by Buchanan in 1905;[45] it has been edited by Hurtado and Palencia;[46] Valbuena Prat edited the play three times;[47] and we have prepared an edition for publication in the near future.[48] Professor George Haley, in connection with his work in progress on the theater in Salamanca in the early years of the seventeenth century, has provided in a letter dated March 27, 1972, the following information concerning the play's performance: "A play which was almost certainly Mira de Amescua's *El esclavo del demonio,* as I hope to demonstrate in a forthcoming study, was performed under a different title at Salamanca in 1605." Certainly the most tragic performance was given in Seville's Coliseo on Wednesday, November 12, 1698.[49] A serious fight among students earlier in the day caused the official in charge of the *cazuela* (women's gallery) to lock it as a precaution against infiltration by scandal-minded youths during the performance. After he locked the solitary exit door, the official left, intending to return to reopen it at the conclusion of the play. The spectators knew well that the Coliseo had twice burned down, and, as the long *comedia* did not end until after dusk, when fireworks were used for stage effects in the third act, and smoke from torches was noted at the exits of the *corral,* a woman shouted that the theater was burning. Her co-spectators panicked so that before the official returned with the key to release the women, several were killed in their frantic attempt to escape. Estimates of the women killed run as high as twelve. The next day a prohibition was issued against further staging of plays in the Coliseo or in any other part of Seville.

El esclavo del demonio is based on the Portuguese hagiographic legend of Frei Gil de Santarem (b. *ca.* 1190), whose story is related clearly to the Faust legend. Having sold his soul to the Devil in exchange for knowledge of the secrets of necromancy, the Fray Gil of legend repents following two encounters with a supernatural vision and, through the intervention of the Virgin, recovers his signed agreement, nullifying the impious pact. Mira could have been inspired by the published version of Fray Hernando del Castillo in the *Primera parte de la historia general de Sancto Domingo y su Orden de Predicadores* (Madrid, 1584)[50] or by the version included in the *Adición a la Tercera parte del Flos Sanctorum* (Huesca, 1588)[51] whose author, Alonso de Villegas, indicates the work of Fray Hernando as his own source.

When Marcelo announces his intention of marrying his elder daughter, Lisarda, to don Sancho of Portugal, at the same time approving the request made by her sister, Leonor, to enter a convent, he runs afoul of some strong-willed opposition. Lisarda not only refuses to accept her Portuguese suitor, but insists that she will marry don Diego de Meneses, who happens to have killed her brother, Marcelo's only son. The pious Leonor suggests that Marcelo, who has cursed his rebellious daughter, seek the intervention of saintly don Gil to dissuade don Diego from his interest in Lisarda.

Shortly thereafter, don Diego receives a note from Lisarda in which it is proposed that they flee together that very night. Later, while half-way up a ladder leading to Lisarda's room, Diego is spotted by don Gil, whose words are so potently persuasive that Diego immediately descends, repents, and departs. Exultant in the pride of having saved a soul, don Gil suddenly feels tempted by the ladder which don Diego has left. After a brief battle with his conscience, his latent prurience emerges victorious and Gil climbs the ladder. When he has ascended, the ladder is taken down by don Diego's servant, Domingo, unaware of his master's departure, who proceeds to sleep during the vigil with which he has been charged. When the vacillating Gil has second thoughts about his evil plan, the absence of the ladder and words he hears spoken by the sleeping Domingo, heavily tinged with fatalistic reminiscences of the doctrine of predestination, lead him to believe that his soul has already been damned.[52] Soon after, Gil emerges with Lisarda. As he reveals his identity, he deceitfully tells Lisarda that he was put up to this infamy by don Diego. The first inclination of the dishonored girl is to return to her home, but Gil urges her to follow him into a world which will deny them nothing now that God has released them from his hand. Seeing in this event the fulfillment of her father's curse, and considering herself to have been cruelly deceived by don Diego, Lisarda allows herself to be taken away, swearing vengeance on the wrongfully accused author of her disgrace.

The following morning, as Marcelo tells Leonor that she will have to forsake her plans for a religious life and marry in Lisarda's place, a servant arrives with the discarded note that Lisarda had sent to don Diego. Everyone infers that she has been abducted by her former suitor. Thus it is with stupefaction that they receive a visit from a repentant don Diego, anxious to achieve peace with the family he has offended and to secure the hand of Lisarda in marriage. Convinced that the lovers are already together and that it would be better for Lisarda to be Diego's wife than his concubine, Marcelo agrees to the marriage but refuses to attend the ceremony or ever again to set eyes on Lisarda. As father and daughter prepare to depart for their country home, the details of the play's subplot are advanced. Don Sancho of Portugal has come secretly to verify his fiancée's beauty. Upon seeing Leonor, he falls in love with her, although he realizes that she is not his intended bride. When don Diego arrives with a carriage to pick up Lisarda according to the agreement he thought he had concluded with Marcelo, he finds the house empty. Considering himself to have been deceived by Marcelo, Diego closes the first act with the promise that he will steal Lisarda from her father's grasp.

As Act II opens, Gil and Lisarda, both dressed in men's clothes, are bandits. Lisarda, now the more violent of the two, reveals her intention to kill don Diego, who owns a small forest close to Marcelo's summer home. When the noise of approaching travelers reaches them, they don masks. Marcelo, Leonor, and their servant Beatriz are their victims! While Gil lasciviously admires Leonor's beauty, Lisarda announces her intention to kill them both. Following magnanimous offers, first by Marcelo and then by Leonor, each to die in exchange for the freedom of the other, Gil, who is anxious to enjoy Leonor's favors, proposes that they be allowed to ransom their lives with gold. Marcelo offers a coffer which contains the jewels of his daughter Lisarda, who in an astonishing change, kneels and begs him to bless her as if he were her father. After he complies and is allowed to leave with Leonor, Lisarda reveals that she is not repentant as yet but that she wanted to request pardon "para tenello alcanzado / cuando mudare la vida" ("to have it attained / when I change my life," ed. Castañeda, vv. 1391–92).

As Lisarda goes off to bury the coffer, Gil soliloquizes on the ardent passion awakened in him by Leonor. When he ventures to offer his soul for a chance to make love to Leonor, the Devil instantly appears to negotiate a traditional pact: he will teach necromancy to Gil and arrange for him to have Leonor, on the condition that Gil will renounce God and agree to be his slave. Opining that he has already complied with virtually all the conditions imposed by the Devil, who claims ironically to be named Angelio, Gil readily accedes. As Gil is escorted off-stage by two other slaves, Lisarda returns. Gil is presented to her with the traditional "S" and "clavo" branded on his forehead, and in her presence, the new *esclavo* reads aloud the text of the pact. When alone with Gil, Lisarda expresses interest in learning necromancy. She is not bothered by the need to renounce God, but she would be unable to renounce the Virgin Mary, on whom she will have to rely if she decides to repent.

A shepherd named·Constancio arrives to announce that a slave, who is captain of a group of bandits, has abducted his daughter Lísida. As a group prepares to leave in pursuit of the bandits, the amorous subplot is complicated and confused by the arrival of the Prince of Portugal, whose name, coincidentally, is also don Sancho. He is recognized by the first don Sancho, who becomes jealous as he sees his prince attracted to Leonor. The Prince has come officially to solicit the aid of the saintly don Gil for his ailing father, the King of Portugal. Captured by the bandit Gil, don Diego attempts to save himself by employing the same words once used on him with such miraculous effect by his captor, but to no avail. Lisarda returns, recognizes don Diego, aims a pistol at him, and pulls the trigger — but the gun miraculously does not fire. Impressed by this and concerned with her ultimate repentance, Lisarda pardons don Diego. She next frees the captive Lísida and gives to her the coffer which had been taken from Marcelo. Lisarda's repentance progresses rapidly as she concludes the second act by ordering the peasant Arsindo to brand her and sell her for thirty *escudos* to the landowner of that area, her own father.

As the inconstant Leonor confesses to Beatriz that she almost became enamored of the second don Pedro, Marcelo arrives to confirm plans for her marriage to the first one. The search party returns with two captives, don Diego and Domingo. Marcelo orders them imprisoned. Arsindo arrives with Lisarda, dressed as a slave with her face branded beyond recognition. Impressed by her humility, Marcelo buys her. Back in the mountains, the Prince has been captured by Gil. To disabuse don Sancho of the false idea he has of the miracle worker he has been seeking, the "saint" reveals his identity and, before freeing them, relieves his captives of their horses and a valuable chain. When Gil reminds Angelio that he still has not fulfilled the promise to deliver Leonor, the figure of a woman leads him to a cave. Upon emerging to enjoy Leonor by the light of day, Gil discovers that he is accompanied by a skeleton draped with a mantle. Disillusioned, he wants to revoke his pact and requests the return of his signed agreement. When Angelio refuses, Gil invokes the aid of the only divine agent he has not renounced, his Guardian Angel. In an airborne battle made possible by stage machinery, the Angel wrests the parchment from the Devil and returns it to Gil, redeeming the sinner who promises to astound the world with his penitence.

A sudden shift of scene reveals that Prince Sancho, now hopelessly in love with Leonor, has attempted to pass himself off to Marcelo as the fiancé originally intended for his daughter. The lamentations of the real fiancé are silenced immediately, however, by news that the King of Portugal has died. The scheming Prince now reveals his identity and receives the hand of Leonor, who will be Portugal's next queen. The subplot having been happily resolved, the penitent Gil enters with don Diego and Domingo. His full confession establishes don Diego's innocence and recounts the perdition, repentance, and salvation of Lisarda, who is discovered, more beautiful than ever, kneeling in death. Gil departs to join the Dominican Order, a grave is prepared for Lisarda, and Leonor leaves to occupy the Portuguese throne.

From the summary, it is obvious that the tedious subplot detracts substantially from the *comedia's* dramatic coherence,[53] and the acts of penitence which won salvation for Gil in the hagiographic sources are missing here. These items may have been obstacles to a favorable acceptance of the play which, ironically, was apparently performed far less frequently than its less magnificent but better organized recasting, *Caer para levantar.* It is the starkness, the force, the sudden — sometimes dramatically unjustified — transformations, and the generous absolution of sin and glory of salvation which account for the grandeur and fame of this uneven *comedia de santos.*

3. *El mártir de Madrid (The Martyr of Madrid)*

This play, which has never been published, exists in one stringently censured Biblioteca Nacional manuscript copy (Ms. Res. 107) on which are inscribed *aprobaciones* spanning the years 1619–41 to authorize productions in Madrid, Zaragoza, and Granada, and in the 1974 dissertation edition of Henry A. Linares.[54] As noted by Cotarelo[55] and Ruth Lee Kennedy,[56] *El mártir de Madrid* is an intermediate link in a long chain of rather mediocre plays on the same general theme beginning with Lope de Vega's *Los mártires de Madrid,* and including *No hay reino como el de Dios (There Is No Kingdom Like God's),* a collaborative venture by Cáncer, Moreto, and Matos,[57] and ending with *La gran casa de Meca (The Great House of Mecca),* possibly by Antonio Granada y Vanegas. An account published in 1601 by the historian Antonio Herrera y Tordesillas (1559–1625) of the martyrdom in 1580 of a Madrilenian named Pedro has been convincingly proposed by José M. Bella as Mira's direct source.[58]

The action opens with a violent scene in which Álvaro Ramírez beats one son, Pedro, while another, Fernando, tries to calm his father's ire. A bailiff interrupts the family squabble and attempts to arrest Pedro for crimes he has committed, but the culprit escapes from Madrid and flees to Valencia, where he presents himself in the house of Clemencia, his brother's fiancée. To his surprise, he is taken for Fernando by Clemencia who, nevertheless, notes that his is not the face of a picture alleged to be of Fernando. Considering herself to have been deceived, she plans to elope to Barcelona with another lover, don Juan. Pedro thwarts Clemencia's willing abduction by wounding don Juan and by replacing him, his deceitful substitution made the easier by Clemencia's enjoinder that her companion not talk as they set out for Barcelona.

Fernando arrives in Valencia that night to find a wounded don Juan. Apprised of Clemencia's abduction, Fernando sets out in pursuit. On the road to Barcelona, Pedro has shown his face to Clemencia, who still thinks he is Fernando. When the real Fernando overtakes them, however, Clemencia identifies him through the picture and Pedro's treachery is discovered. As the brothers begin to fight, both are wounded and, along with Clemencia, who is dressed in male attire, are taken captive by Moorish pirates.

In Algiers, the three prisoners are entrusted by the Moorish princess Celaura to the care of the servant Trigueros, who is posing as a *morisco* captured in Spain. Álvaro journeys to Algiers in an effort to ransom his sons. Although the Moorish king is willing to permit him to ransom both, Celaura, who has fallen in love with Pedro, succeeds in convincing her father to free only one. As she expected, after a battle with his paternal conscience, Álvaro decides to ransom Fernando. Pedro, outraged by this decision, renounces his faith in Christ.

In Act III, Álvaro, Fernando, and Clemencia are fleeing from a Moorish skiff manned by Pedro, who now goes by the name of Hamete. Pedro captures and returns with his prisoners and cruelly advocates severe punishment for them. Trigueros, charged with guarding the prisoners, is overheard confessing that he has always been a Christian. He is condemned to death by Pedro. This example of a poor servant who prefers death to renunciation of his faith makes a deep impression on Pedro and sets in motion his ultimate repentance. Following a long speech in which Pedro states his origins and proclaims his faith in Christ, the King orders him crucified. Even in the throes of death, Pedro continues to preach his Christian faith in front of Álvaro, Fernando, Clemencia, and the Moors. Impressed by his constancy and valor, the King frees the Christian captives and magnanimously orders Fernando to wed Clemencia.

4. *La mesonera del cielo (The Innkeeper of Heaven)*

Printed first under this title in *Parte XXXIX* of the *Escogidas* (Madrid: Fernández de Buendía, 1673) and subsequently in several *sueltas* under the title *El ermitaño galán, y mesonera del cielo (The Gallant Hermit, and . . .)*, this hagiographic *comedia* was edited critically in the dissertation of Karl Gregg[59] and published in a modern edition by José Bella in 1972.[60] From the middle of the eighteenth century, the title found in the *sueltas* was frequently confused with Juan de Zabaleta's *El hermitaño galán,* published in *Parte X* of *Nuevo teatro de comedias varias de diferentes autores* (Madrid: Imprenta Real, 1658). As Cotarelo demonstrated in 1931,[61] the two plays are independent creations inspired by a common source, Pedro de Rivadeneyra's *Flos sanctorum.* On the basis of a study of the play's versification, Gregg proposes 1620?–1632?[62] as a probable range for its date of composition.

In Alexandria, on the day of his planned marriage to Lucrecia, Abraham decides not to go through with the wedding, contending that a woman's beauty would be an obstacle to his service to God. When Lucrecia hears of Abraham's change of heart and of his decision to depart into the wilderness, she courageously resolves to follow him and regain his love. In a parallel theme, Alejandro seeks the hand of María in marriage. Artemio, her uncle and guardian, renders a conditional consent, contingent upon the approval of his brother Abraham. The love intrigue is filled out by Leonato, who learns in Thebes that his beloved Lucrecia has departed for Alexandria to marry. Disconsolate, Leonato sets out for Alexandria.

Artemio, María, and Alejandro find Abraham soliloquizing on the happiness he has found in the wilderness. Although grieved to learn that Lucrecia has become lost while searching for him, he insists on the impossibility of their marriage, since he is not capable of serving two masters: God and love. While overtly he neither approves nor disapproves of the marriage of María and Alejandro,[63] his words on matrimony and the example of his own life lead María to renounce plans to marry Alejandro and to follow Abraham into the mountains to serve God at his side. Alejandro, in his turn, pursues María as the first act ends, thinking less at this point of marriage than of simple physical possession.

Two years of hermit-like existence have been shared by Abraham, his servant Pantoja, and María, when Satan appears and attempts to rekindle Abraham's passion. After a conventional account of his fall from heaven, only lightly masked in metaphor, helps Abraham to recognize the identity of his visitor, Lucrecia, having spent all this time searching for Abraham, falls on a hillside and rolls, bloodied and unconscious, to Abraham's feet. Crafty Satan leaves them alone, and during Lucrecia's unconsciousness, Abraham fights back temptation. She does not recognize him when she revives, but he gradually reveals his identity through veiled references to their broken plans and his flight to the wilderness. He counsels Lucrecia to leave the wilderness and take another husband, but when he fully reveals his identity, she resolves never to cease her efforts to win him back. Unsuccessful in his attack on Abraham, Satan now sets his sights on María. At his incitation, Alejandro, who has been pursuing María, enters through her window, conquers her resistance, and seduces her. His lust satiated, Alejandro abandons the fallen woman who, reminiscent of other sinners in Mira's theater, resolves as follows:

... voy, perdida el alma,	... I'm going, now that my soul has been lost,
a que se pierda el cuerpo.	to have my body lose itself.

(ed. Bella, vv. 2167–68)

As Satan exults in his victory, Abraham and Pantoja discover María's absence and set out to find her.

Alejandro has returned to Thebes where, to relieve him of his melancholy, his friend Mardonio proposes a visit to the inn, where an exquisitely beautiful new girl has been working for the last two months. Alejandro begrudgingly accompanies Mardonio and recognizes the girl as María. The innkeeper Álvarez exclaims with gratitude: "el cielo me la ha traído al mesón" ("heaven has brought her to my inn," vv. 2493–94). From that statement to the play's title is a simple linguistic step made three times in this scene, but the alteration also prefigures María's salvation. When Alejandro realizes that his perfidy has forced her to the depths of prostitution, he again offers her his love. But María, hesitant to be discarded once more and pessimistic about the firmness of promises, spurns Alejandro.

The scene shifts back to the mountains, where Leonato has finally found Lucrecia, now dressed in animal skins. She gives his amorous pretensions some hope by telling him that she could never think of another man as long as Abraham, whom she considers to be her husband, is alive. Leonato draws his sword and leaves in search of Abraham.

In an attempt to verify what he has been told about María, Abraham, disguised as a soldier, calls at the inn and asks to have a room with her, hoping to effect her repentance and to have her become "la mesonera del cielo." Once they are alone, María offers to take Abraham's shoes off so they can get into bed. When she brushes his hair aside she recognizes her uncle. Through a long speech which holds out to her the promise of redemption, Abraham persuades her to return to the mountain with him.

After their departure, swordplay erupts at the inn when Alejandro is unable to find María, with whom he has again fallen sincerely in love. Álvarez tells of María's visitor, whom Alejandro correctly assumes must have been Abraham. With a common goal, Álvarez and Alejandro leave in pursuit of María and Abraham. Satan appears briefly to express his bewilderment at how a public sinner like María could ever escape from his grasp. He boasts that he will again ensnare her, but in a face-to-face confrontation he is unable to incline her to think again of Alejandro, and María resoundingly rebuffs him as she offers herself to Christ. Álvarez, Alejandro, and Leonato all arrive with the intention of killing Abraham, but their attitudes are transformed instantaneously when they find María dead, kneeling penitently at a cross. Abraham counsels Lucrecia to marry Leonato, but she decides instead to stay and live in the wilderness. Leonato returns to Thebes, Álvarez to his inn, and Alejandro decides to live as a hermit with Abraham.

Mira has handled daringly and well the difficult portrayal of a public prostitute and the sudden changes which first threaten to damn her soul and then effect her redemption. He has studied carefully the contrasts between Abraham's worshipful view of nature and his servant's consuming interest in food and drink and, more important, Abraham's strength and resistance to temptation as compared to the weakness of those who surround him. Valbuena Prat finds that *La mesonera* contains "unbridled romanticism and strong contrasts"[64] and considers it second only to *El esclavo del demonio* in Mira's hagiographic theater.[65]

5. *El santo sin nacer y mártir sin morir*
(The Saint Without Birth and Martyr Without Death)

Medel lists a play entitled *San Ramón*[66] as Mira's and attributes *El santo sin nacer y mártir sin morir*[67] to Dr. Remón. The latter title was published anonymously in *Doce comedias de varios autores* (Tortosa, 1638), but it is attributed to Mira in an eighteenth-century manuscript (Biblioteca Nacional Ms. 14.834). Most hagiographic plays suffer from loose dramatic structure because of the necessity to provide the full, panoramic view of the documented events leading to the protagonist's canonization. *El santo sin nacer* is no exception. In its portrayal of the life of St. Ramón Nonato, thirteenth-century Mercedarian, it develops at least one virtually independent plot in each act and is replete with surprising, if not totally unjustified, whirlwind changes in the attitudes and actions of its characters.

The curtain rises on a duel in Barcelona between the noble Cardón and the jealous Leonida who, in male disguise, having confirmed suspicions that she has a rival, is attempting vengeance on her lover. King Pedro of Aragón puts a stop to the fight, discovers Leonida's identity, and hears her complaint. After Cardón had asked for her hand in marriage, she discovered that he was involved with a humble woman named Raimunda. Since Leonida's brother, a count, was in Flanders, she had donned his clothes and found Cardón courting Raimunda. Leonida departs after demanding that the King either grant her justice or send Cardón to continue his fight with her. Cardón then confesses his duplicity to the King but begs to be allowed to marry Raimunda, who is pregnant with his child. The King first orders that Cardón marry Leonida and make amends to Raimunda with money, but the Queen intervenes on Raimunda's behalf and the King finally accedes, although he imposes exile of a month from Barcelona on the couple for having married without his authorization.

Leonida, now dressed as a bandit, learns from her servant Aristo that the King has retracted his initial decision in her favor. Furious, she insanely swears to terrorize the countryside. After ludicrous encounters with a merchant and then a group of peasants, whose lives are saved because Aristo convinces them that they should humor his mistress, Cardón bursts frantically on the scene in search of help for Raimunda, who is dying in childbirth. Leonida physically overpowers her erstwhile lover from behind, ties him to a tree, and goes off to look for Raimunda. Upon her return, having buried the mother, Leonida carries the newborn son, whom she names Raimundo. She offers to be the child's stepmother, but, to hurt Cardón, she will refuse him Christian baptism. Leonida states that she will marry Cardón and then immediately become a widow by killing him. She then decides to kill the child also, but as she prepares to hang it from a tree, stage machinery whisks her and the infant away amidst spouting flames. An angel appears, announces that Raimundo will have a distinguished place in heaven, and unties the bound father. In a final tableau, the allegorical figure Religion, dressed in the Mercedarian habit, is seen holding in her lap an infant dressed as a cardinal.

In the rustic Catalan setting of Act II, Raimundo, several years following his miraculous escape from death, is a young shepherd in Tirso's service. The spectators learn that twenty-two or twenty-three years ago, a woman dressed as a bandit abandoned a newborn baby in the village, saying that his name was Ramón Non Nat "porque no naciera" ("because he shouldn't have been born"). Later references inform us that Leonida died a nun and that Cardón was virtually insane at death over not being able to find his son. As a result of rivalry with a lecherous count and a wealthy rancher for the hand of Paula, Tirso's daughter, Raimundo feels irreparably dishonored and departs for Barcelona, intending to enlist in the army of King Jaime for his campaign against Valencia. Paula, spurning the suits of her affluent pretenders, leaves in pursuit of Raimundo.

In Barcelona, where Pedro Nolasco (founder in 1223 of the Orden de la Merced, whose purpose it was to ransom prisoners) is giving his blessings to King Jaime's mission, Raimundo is found unsuitable for military service by a captain; when he vows to be a soldier and fight in spite of this rebuff, he is visited by the allegorical figure Obedience, who offers him the opportunity to wage war as a soldier in the company of the Virgin Mary, whose Mercedarian order had been founded twelve years ago. Obedience informs him that Paula, who is currently pursuing him, will die a saint.

In Act III, having served for a decade as an exemplary Mercedarian, Raimundo is in Algiers to ransom Christian captives. Coincidentally, for ten years the Moorish King has unsuccessfully courted a Christian captive, who turns out to be none other than

Paula who, accosted by bandits while on her way to Barcelona in pursuit of Raimundo, was then captured by Moorish pirates while swimming off the Catalan coast. Through the years a vision of Raimundo, dressed as a priest, has kept her from renouncing her faith. Now, she decides to resist no more. She will renounce her Christianity and give herself to the King, in return for his promise to avenge her dishonor by impaling Raimundo. Just then, however, the jealous Queen finds her rival and inflicts a fatal dagger wound on Paula. Raimundo hears her confession, absolves her of her sins, and she dies a saint. Accompanied by a coarse and ill-spoken lay priest named Cerrato, Raimundo goes about among the captives, preaching and strengthening them against the temptation to abjure their Christian faith. The irate King has Raimundo's lips drilled through and closed tightly with a heavy padlock. Miraculously, however, Raimundo goes on preaching.

The scene now shifts back to Spain, where Raimundo's subsequent activities are reported. After his miraculous preaching in Algiers, he was summoned by the Pope to Rome and raised to the status of Cardinal. He returns ill from his journey and dies almost immediately, proclaimed in the play's final lines to be truly *El santo sin nacer y mártir sin morir.*

Cotarelo's judgment of this long and disjointed play seems particularly perceptive: "This *comedia,* from an artistic point of view, has neither head nor feet; but there is much force and vigor in the emotions it portrays and it seems to me it achieves the devout purpose at which it aimed."[68] The very truculence of some of its scenes and characters, albeit not integrated into a dramatically coherent whole, is in itself a recurrent characteristic of Mira's theater.

6. *Vida y muerte de la monja de Portugal*
(Life and Death of the Nun from Portugal)

Printed only twice, in *Parte XXXIII* of the *Escogidas* (Madrid: Fernández de Buendía, 1670)[69] and, according to Durán, in an eighteenth-century *suelta,*[70] this play provides a saintly end to the life of a famous historical nun whose fraudulent sainthood was finally uncovered by the Inquisition.[71] The historical figure, Sister María de la Visitación, Prioress of the Convent of la Anunciata in Lisbon, whose lies and frauds duped such an eminent figure as Fray Luis de Granada, is here replaced by an innocent young beauty who became the object of Satan's persecution. The play's action begins prior to the sailing of the ill-starred Invincible Armada (1588) and closes after a report in Act III of its disastrous defeat, one of the darkest moments in Spain's military history.

Mira here again blends swashbuckling elements into an essentially hagiographic plot, which opens with a duel between don Juan and don Diego, both claimants to the hand of the beauteous María. When the fight is broken up, Juan is condemned by his father for constant trouble-making, informed that he is no longer welcome in the family home, and told that he must leave Spain. Alberto, Juan's father, will arrange for him to sail in the Armada under the command of the Duke of Medina. Except for the looming intervention of Luzbel (Lucifer), the entire first act would pass for the initial phase of a stock Golden Age love intrigue.

Luzbel appears to María in sailor's uniform and deceitfully tells her that Juan is embarking on a ship bound for Seville, where he will marry a beautiful Andalusian. María's maid Teresa, aware of her mistress' preference for Juan, guesses that such bad news could be brought only by Satan. The scene suddenly shifts to the coastal city of Belem, where the Duke and Duchess of Viseo, while on the beach in the company of fishermen, see a boat founder and sink in a sudden storm. The fishermen save a beautiful woman, who turns out to be María. In a long speech, María tells the Duke and Duchess of the cosmic portents which accompanied her birth on a March 14. Her mother died in childbirth, comets appeared whose effects were noted in Spain and England, she tore asunder the breasts of three wet nurses, and she was finally nursed by a "pious goat." Although her great beauty motivated the pretensions of a multitude of men, she loved but one, and he deceitfully left her to marry another in Seville. María confesses having set sail in his pursuit when a storm caused her shipwreck. Now, to show thanks for her rescue, María says she will become a Dominican nun. The Duchess offers to facilitate this through a cousin, doña Vitoria, who is Prioress of the Convent of the Consolation in Lisbon.

Several years have transpired as Act II begins. Diego, still enamored of María, has just returned to Lisbon after an absence of two years. Juan has been in Madrid and Naples, and María has entered the convent, where she is revered for her perfection. Inside the convent, Luzbel, with the aid of his allegorical henchmen, Vainglory, Flattery, Adulation, and Delight, works to discredit the saintly

María. While she sleeps, Delight provides musical accompaniment and Vainglory, Flattery, and Adulation paint a representation of the wounds of the crucified Christ on her body. When the prioress doña Juana and Teresa return, Luzbel has the sleeping nun levitate before their eyes. He also tries to tempt her to leave the convent by appearing to her in the form of Juan, but the allegorical figure Disillusionment uncovers his deceit.

The Duke of Medina has just arrived in Lisbon with the Armada, and Mira, who misses few chances to underscore his patriotic belief in Spain's important role in the international extirpation of heresy, has Luzbel proclaim in dismay that this impressive military strength is all directed against him. The last act contains some interesting comments on the defeat of the Invincible Armada. Juan was a participant and, now home and living in seclusion because of the grief caused by news of María, he is willing to discuss the ill-fated expedition only to a certain point. Some, he says, will attribute the disaster to bad weather, others to poor administration. He will offer no personal opinion, saying simply that the event will have its own chroniclers.

What most distresses Juan, however, is news that the Holy Office of the Inquisition has found María guilty of fraud and that its General Inquisitor, don Alberto de Austria, has imposed the severe punishment of confinement to a cave with minimal sustenance of bread and water. Luzbel, furious because María has not yet succumbed, plans a last onslaught on her honor. He forges notes to Juan and Diego, through which it appears that María has urged each of them to scale the convent wall that night to take her away. He permits himself to be seen by the scandalized Prioress, to whom he imparts the lie that two gallants have nightly been visiting the supposedly penitent María. This allegation causes the Dukes of Viseo and Berganza to come personally that night to verify the accusation. When they recognize don Juan and don Diego, who are unsuccessful in overcoming María's virtuous penitence, they order her punishment doubled and her sustenance cut in half. Unable to withstand this latest cruel turn of fate, María faints. She revives when called by the child Jesus, who beckons to her from a cross. When she kneels at the foot of the cross, Jesus promises her the same reward as that given to Mary Magdalen. Luzbel knows instantly that he has been thwarted, and, discredited and frustrated, he sinks through the stage into his eternal flames. As María expires, all realize that she had been throughout a victim of Satan's persecution.

The account of the Portuguese nun was widely disseminated in Spain around 1580 and much was written on the subject. It would be difficult, however, to determine which of several available texts served as sources for the highly embellished intrigue, most of which must certainly have derived solely from Mira's fertile imagination.

CHAPTER 7

Teatro Menor

SPANISH *teatro menor* is normally equated with one-act plays. This holds true in the present chapter, with the exception of a single two-act nativity play. These short plays are divided into the religious and the secular, and, although the losses through the centuries of Golden Age plays of all types have been staggering in number, we would not be surprised if Mira's extant *teatro menor* is truly representative of the proportions of his original contribution to this general area. Fourteen religious *autos* attributed to Mira are available for study, while there exist but two *loas* (introits, or introductions in verse) and a single secular *entremés* (one-act interlude, comic and popular in nature).

I Autos

The Medieval moralities and mysteries gave way in Spain to a form whose generic name is *auto*. Within the general framework were three main categories: *autos de nacimiento* (nativity plays), *autos sacramentales* (Eucharistic plays), and *autos marianos* (Marian plays). One of the distinctive characteristics of the genre is its use of allegorical and symbolic figures. We have three of Mira's *autos de nacimiento (Coloquio del nacimiento de Nuestro Señor, Los pastores de Belén,* and *El sol a medianoche, y estrellas a mediodía)* and one *auto mariano (Nuestra Señora de los Remedios).* It is especially in the first category that we find Mira at his pastoral best. With little thematic liberty possible in the dramatization of Christ's birth, the ingenuous dialogue of Mira's shepherds is delightful, and it is interesting to note his incorporation of *comedia* conventions and techniques in his dramatic celebration of this supreme religious moment.

The remaining ten works are *autos sacramentales,* whose purpose it was to deal not with a known Biblical event, but with dogma. As Wardropper points out, "Corpus Christi, from the beginning, was celebrated first to honor a dogma and a sacrament, and only to a subordinate degree to recall the Last Supper, the historic event on which the Eucharist is founded."[1] Toward the middle of the sixteenth century, the *autos sacramentales* became an integral part of the celebrations of Corpus Christi, instituted by Pope Urban IV in 1264. They reached their artistic and doctrinal apogee in the hands of the undisputed master of the genre, Pedro Calderón de la Barca (1600–81). In the less able hands of Calderón's successors, however, the difficult use of the allegorical and the symbolic gradually lost touch with reality, and this sin against the Neo-Classical sensibilities of the eighteenth century eventually led Charles III to effect the total prohibition of the genre in a royal edict dated June 11, 1765.

Mira's *autos* have suffered the same critical neglect which has been the lot of his *comedias*. When dealt with at all, his contributions to this important genre usually have been simplistically categorized and judged. Schack, in 1845,[2] offers but brief and superficial comments on *El sol a medianoche (The Sun at Midnight)* and *La mayor soberbia humana (The Greatest Human Presumption)*. Mariscal de Gante comments on none of Mira's *autos* and limits his consideration of Mira to a one-sentence judgment in which he is classified as inferior to Lope, Tirso, and Valdivielso.[3] Pfandl[4] does not even place Mira among the most important authors of *autos*, while Moreto, whose known production in the genre is limited to a single title, is included, along with Lope, Calderón, Tirso, and Valdivielso. Valbuena Prat[5] is a proponent of the theory that Mira represents a bridge between the *autos* of Lope and Calderón. Wardropper, elucidating on the same general idea, comments: "Even Mira de Amescua, whose modification of the sacramental tradition paved the way for Calderón, failed to integrate his brilliant innovations into convincing sacramental plays."[6] In support of Mira, Lugo Aponte de Luis, in 1963, stated that, in her opinion, after Calderón, he was the dramatist who contributed most to the creation of the *auto sacramental*.[7] Scholars who deal with the *auto* either label Mira as a servile member of Lope's school or as a bridge or transition between Lope and Calderón. In neither case have they supported their conclusions with serious textual study of Mira's *autos*.

In two recent dissertations devoted to Mira's *autos,* however, we find presented a convincing case for Mira's distinctiveness. In 1971, Phyllis Irene Patteson Mitchell[8] delved into a study of the available corpus of Mira's *autos* in an attempt to substantiate the theory that they represent an important intermediary step between those of Lope and those of Calderón. She convincingly demonstrated that Mira adapted techniques from the *comedia* and that he broadened the traditional doctrinal function of several of these plays by basing their plots on political issues of current national concern. James C. Maloney, who in 1973 provided critical editions of three of Mira's *autos,*[9] also has noted the political thrust of these works and considers this blend a merit as well as a distinctive characteristic of Mira's *autos.*

A summary of *autos* attributed to Mira through the centuries enables us to propose with some degree of confidence a canon of these works. In 1735, Medel[10] attributed ten *autos* to Mira, the texts of all but one of which, *Ronda y visita de la cárcel (Patrol and Visit in the Jail),* are currently available components of Mira's canon. Among the thirteen *auto* titles attributed by Mesonero Romanos to Mira in 1852[11] are the ten supplied by Medel and three not previously mentioned: *Los mártires del Japón (The Martyrs of Japan), Los mártires de Madrid (The Martyrs of Madrid),* and *San Lázaro (St. Lazarus).* Barrera,[12] in 1860, deletes two titles from this list and adds five, including *La fe de Abraham (Abraham's Faith).* Cotarelo[13] is the critic who attributes the largest number of *autos* to Mira, seventeen. His list represents our final canon with but one exception: *La viña (The Vineyard),* which he mentions, seems obviously to be an alternate title for the *Auto del heredero del cielo (Auto of the Heir to Heaven).* Flecniakoska,[14] in 1961, limits his attributions, one of which he considers very doubtful, to the thirteen *autos* which he has been able to read. In her perceptive 1971 doctoral dissertation, Mitchell considers the same thirteen titles, which include all of those which we have examined with the exception of *El pastor lobo (The Wolf Shepherd).*

Of the total of twenty different *auto* titles connected with Mira's name, we believe it possible to excise four with certainty. In addition to *La viña,* erroneously considered by Cotarelo to be a separate title, *La fe de Abraham* could possibly be another name for *La mesonera del cielo,* especially in view of Barrera's compulsion to provide double titles and in view of the confusion elsewhere in

his coverage of Mira, illustrated by his listing *El arpa de David* as
an *auto*.[15] As noted by Alenda,[16] *El arpa de David* could be confused with another *auto* of similar title ascribed to "tres ingenios"
and listed by Huerta as anonymous. *San Lázaro,* listed by Mesonero Romanos, may be a shortened form of the alternate title for
El rico avariento, which is also included in Mesonero's list of
comedias. Although Alenda notes that both *Los mártires del Japón*
and *Los mártires de Madrid* are reported by Moratín to be
comedias,[17] Cotarelo claims that the former is cited as an *auto* in
the *Catálogo* of the manuscripts of the Osuna Library;[18] he also
states that the play appears never to have been accessioned with the
rest of that collection when it became the property of the Biblioteca
Nacional. *Ronda y visita de la cárcel* was mentioned by the first
four cataloguers of Mira's *autos;* and Shergold and Varey document its presentation in Madrid in 1641.[19] Until further evidence
becomes available, therefore, we feel compelled to consider *Ronda
y visita de la cárcel* and *Los mártires del Japón* as lost Mira titles
which some day may be added to the fourteen *autos* which we have
been able to study.

A.   Autos de Nacimiento

1. *Coloquio del nacimiento de Nuestro Señor*
   (Colloquy of the Birth of Our Lord)

Published first under the above title in *Autos sacramentales con
cuatro comedias nuevas y sus loas, y entremeses* (Madrid: María de
Quiñones, 1655), this work was published again two decades later
under the title *Auto del nacimiento de Nuestro Señor* in *Autos
sacramentales y al nacimiento de Christo, con sus loas y entremeses*
(Madrid: Antonio Francisco de Zafra, 1675). An oddity in that it
consists of two acts, this nativity play is another example of Mira's
charming blend of the devotional and the popular, written with evident influence of *comedia* technique and motifs.

While her husband Joseph sleeps, Mary informs us that she is
reading the chapter of the Book of Isaiah in which the virgin birth
of the Lord is prophesied (Isaiah, 4:14). The angel Gabriel appears
and informs Mary that she herself has been selected by God to bear
Jesus. When she expresses surprise because of the vow of chastity
which she and Joseph have observed, Gabriel tells her that the Holy
Ghost will come upon her and conceive in her the Son of God. As a

proof of this miraculous divine power, he tells Mary that God will give a child to her elderly cousin Isabel, who had been considered sterile (the story of St. John the Baptist's birth to Elizabeth is told in Luke, 1:36–80). With permission granted by Joseph, Mary journeys to her cousin's home to bear witness to this miracle.

The remainder of the first act is devoted to one of Mira's delightful rustic scenes. Bato, an ignorant shepherd and the play's *gracioso,* appears with a rope, announcing his intention to employ it to hang Gila, his wife. He has no evidence, but his suspicions parallel Joseph's and his jealousy and resultant inclination to avenge imagined stains on his honor parody similar behavior dramatized in serious honor plays.

Act II, which carries the subtitle "los celos de San José" ("the jealousy of St. Joseph"), opens with apprehensions expressed by Mary. The sight of her pregnancy has obviously saddened Joseph, but she still does not dare reveal to him the divine mystery. Joseph, who tells Mary that his preoccupation is the result of the census edict which requires a journey to Bethlehem, is secretly bewildered by this result of Mary's three-month visit with Isabel. As Mitchell notes,[20] one can see blended into this portrayal of jealousy which the Biblical Joseph fights to control, folk traditions and jokes about cuckolds as well as reminiscences of the wronged husband of the *comedia.* The visitation of an angel and his explanation of Mary's divine mission set Joseph's heart at ease. Before the baby is born, Mary and Joseph depart for Bethlehem, where they are forced to sleep in the doorway of a stable.

The scene shifts back to the shepherds, who are complaining of the bitter cold. They stop to eat a rustic repast replete with garlic and wine. As they end their meal the shepherd Bras arrives with news of the appearance of a winged angel. As Bato reflects that the angel could perhaps fly away with Gila, St. Gabriel appears on high and announces the birth of Christ. Immediately, the shepherds set out to see the child and discuss the gifts of butter, honey, a shepherd's jacket, and a lamb, which they will offer him. Upon their arrival, Bato offers to leave his shepherd's life and thenceforth serve Mary and Jesus, after ingenuously admitting that he, at that age, was not as good looking as the newborn babe. He does not miss the chance to note, however, that one reason for serving Christ is that he will thereby be able to get away from his wife. As the gifts are presented, the music strikes up and Gila announces that they will dance till dawn.

2. *Los pastores de Belén (The Shepherds of Bethlehem)*

Paz y Melia catalogues two seventeenth-century manuscript versions of this *auto* in the Biblioteca Nacional (Mss. 16.431 and 15.211).[21] As Mitchell observes,[22] this nativity play is written exclusively from the point of view of the shepherds; the Holy Family in no way intervenes in the action and simply appears in a final tableau.

As the play begins, word of Christ's birth has just reached the six shepherds who provide all of its action. Mengo, the *gracioso*, states presumptuously that any child ever born to him will resemble the one just born to Mary in Bethlehem. As the shepherds merrily wend their way toward Bethlehem, they meet the head shepherd and invite him to join them in their journey to see the child Saviour. Mengo's suggestion — that they locate the mother and her infant by enlisting the aid of a local midwife — is treated with derision by Flora. There follows an ingenuous discussion of the Virgin birth and the apparent paradox of redemption through death.

The *auto* ends as the Holy Family is found and the shepherds bestow on Jesus their simple but heartfelt gifts. Gil offers white wool; Flora, a medal; the head shepherd humbly claims that he has nothing to give, since Christ is already the owner of all his possessions. Menga offers some sweets and butter, even over her husband's reminder that she was expected to sell them. Finally, even Mengo presents an offering, his shepherd's sling. In this spontaneous flow of gifts to Jesus, Menga does not want to see His Mother forgotten. She offers her own trousseau to Mary as the head shepherd closes this delightful play with Christmas wishes to the audience.

3. *El sol a medianoche, y estrellas a mediodía*
(The Sun at Midnight and Stars at Noon)

This *auto de nacimiento,* under the title *Auto famoso del Nacimiento de Christo nuestro bien, y sol a medianoche,* was first published in *Navidad y Corpus Christi festejados* (Madrid, 1664) and then appeared twice as a *suelta,* the first published by Juan Sanz about 1715[23] and the next by Antonio Sanz (Madrid, 1733). Here again Mira capitalizes on a theme still fresh and relevant in the memories of his audience: the ransoming of prisoners held captive by infidels. The allegorical figure *Naturaleza Humana* (Human Nature) bears the brand of slavery which marks her captivity in the dominion of *Pecado* (Sin), whose Turkish attire identifies the allegorical captor with his feared Mediterranean referent. *Naturaleza Humana* hopes that her ransom will be provided by her *Redemptor increado* (Unborn Redeemer) when the weeks foretold by the prophet Daniel for the Messiah's birth have been accomplished.

Human Nature stoutly resists the amorous advances of her captor, who promises her worldly riches in exchange for her love. St. John the Baptist arrives to proclaim the coming of Christ. His arrival has been witnessed by Sin, who sends the vices of Pride, Gluttony, Avarice, and Lust, also dressed as Turks, to arrest this intruder. When the frustrated vices report back on their lack of success with the elusive shepherd, they find their King abjectly kneeling before Human Nature and proceed to berate him for these attentions to a base slave.

At this point, the scene shifts to Bethlehem, where Mary and Joseph are vainly seeking shelter for the night. After being turned away first by two friends of Joseph, and then by two greedy innkeepers, they take refuge under the dilapidated city gate. The scene again changes brusquely, as we see the play's *gracioso* Mendrusco who, with Silvia, is shivering from the cold and the snow. Just then, Silvano, trying to elude a group of friends who are playfully in pursuit, trips and lets loose a frying pan full of *migas* (bread crumbs fried in oil and garlic), which are recovered and devoured by Mendrusco. When he returns the empty pan and boldly requests wine to wash down the *migas,* they good-naturedly toss him a *bota.*

In the midst of this exuberance, an angel appears and announces the birth of Christ. The scene now shifts again and shows the Virgin Mary, seated on a throne with the Christ child in her arms and a subdued Sin at her feet. St. John and Human Nature also kneel at her feet as the shepherds arrive, led by their eloquent spokesman Belardo, who announces the simple, rustic gifts which each of the shepherds will offer to the Christ. Each then personally presents his or her gift with simple but devout words. Mendrusco's walking staff, the last gift, is followed by dancing and a song, whose message illustrates the play's title — Christ's birth truly represents the midnight appearance of the sun.

B.   El Auto Mariano

Nuestra Señora de los Remedios (Our Lady of Remedies)

This Marian *auto* existed only in two seventeenth-century manuscripts until it was edited in 1970 by Sister M. Carmel Therese Favazzo,[24] who proposes the span of August 16, 1624 to spring, 1632 as the probable range for the date of composition. This *auto* shares some thematic similarities with Francisco del Castillo's epic poem, *Nuestra Señora de los Remedios de la Merced de Madrid* (Madrid, 1619), whose approbation Mira signed; both works appear to have been inspired directly by Alonso Remón's *Historia de la imagen de la Madre de los Remedios,* published first in 1617 and subsequently condensed and summarized in Chapter II of the *Historia general,* published posthumously in 1633. While Castillo's poem emphasizes intense religious devotion, however, Mira's *auto* significantly stresses ardent patriotism.

The play's action revolves around the fortunes of the image of Nuestra Señora de los Remedios, particularly its journey from Holland to Spain in 1572. According to legend, the twelve-inch-tall statue was made by St. Luke. Its presence in the Netherlands can be traced to 605 A.D., almost one thousand years before its entry into Spain. An intermediate step, one which is omitted in Mira's *auto,* consists of having the image go first to Cuenca, where it worked many miracles before the members of the local Mercedarian Order decided in 1573 to send it to a destitute monastery of theirs in Madrid. Through the year 1632, Remón claims that the statue worked some 600 miracles. In 1836, when transferred to the Monastery of St. Thomas, its popular devotion waned. It subsequently was placed in the baptistry chapel of the Church of Santa Cruz, and it disappeared during the Spanish Civil War of 1936–39.

The cast contains three allegorical figures (Ambition, Heresy, and Faith), a Guardian Angel, a Spanish soldier, and a peasant. As the play opens, the Guardian Angel is begging Ambition not to hurt the image of Nuestra Señora de los Remedios in Holland, where everything Catholic is being profaned. A Spanish soldier, fleeing after having killed two military officers, meets a peasant who is looking for crosses and religious statues because the Prince of Orange pays well to have them burned. While searching for firewood, the soldier is told by divine music that there is a treasure inside a cypress tree. With the first blow of his axe, the image of Nuestra Señora de los Remedios appears. The peasant returns with an armload of crosses, statues, and rosaries and takes Nuestra Señora too. When the soldier notices it is missing, he learns that the peasant has sold the image to Heresy, who has thrown it, along with the other religious objects, into the flaming mouth of a dragon. The intrepid soldier leaps in and recovers the statue, undamaged except for a heat blister on its forehead and some smoke on its face.

As the soldier plans to return to Spain with the image, Ambition and Heresy plot to follow him and offend Our Lady. They invoke a storm and a large ship to frighten the soldier in his little boat, but the image is held aloft by its faithful possessor, and the ship disappears. Heresy, thoroughly defeated, is seen riding a dragon, bound for Brazil (lost to the Dutch in May, 1624, and regained by Spain and Portugal on April 30, 1625), and the *auto* ends as the image arrives in Spain to receive the immediate devotion of the *Reyes Católicos,* Ferdinand and Isabel.

Mira has here given us more than simply a religious play. The work's political and patriotic overtones are very evident. It may be noted that Mira has devoted a full-length play[25] to the death of the cruel, anti-Catholic Prince of Orange, to whom the peasant alludes in this *auto.* It is not unlikely that Mira's dramatization of the statue's transfer to Spain and resultant fame in Madrid did serve to fan the embers of national pride when Spanish soldiers were attempting to suppress the Protestant rebellion in the Netherlands.

C. Autos Sacramentales

1. *El erario y monte de la piedad* *(The State Treasury and Mount of Piety)*

Although this *auto* is generally known by its short title, *El monte de la piedad,* Flecniakoska[26] has argued convincingly that its full title, used by the manuscript's scribe at the end of the play, more accurately reflects the content and should be restored. In 1973 Maloney provided a critical edition[27] of this *auto* from two Biblioteca Nacional manuscripts (Mss. 15.490 and 15.305); it appeared in published form in 1975.[28] Its action, which is based on the unsound economic situation which gripped Spain under Philip III and Philip IV, serves as an intriguing context for one of Mira's typical doctrinal attacks on heresy.

Heresy and La Gentilidad (Heathendom), after an inconsequential struggle for supremacy, welcome Africa, which represents Mohammedanism, into their midst. Having already been successful elsewhere in the world, they now intend to spread their destructive influence in Spain. Heresy conceives the plan of introducing *moneda falsa* in this bastion of Christianity. The *auto's* theme is built upon the dual significance of this *moneda falsa*. Literally it means "false currency"; symbolically it refers, as Heresy notes, to "erroneous opinions." Its introduction will therefore create both economic and spiritual confusion. To the contemporary Spaniard, this allusion to monetary matters evoked the painfully personal effects of the inflationary spiral created in Spain by royal tampering with *vellón,* coinage of copper and silver alloy.[29]

In spite of an exponentially increasing national deficit, both Charles V and Philip II resolutely resisted the temptation to devalue this currency; but, as Earl J. Hamilton notes, "forces were at work during their reigns that rendered debasement inevitable as soon as a weak ruler ascended the throne."[30] The process was actually initiated toward the close of the reign of Philip II, when tremendous financial pressure forced him to permit the coinage of sufficient additional *vellón* to threaten its parity. Under his unbridled successors, the situation dramatically worsened. In 1599, Philip III, maintaining that the silver content of *vellón* was useless, authorized its coinage from pure copper. An ordinance of June 13, 1602 provided for a fifty percent reduction in the weight of copper *vellón,* and restamping in 1603 doubled the face value of this currency. Although the Cortes foresaw the danger of these policies, they were ineffectual in curbing Philip III, and especially Philip IV. The prevailing inflationary situation soon prompted the smuggling of counterfeit *vellón,* a condition which finally brought about, on February 2, 1627, a transfer of the jurisdiction in trials of *vellón* smugglers to the courts of the Inquisition; eventually, on September 13, 1628, the ordinary death penalty for this crime was replaced by burning at the stake.

Constant references to the disastrous contemporary economic situation thus became meaningful to the audience on two levels: the practical and the doctrinal. Asked to combat the introduction of false currency are the allegorical figures *Justicia* (Justice) and her lady-in-waiting, *La Piedad* (Piety), who represent respectively Old Testament rigor and New Testament forgiveness. Two more allegorical figures, *Nobleza* (Nobility) and *Simplicidad* (Simplicity), are derivations from the *comedia*. Nobility appears as a *galán* and becomes enamored of Justice, whose favor he seeks through the intervention of Simplicity, his servant and the play's *gracioso*. Simplicity reports the effects of Heresy's project: the bread being sold in the plazas contains bran, and the available wine is neither cheap nor pure. He further comments that everything was inexpensively priced when God loved Adam but that now everything costs twice its value.

Heresy unsuccessfully attempts to obtain gold and silver from Simplicity for inflated *vellón*. He also argues briefly with the *gracioso* concerning transubstantiation. Justice appears with several *premáticas* (decrees) designed to relieve the nation's plight: the punishment of smugglers of false currency will be placed under the jurisdiction of the Inquisition; another seal will be used to distinguish authentic coins from counterfeit ones; a state treasury will be filled with the riches of the Church; and interest on investments of the faithful will produce a hundredfold return. Justice signs all of the documents and then yields her authority, based on Old Testament rigor and justice, to Piety, who will be governed by New Testament clemency.

Heresy, still unable to accept the doctrine of transubstantiation on faith alone, has asked Piety to provide some concrete proof. She does, in the form of a seven-headed dragon upon which she enters mounted, representing symbolically the submission to which she has forced Satan. She invites all present to gather at her Mount and dine on the divine elements. A cloud opens to reveal the Eucharist as the play ends.

Cotarelo is critical of the allegory which is not, in his opinion, well developed because of the mixture it contains of extraneous and foreign details.[31] We must disagree with Cotarelo's negative evaluation and side with Maloney, for whom this *auto* represents an "admirable synthesis of historical and religious phenomena,"[32] and with Mitchell, who comments: "This concentration on the Spanish situation seems to reflect an awareness of the needs, interests and ambitions of the audiences which the strongly traditional nature of the *auto* had previously prevented dramatists from exploiting."[33]

2. *La fe de Hungría (The Faith of Hungary)*

Attributed to Mira in the Medel catalogue,[34] this *auto* existed in a sole Biblioteca Nacional manuscript copy (Ms. 15.318) until it was edited in 1973 by Maloney.[35] John J. Reynolds, who is also preparing a critical edition, has shown it to be the inspiration of Moreto's only known venture into the genre.[36]

As the action opens, Alberto, young Archduke of Austria, exasperated over Hugo's refusal to accept the doctrine of transubstantiation, draws his sword and a duel begins. This *comedia*-like scene is interrupted by the arrival of Matilde, Alberto's sister and regent who, when told of the reason for the fighting, admits having observed that Hugo, who came from Hungary to serve in her household, has for several days demonstrated that he does not have "Catholic feeling for the Divine Sacrament of the Eucharist." When Hugo aggressively announces his intention to go through Europe disillusioning all who believe in the mystery of the Eucharist, Matilde summarily exiles him from Austria.

Ignoring his exile, and counseled by Onorio, who represents Satan, Hugo agrees to carry secretly a consecrated Host into a raging fire. He will be protected, Onorio assures him, by its miraculous properties, and he will then be able to pass the miracle off as his own. Onorio and Hugo arrive at a rustic church as its sacristan, Damián, is attempting to exorcize storm clouds.[37] When Hugo offers a ruby in exchange for a consecrated Host, the sacristan detects that his visitors are heretics and tricks them by delivering an unconsecrated Host. Thus, when Hugo walks into the fire he is severely burned and forced to retreat immediately. Anything but repentant, he is more obstinate and vengeful than ever. Matilde exiles him again.

Since the Host carried into the fire was itself burned, Onorio suspects the trick played upon them by the sacristan. Hugo next plans to avenge himself directly on the Holy Sacrament. He steals a consecrated Host from the same church, but as he leaves the sanctuary he can hardly walk and feels himself burning. Onorio provides Hugo with a dagger with which to wound the Host, but on two occasions Hugo's raised arm is paralyzed and he cannot strike the blow. On his third attempt, his arm is held back by St. George, patron saint of the church from which the Host was stolen.

Infuriated and frustrated, Hugo flings the Host into a flaming furnace. St. George is seen going in after it, and angelic music emanates from within. Matilde, who has been hunting with Alberto, is met by the sacristan, who reports the theft of the Host. When told that the Host is in the furnace, Matilde is the only one with faith sufficient to enter and remove it from the flames. Hugo, still obstinate in his disbelief, even after witnessing this miracle, meets his end as Matilde fatally wounds him with her crossbow. Hugo makes full confession before dying, and St. George promises a happy succession to Matilde as the *auto* ends.

Although the defense of the doctrine of the Eucharist is central to the play's action, the Eucharist itself is not presented in this *auto* and this is one of the few *autos* which has no completely allegorical figures. Cotarelo[38] perceptively notes the contradiction in Hugo's dependence on protection from a consecrated Host, the denial of whose power is his constant thesis.

3. *El heredero del cielo (The Heir to Heaven)*

Flecniakoska[39] cites as the earliest of three volumes in which this *auto* was published, *Fiestas del santísimo Sacramento* (Zaragoza, 1643). It was later published with the shortened title, *Auto del heredero,* in *Autos sacramentales* (1655), which is the edition we have consulted.

Delightful in its naïve expression, this *auto* leads to the final celebration of the Eucharist by the allegorical dramatization of the problems which develop when the vineyard inherited by the Son (Jesus Christ) from his Father is leased to three tenants: Envy, Judaism, and Heathendom. They connive and plan to refuse to pay the established rent of one tenth of the produce. The Son returns incognito to inspect things and competes with his tenants for the prize of a crown of flowers in a game in which each in turn is blindfolded and must guess the identity of the others as they clap their hands. He is declared the winner by the Guardian Angel, but Envy immediately substitutes a crown of thorns for the prize which he has received. While the Son is off-stage trying to win over Heathendom, Envy discourses on the Last Judgment.

Returning by ship, the Father commissions St. John the Baptist to collect the rent. Envy and Judaism are attempting to kill the collector as the Son returns, having converted Heathendom. Judaism strikes the Son with a vine which is transformed into a cross and bears the Heir aloft. The appearance of the Christ child with the Holy Sacrament, and its adoration, conclude the *auto*. Cotarelo[40] lists an *Auto de la viña* as a separate work, but the constant identification in this *auto* of "the inheritance" with "the vineyard" tends to support the claim of Valbuena Prat[41] that the *Auto de la viña* is simply another title for the *Auto del heredero.*

4. *La jura del príncipe (The Oath to the Prince)*

Cotarelo[42] suggests that this may have been the last dramatic work written by Mira before his departure from Madrid to take up his duties as Archdeacon of the Cathedral of Guadix, a post which he assumed on June 16, 1632. Flecniakoska[43] has transcribed the manuscript version, dated 1633, which is found in Paris in the Institut Hispanique (Ms. 17.098), as has Elba Lugo Aponte de Luis for her 1963 dissertation.[44] *La jura del príncipe* was edited critically by José M. Bella[45] in 1972 and by Maloney[46] in 1973. As Flecniakoska convincingly demonstrated in 1949,[47] Mira uses the historic oath of allegiance sworn by the provinces to the young Baltasar Carlos, son of Philip IV, on March 7, 1632, as a thematic nucleus for this *auto sacramental,* which was probably presented for Corpus Christi in Madrid on June 13, 1632.

Heresy, dressed in Hungarian garb, arrives from the islands of the north where he has his palace and court. He is angry with the Hapsburgs for their belief in transubstantiation and their devotion to the Eucharist. He intends to abolish these articles of Catholic faith in Spain and Austria and to introduce a long list of heretical sects.[48] The figure Spain, which symbolizes all of the Spanish people, worried by the aggressive mood of Heresy, attempts to communicate her fears to her King through his favorite, Diego, who represents St. James, patron saint of Spain. The King, representing both Philip IV and God, urges her not to grieve and reminds her of glorious past triumphs which include shaking off the Saracen yoke. He then instructs her to affirm her faith by convoking the Cortes to pledge allegiance to Prince Baltasar Carlos. In the play's obvious parallelism, Spain is grateful to Philip (God) for the gift of his son Baltasar Carlos (Christ). Spain has already prepared for the oath and lists the distinguished representatives, some of them saints, from all parts of the realm. The allegorical figures Heresy and Deceit team up against Faith and Truth in a musical dialectic. Heresy and Faith request their respective companions, each with his own guitar accompaniment, to sing their respective glories. The contest between Faith and Heresy finally touches the central issue: the doctrine of transubstantiation. A deadlock results.

Deceit, when ordered by Heresy to introduce dissension in Spain and to spy on the nation's activities, expresses fear of the Inquisition. When the ceremony of the oath is about to begin, the Biblical Paul reads the passages from his Letters to the Corinthians and the Ephesians which deal with the body and blood of Christ at the Last Supper, and John cites the corresponding Gospel passage. Not only does Heresy fail to be converted by these authoritative readings but, in his sacrilegious fury, he draws his sword on Spain. Just then, however, a curtain is drawn, revealing the Prince, the Chalice, and the Host. Heresy attempts to cover his ears and eyes but cannot avoid the sight of the holy sacraments. Since the magnitude and pomp of the ceremonies preclude their dramatization on stage, Spain narrates to Heresy the impressive list of participants, including 2 infantes, 72 prelates, 13 grandees, and 12 magistrates and counselors, who file in to swear their allegiance. Peter, acting as majordomo, first exacts the oath from all and then promises that the Prince will govern in peace, grace, and justice.

Heresy announces his return to the Danube, implying that he will attempt to seek converts in Germany and Austria on his way home to Hungary. Although further action is not dramatized, a final stage direction calls for a tree on which are hung portraits of the rulers of the House of Austria, and at whose feet lies the vanquished Heresy. Maloney speculates that Mira may have had the specific purpose of using this *auto* to remind the Cardinal Infante Fernando, about to be sent by Olivares to Flanders, to be aware of the Protestant threat in the north.[49]

5. *La mayor soberbia humana de Nabucodonosor* (*The Greatest Human Presumption of Nebuchadnezzar*)

Printed only once, in *Navidad y Corpus Christi festejados* (Madrid: Fernández de Buendía, 1664),[50] this is one of several Golden Age dramatic renditions of scenes from the court of Nebuchadnezzar as told in Daniel 2–5.[51] Mira here attempts to highlight, in Mitchell's words, "the destructive effect of the sin of pride."[52] Mitchell further notes that although the play contains no allegorical figures, the symbolism through which its principal character, Nebuchadnezzar, represents Man in general, is obvious. Schack's[53] judgment of this *auto* is basically favorable. Cotarelo[54] concedes that it is well written but then somewhat paradoxically characterizes it as an insipid Old Testament drama to which a Eucharistic dénouement has been appended.

King Nebuchadnezzar, perplexed by the question of how long his reign will last, requests assurance of his greatness from his court and then falls asleep. He dreams and sees a gigantic, golden statue rise. He asks if it is a second Babel attempting to reach the sky, but receives no answer. Upon awakening, he summons some wise Chaldeans to interpret his dream. When they arrive, led in by the *gracioso* Faisán (pheasant), who himself is dressed as another wise man, they find that Nebuchadnezzar unreasonably expects them to interpret his dream though he cannot reveal to them what he dreamt. Unable to comply with his wishes, they are condemned to die. Faisán then offers a ludicrous interpretation for which he narrowly escapes death himself only by doffing his costume and reminding the king that the order to kill the wise men could not have included him, since he is an idiot.

Daniel is next brought forth. Without hesitation he describes and interprets the gigantic statue as a symbol of the supremacy of Nebuchadnezzar and his Assyrians over the great nations of the world; but he also mentions a stone which falls from a mountain and shatters the clay of the statue's legs. Daniel refuses the offer of the grateful Nebuchadnezzar to name him prophet but is appointed Prince of Babylon. Nebuchadnezzar, again confident and with burgeoning presumption, now plans to resume construction of the famous Tower of Babel, symbolized by the statue, which was begun by Nembroth, his grandfather. He also becomes so obsessed with his magnificence that he is no longer content to be referred to as King. He wants everyone to address him as God.

The King of Jerusalem and the two young Jewish princes, Azarías and Ananías, prisoners of Nebuchadnezzar, have been told by Daniel that the captivity of the Jews will last for seventy years. To add to his humiliation, the King of Jerusalem has been required to continue to wear his gold crown while in captivity. When Faisán reports the customary arrival of beggars seeking alms, Nebuchadnezzar announces a policy change: since he is now a god, they must henceforth do their begging at a scented altar and worship him, sacrifice to him, and wail as they state their needs.

The *auto's* structure is loose at this point, as isolated events transpire or are reported with insufficient prior exposition. A servant reports that the statue is growing fast. The Biblical furnace is suddenly mentioned for the first time, and the King of Jerusalem and the two prisoners are ordered thrown to its flames. Faisán brings word that sweet smells emanated from the fire when the three Jews were thrown into the furnace. Upon reopening it, not three but four were there, all unharmed. As he hears this news, Nebuchadnezzar again falls asleep. This time his dream, subsequently interpreted by Daniel, indicates that he will suffer a seven-month transformation into a beast in punishment for his sins. The conversion is immediate. With an eagle's head, feathered arms, scales on his chest, and a lion's back, Nebuchadnezzar, on all fours and with a rope around his neck, is being led around stage by Faisán. Unable to do more than whine and look toward heaven, the transmuted Nebuchadnezzar makes it obvious that he wishes to be trod upon by the King of Jerusalem. The Jewish king uses the wheel of fortune image dear to Mira in accounting for the fall which his former captor has so deservedly taken. Daniel then offers to help Nebuchadnezzar if he will make three promises: to be charitable, to be merciful, and to believe in the true God. When the quadruped shakes its head affirmatively on all three counts, the spell ends. As Nebuchadnezzar removes the eagle's head, his words indicate a complete spiritual change:

Pues asombró mi pecado,	Since my sinfulness astounded,
asombre mi penitencia. (p. 48)	now let my penitence astound.

Following rapid calculations by Daniel that just seventy weeks separate them from man's redemption through the coming of the Messiah, a thoroughly repentant Nebuchadnezzar, dressed in his initial finery, but with a chain around his neck, announces that the jails are to be emptied and that the poor are to be invited to sack the palace of his treasure, with the single exception of the goblets which had been looted from the temple in Jerusalem. He then earns divine pardon by a full confession of his sins. In the play's final scene, Daniel uncovers two altars. From the first, a representation of Death in the figure of Satan tumbles down its slide. The play ends as the second is shown to contain the Eucharist.

6. *El pastor lobo (The Wolf Shepherd)*

An *auto* of this title is attributed to Mira by Medel,[55] García de la Huerta,[56] and Barrera.[57] Although Cotarelo reports having no knowledge of it other than its appearance in Medel's list,[58] and al-

though Mitchell does not include it among the *autos* of Mira which
have been preserved,[59] it was published, attributed to Lope, under a
longer title, *El pastor lobo y cabaña celestial (The Wolf Shepherd
and Celestial Bower),* by Pedroso in 1865[60] and again by Menéndez
Pelayo in the Academy edition of Lope's works.[61] Since don Marcelino states in his prefatory remarks: "This *auto* has been from
time to time attributed to Mira de Amescua,"[62] it seems likely, not-
withstanding the still perplexing assignment of authorship, that this
is the work whose text Cotarelo and Mitchell were unable to find.

As Menéndez Pelayo points out, the allegory of the wolf and the
lamb, on which this *auto* is based, was one of the themes most frequently used for Corpus Christi celebrations. He may be correct in
refuting Mira's authorship, but since the only support offered for
his attribution of this poetically beautiful *auto* is his comment that
its "style shouts out that it is Lope's,"[63] we are reluctant to consider the matter closed, especially after recalling don Marcelino's
own quandary in distinguishing between the styles of Mira and
Lope (see page 160). According to Sánchez Arjona,[64] an *auto*
entitled *El pastor lobo* was performed in 1624 at Seville's Corpus
Christi celebrations by the company of Andrés de la Vega.

The action of this *auto* is simple. Satan, disguised as the Wolf
Shepherd, has lascivious designs on the Ewe Lamb, the favorite of
the Lamb Shepherd (Christ), and symbolic representation of the
Soul. As a reflection of the stock elements of the *comedia,* the
Lamb Shepherd is described as a dashing *galán* and Satan's envy is
couched in terms of human jealousy. His allegorical henchman
Appetite abducts Ewe Lamb, who has just been joined in marriage
to the Lamb Shepherd. Captive in a mountain bower, Ewe Lamb
resolutely resists Satan's advances and rejects his offers of wealth
and power. The Lamb Shepherd, disguised as a livestock trader,
stealthily gains entrance to Satan's lair and rescues Ewe Lamb; on
their return journey they pause at the River Jordan where He
washes away her sins.

The pursuit of the furious Wolf Shepherd is halted in the bower
of the Lamb Shepherd at the top of another mountain as Christ
climbs onto a cross and impales Himself on its nails. From the
cross, Christ invokes fire which destroys the bower, visible in the
distance, where Ewe Lamb has been held captive. When a curtain is
drawn to reveal the Eucharist, the Wolf Shepherd is defeated. As he
slinks away, he threatens Ewe Lamb with a similar abduction in the

future if she is guilty of sinning. In the play's closing lines, she exultantly assures him that, now a bride of God, she will never leave the eternal glory which she has finally attained.

7. *Pedro Telonario*

Pedro Telonario enjoys the distinction of having been, until 1972,[65] Mira's only *auto* correctly attributed to him in a modern edition. Although listed by Medel,[66] it appears to have existed only in manuscript (Biblioteca Nacional, Ms. 16.636) prior to Valbuena Prat's 1926 edition.[67] The accessibility of this *auto* probably accounts for the fact that it is Mira's only venture in the genre to be analyzed by Wardropper.[68] It seems unfortunately evident that much generalization on Mira's sacramental theater has been based on a consideration of *Pedro Telonario* as a representative sample. In our opinion, this *auto* is surpassed in quality by several others which, again unfortunately, are not yet available in modern published editions.

The action opens with a verbal duel between the allegorical figures Avarice, who is dressed as a Turk, and Charity over Pedro Telonario, reputed to be the wealthiest, as well as the cruelest and most avaricious citizen of Alexandria. While Avarice aspires to be Pedro's master, Charity, who appears as a woman, hopes to win him as a lover. Symbolically, the two figures represent conflicting forces in Pedro's own subconsciousness. Pedro, in considering written petitions which have been submitted to him, is an obvious caricature of cruelty, cynicism, and avarice. A widow is unable to repay her debt of 100 ducats. Claudio, Pedro's servant, begs that she be given a month's grace, but the plea is refused by Pedro, who · cynically remarks that no widow really regrets the death of her husband. A sick priest, also Pedro's debtor, requests an extension of a few days and is denied by Pedro.

Pedro boasts that he has never given alms, nor will he ever. This affirmation buoys the spirits of Avarice, who gloatingly anticipates victory. Claudio attempts to reason with his master, citing Christ's preachings on charity, but Pedro admits that he becomes possessed by Satan every time he sees a poor person. Pedro orders his servants Avarice, Gluttony, and Sloth to set the table for a lavish meal. As he prepares to eat, Claudio reminds him that the crops of Alexandria have been blighted and asks again for alms of food for the poor. As reward for this intercession, Claudio is banished from

Pedro's household, his place being taken by the hypocritical Livio, who flatters Pedro on his miserliness.

When asked if he wants music during dihner, Pedro's response again caricatures his avarice. He refuses to pay the musicians for doing what they enjoy; they should pay him for listening, he declares! In the middle of his opulent feast, a poor woman named Flora arrives to beg for water and is turned away. Led by Charity, however, some pilgrims have also slipped through the door. As they sing of their pilgrimage to the shrine of Santiago, they bring upon themselves verbal vilification from Pedro, who unwittingly hurls bread at them.

Nevertheless, as he instantly realizes, he has finally given something, albeit of small practical significance. While he sleeps, overcome with melancholy caused by his unprecedented act, it is now Charity's turn to gloat, having wrung alms from Pedro, even if only in the form of begrudgingly given bread. An ensuing altercation between Avarice and Charity is interrupted by the allegorical figure Justice; mounted on a throne with an angel on one side and a devil on the other, she calls Pedro to his final judgment. Avarice, in the role of prosecutor, itemizes Pedro's many sins. The chastened sinner is able to boast of no virtues in his own defense, but Charity balances his sins with the alms of bread which he gave. It is through bread, she reminds us, that God works miracles. Pedro is acquitted but instructed by justice henceforth to be generous and to do saintly works.

All of this appears to have been a dream from which Pedro awakens a changed man. He recalls Claudio to help convert his home into a refuge for the poor. Having given to the needy all of his possessions, Pedro wishes to sell himself as a slave. Carlos, French captain of a ship bound for Europe, is willing to pay the price of 2,000 *reales* asked by Claudio, but Pedro will not agree to be sold for more than 29, one less than the number paid for his Redeemer. Carlos gives Pedro 100 *reales* to buy provisions of fruit and bread for the ship. Christ then appears, disguised as a pilgrim and begging for alms to help him on his journey to Jerusalem. Pedro offers himself, having nothing more of his own to give. When dancing and singing gypsies arrive, however, begging for alms in the name of God, Pedro gives them the 100 *reales*. Repentant because he has given what was not his to give, Pedro wanders into a garden where his new owner arrives to find him dead, surrounded by the saintly smell of flowers. Avarice appears once more to dispute with Charity over Pedro's soul, but a curtain is drawn to reveal the Eucharist. Pedro, whose charity has earned him salvation, is seen kneeling at the feet of Christ as the *auto* ends.

As critics have noted, the appearance of the Eucharist in this and other of Mira's *autos* is not well integrated nor well prepared for by the play's developing action.[69] Subtlety is lacking in *Pedro Telonario,* whose charm rests, according to Valbuena Prat, in its "great tenderness and ingenuous devotion, with all the primitivism of a medieval morality play."[70] To Valbuena, Pedro's repentance and the greatness of soul with which he works toward goodness as impetuously as he had formerly embraced evil is reminiscent of Lisarda in *El esclavo del demonio.*[71] Wardropper provocatively suggests that, in spite of the allegorical apparatus, this work was conceived as a *comedia* rather than as an *auto.*[72] We find it hard to agree with him, however, when he states: "Pedro does not repent, he doesn't consciously act with charity, and nevertheless he is saved."[73] Although Avarice and Charity make an ongoing issue of the importance of the alms of bread, thrown, as Wardropper notes, "because he didn't have another projectile handy,"[74] Pedro's obedient response to Justice's instructions, in itself a living repentance, seems obviously to be a factor of no small significance with regard to his ultimate salvation. José Bella, in a recent article,[75] has shown that both *Pedro Telonario* and Felipe Godínez's *El premio de la limosna y rico de Alejandría (The Reward of Alms and the Rich Man of Alexandria)* follow closely the earliest account of the frequently retold medieval story of San Juan el Limosnero, patriarch of Alexandria, who died in his native Cyprus around 620 A.D.

8. *El Príncipe de la Paz (The Prince of Peace)*

Salvá, in one of the catalogues of his London bookstore,[76] announced for sale a manuscript dated 1629 of the *Auto del Príncipe de la Paz y transformaciones de Celia,* written for Madrid's Corpus Christi celebrations and attributed to Lope de Vega. Menéndez Pelayo did not believe that manuscript, now located in the British Museum, to be the one attributed to Mira de Amescua; although the *auto* is also attributed to Mira in the catalogues of Medel[77] and García de la Huerta.[78] It is, however, included in Menéndez Pelayo's edition of Lope's works[79] because of its considerable poetic merit. On the play's authorship, Menéndez Pelayo remarks:

"The question of attribution is in no way easy to resolve, because the style of Mira de Amescua is closer to Lope's than that of any of our other dramatists; but the poet from Guadix usually shows himself to be more exuberant and laden with lyric pomp than the Madrilenian — qualities which we seem to see in some scenes of this *auto*."[80] Don Marcelino used the British Museum manuscript as the basis for his text. Flecniakoska[81] attributes this *auto* to Mira, although hesitatingly.

Celia, who represents the soul, and whose name, as we are later told by Christ, is a near anagram for *cielo* ("heaven"), has just been won over completely by the Prince, who represents Christ. Prior to the marriage they contemplate, she begs him to transform her into a state of pure innocence in the form of a rustic woman to whom worldy pleasures and values will be abhorrent.

In preparation for their wedding, Celia announces to her servants, the allegorical figures Discretion, Honor, and Concern, that the entire household must be converted to purity and innocence. To that end, all ostentation will be eliminated, her palatial home will be converted into a poor hut, and her servants' names will be changed as follows: Concern will henceforth be Neglect, Discretion will be called Ignorance, and Honor will be known as Contempt. Everything will be the opposite of its former state. In a passage which parodies the famous "Rey don Sancho, Rey don Sancho" *romance*,[82] the Guardian Angel warns Celia of the fall from heaven and escape from earth of the treacherous Devil, here named Lucero, who is reputed to be en route to Celia's house disguised as a lion.

When Lucero arrives, dressed in black, with a star-strewn mantle, and wearing a lion's head, he is informed by Neglect, whom he finds sleeping in the doorway, that his mistress has married Christ, the Prince of Peace, in order to put an end to the amorous pretensions and pursuit of another persistent lover. Unsuccessful in an attempt to burn Celia's home, Lucero next plans to disguise himself as the Prince and take his place as her husband. The omniscient Prince reveals the Devil's plan to Celia, and when Lucero arrives, visually identical to his divine adversary, he finds himself confronted by Concern with an anachronistic shotgun.[83] In the midst of Lucero's efforts to convince Celia and her household that he is the Prince, the real Prince appears. Christ, who with quiet confidence allows his rival to state his case, decides finally to intervene.

In open competition, the Devil promises gifts and riches to Celia while Christ counters with the offer of travail, sadness, and proofs of love and faith. Celia declares Christ the victor, and, having uncovered Satan's deceit, she calls for slings to drive the lion away. Recognizing still another defeat in his ongoing battle with God, Lucero slinks back to Hell. When Christ mildly chides His bride and tells her that hereafter He wants her to kill Him with love, not with jealousy, Celia asks Him for signs which will in the future help her to see through His rival's fraud. Christ replies that Satan will evoke vainglory, while the authentic Christ will cause submission and humility. As He departs after the assurance that He will always be with Celia, He is presented in the Eucharist.

As Mitchell astutely points out,[84] in addition to the obvious Biblical source of the Song of Songs, Mira seems to have been inspired by mystic poetry, perhaps even specifically by St. John of the Cross's "Aunque es de noche " ("Although It Is Night").[85] She also notes that the relationship of the Prince and Celia has many points of comparison with the traditional *galán-dama* relationship of the *comedia*.

9. *Las pruebas de Cristo (The Examination of Christ)*

According to Sánchez Arjona,[86] *Las pruebas de Cristo* was presented by the company of Adrián López as part of the Corpus Christi celebrations in Seville in 1651. In addition to its existence in a manuscript, copied by Martínez de Mora around 1630 (Biblioteca Nacional, Ms. 16.690) it has been published twice, in *Autos sacramentales* (Madrid, 1655 and 1675). Here again, Mira employs a national institution, the *prueba de limpieza* ("proof of purity"; i.e., freedom from Jewish or Moorish ancestry), as a framework for a Eucharistic play. In Christ's submission to a *prueba de limpieza,* Mitchell[87] sees the possibility that Mira was defending these examinations from attacks directed against them during the reign of Philip IV.

El Hombre (Man), a galley slave of the *Príncipe de las Tinieblas* (The Prince of Darkness or Satan), is urged by *La Esperanza* (Hope) to escape captivity by applying for admission to a military order. In the framework of a contemporary *prueba de limpieza,* the denigrating testimony offered by the *Príncipe de las Tinieblas* and his cohort *Envidia* (Envy) is strong enough to counteract the support offered by the prophet Zacharias and by David. *El Hombre* is judged unworthy of election. He is met by Emanuel (Christ), who attempts to assuage his grief. As *El Hombre* returns disconsolate to his oars, he urges Emanuel to seek the habit which he has failed to obtain.

El Príncipe and *Envidia* attempt to block Emanuel's election as they did *El Hombre's,* but they are unsuccessful. Their ingenuous arguments that the son of a carpenter and of a mother of humble origin cannot qualify for inclusion among nobility are easily invalidated by documented accounts of Emanuel's miraculous deeds. To the chagrin of his adversaries, Emanuel is elected to the Order of Santiago. Fully invested in the habit of the Order, Emanuel frees *El Hombre* from captivity, and the *auto* ends with a standard revelation of the Eucharist.

Mira enriches his allegorical message with allusion to topics beyond the general theme of the *pruebas de limpieza. Envidia,* for example, unable to comprehend the mystery of Emanuel's declarations, relates them to the obscurity of the *culterano* poets:

Tus voces me dan pena;	Your declarations bother me;
vocablos hablas ásperos y ocultos,	you speak words harsh and occult,
que pareces poeta de los cultos,	and seem to be a *culterano* poet
que escribiendo sin vena,	who, writing without inspiration,
en lengua endemoniada,	in demonic language,
haces enigmas, sin que diga nada.	spouts enigmas, without saying anything.

(*Autos sacramentales,* 1675: pp. 45–46)

Mira also touches on the sublimation of vengeance into pardon in a Christian view of honor, one which will be more fully developed in Calderón's *autos.* Although this *auto* is almost devoid of action and movement, it does present with great coherence Mira's utilization of a secular frame of reference to establish Christ's nobility. As Cotarelo notes, Calderón's *Las órdenes militares (The Military Orders)* and the anonymous *Las pruebas del linaje humano (The Examinations of Human Lineage)* deal with the same theme.[88] Mitchell expresses her conviction that Mira's *auto* definitely served as Calderón's model.[89]

10. *La santa Inquisición (The Holy Inquisition)*

Barrera[90] assigns this *auto,* sometimes referred to by the shorter title of *La Inquisición,* to Lope on the basis of its attribution in a manuscript dated 1629 from the Osuna library. The authority of this manuscript has been called into question, however, by the discovery in the Biblioteca Nacional of another, attributed to Mira, which carries the indication that it was staged in Madrid in 1624.[91] Sánchez Arjona surmises that the *auto* entitled *La Inquisición* performed in Seville in 1625 was Mira's.[92] Menéndez Pelayo, who publishes this *auto* in his edition of the collected works of Lope,[93] feels nevertheless that it is definitely in the style of Mira de Amescua,[94] and Flecniakoska unhesitatingly concurs.[95]

Satan here appears as Lion. He calls upon his ally, Night, and after recounting the conventional story of the world's creation and his fall from divine favor, he informs Night that his implacable enemy, the Church . . .

ha formado un Tribunal,	has formed a Tribunal,
ha creado un Santo Oficio,	has created a Holy Office,
tan tremendo y admirable,	so tremendous and admirable,
tan fuerte, tan exquisito,	so strong, so exquisite,
que aun yo estoy temblando dél,	that even I am trembling at it,
porque es eterno castigo	because it is eternal punishment
de mis herejes, si bien	of my heretics, while
es dulce, es blando y es pío.	it is gentle, it is tender, and it is pious.

(*BAE,* CLVIII, 461)

The Inquisition is preparing to try the allegorical figures Heresy and Idolatry; and the five human senses and Fear, who all represent the dreaded *Familiares* (Officers of the Inquisition), are to keep vigil through the night, guarding the cross.

Satan requests that Night prevent the rays of the sun from rising in the east and announcing the day. Hoping thus that the nocturnal medium, in which he is most effective, will assure his success, he plans to keep the senses from erecting the cross by putting them to sleep. His soporific powers work with all but Fear, who is also the *gracioso*. The allegorical figures Faith and Love are finally also successful in awakening the senses so that they can keep their vigil. As Sight spies day breaking in the east, the sun appears, to announce by its presence that the trial may proceed. The music and ceremony of the preparatory Mass make the Devil fearful that his cause will be lost. In effect, St. Thomas Aquinas, serving as *calificador* (qualificator) in the trial, persuades Idolatry to abjure and confess publicly his errors and beg for mercy. The Church pardons Idolatry and grants his absolution. Heresy, the more dangerous of the two offenders, is obstinate in continuing to deny the presence of God in the bread and wine of the Eucharist and is consequently found guilty.

Not a literary work of great merit, *La santa Inquisición* is of historical importance in that, as first noted by Pedroso in 1865,[96] very few *autos* include an apology for the Inquisition. Although other incidental references to the Inquisition are found elsewhere in Mira's *autos,*[97] nowhere else is it central to the theme. *La santa Inquisición* is another instance in which a national institution serves as the thematic framework for a strong affirmation of the doctrine of transubstantiation. Mitchell suggests[98] that Mira perhaps composed this *auto* in 1623 for the purpose of defending the Inquisition from attacks formulated during debates on this controversial institution which took place in 1620–22.

II   *Secular* Teatro Menor

The delightful short pieces which comprise the genre of *teatro menor* are an important part of Golden Age literary production and were written by some of Spain's most outstanding literary figures. Cervantes and Moreto, in addition to their undisputed excellence in other genres, are among the very best *entremesistas.* Agustín Rojas and Quiñones de Benavente, on the other hand, were specialists, the dramatic production of the former being restricted to *loas,* in whose composition he reigned supreme, and that of the latter to *entremeses.*

Since the preservation of these ephemeral works was even more difficult than was the case for full-length *comedias,* we may assume that Mira wrote more than we currently have available; his known extant contributions, however, are limited to two *loas* and one *entremés.* Both *loas*, identically titled *Loa famosa,* appear in the 1655 and 1675 editions of *Autos sacramentales.* One has a very heavily religious orientation, while the other appears to be addressed to an audience of administrative officials. Neither is notable for its poetic inspiration. The *Entremés de los sacristanes (Interlude of the Sacristans),* published also in both editions of *Autos sacramentales,* is the only known example of Mira's secular *teatro menor.* It is indicated in the 1655 text that the *Entremés* was written to be played with the *Auto de la viña,* for which Cotarelo was unable to account.[99] As we have noted on pp. 151–52, this must have been an alternate title for the *Auto del heredero,* which is published with Mira's *entremés* in both editions of *Autos sacramentales.*

Two sacristans, colorfully nicknamed Poca Ropa (Scant Clothing) and Cantalapiedra (Singing Stone), whose macaronic Latin has impressed Marica, gullible daughter of a lawyer, and her maidservant Teresa, pay their ladies a visit when the father leaves the house to discuss a case with a litigant. As Marica likens her witty beau to Virgil and Teresa hers to Ovid, the father and the litigant return home to the consternation of the four lovers. Poca Ropa and Cantalapiedra hide in a rolled-up mat, on which the two men sit. Miraculously unobserved, the sacristans come out of hiding and administer real-life buffets and punches to the father and his guest in a slapstick scene, following which the two men depart.

Before their return, the girls have Poca Ropa get on all fours as if he were a bench and they place Cantalapiedra on top in a position supposed to simulate a kneading trough. When the father and the litigant reenter, Marica contends that she is kneading dough to prepare for a fiesta. The feigned bench and trough lose their composure when their intended dupes announce their intention of placing heavy stones on top of the "stone" trough. All comes tumbling down, and Cantalapiedra humorously cites the second part of the title of Tirso's Don Juan play as he claims to be "el convidado de piedra" ("the stone guest").

Their plot discovered, Marica requests that as a dowry she be given money left by her deceased mother and that she be permitted to marry her sacristan. The father adamantly refuses and, to the accompaniment of singing, the piece ends abruptly.

The use of Latinist sacristan suitors who, when discovered, are asked to assume ludicrous positions and unconvincingly feign being inanimate objects is a stock convention. Mira's Marica may show a shade more animosity and acrimonious disobedience to her father than is usual, but neither she nor any other aspect of this short piece represents a distinctive departure from the typical themes or style of this amusing but superficial genre. If Mira made more contributions to *teatro menor* it is regrettable that they have not survived.

CHAPTER 8

Mira's Popularity and Significance

SUCCEEDING periods reveal, in their appraisal of literary works, something about themselves as well as something about the objects of their criticism, and our understanding of Mira de Amescua and of literary history cannot help but be enhanced by knowledge of the patterns of his reputation and popularity through the years. Until a very recent rebirth of interest in Mira de Amescua, his reputation lay enshrouded in an almost total eclipse which probably began in the last years of the seventeenth century. Interestingly, this centuries-long lack of regard for Mira was in complete contrast to the high esteem in which he was held by several of his most illustrious contemporaries. Lope de Vega, after meeting Mira during a visit to Granada, dedicated a sonnet to him in *La hermosura de Angélica* (Madrid: Pedro Madrigal, 1602).[1] In his important miscellany, *El viaje entretenido,* published in 1603, Agustín Rojas includes Mira's name among those of other well-known contemporary dramatists,[2] and in 1614, Cervantes includes words of praise for Mira and reference to *El arpa de David* in his *Viaje del parnaso.*[3] Even the normally acerbic Suárez de Figueroa, a ruthless critic of the many excesses of Golden Age theater, includes Mira among Spain's best dramatists in his *Plaza universal de todas ciencias y artes* (Madrid: Luis Sánchez, 1615).[4] Cervantes, in the prologue to the first edition of his *Ocho comedias y ocho entremeses* (Madrid: Viuda de Alonso Martín, 1616), praises "the gravity of Dr. Mira de Amescua, singular pride of our nation."[5]

Lope once again mentions Mira in his account of the activities of the 1622 celebrations held in honor of the canonization of San Isidro:

Dame nuevo aliento aquí	Give me breath here,
Delio, porque [a] hablar me atrevo	Delio, to permit me to speak
del doctor Mira de Mesqua,	of Dr. Mira de Mescua,
honor de tu monte excelso.	honor of your sublime mount.
Sus comedias ingeniosas	His ingenious *comedias*
vencen en arte a Terencio	surpass the Latin Terrence's art
latino, con su inventor	as well as that of its inventor,
Rodio Aristóphanes griego.[6]	The Greek Aristophanes of Rhodes.

Lope's final praise of Mira is found in his *Laurel de Apolo* (1630):

> Oh Musas, recibid al doctor Mira,
> que con tanta justicia al lauro aspira,
> si la inexausta vena
> de hermosos versos y conceptos llena,
> enriqueció vuestras sagradas minas
> en materias humanas y divinas.[7]

> Oh muses, receive Dr. Mira,
> who with so much justice aspires to the laurel,
> if the inexhausted vein
> full of beautiful verses and conceits,
> enriched your sacred mines
> in human and divine matters.

Pérez de Montalván, contemporary dramatist and first biographer of Lope de Vega, mentions Mira in 1632 among the Castilian dramatic poets in the following terms: "Dr. don Antonio Mira de Amescua, great master of this most noble art, both in its divine and human elements, since his singular eminence is successful both in *autos sacramentales* and in secular *comedias*."[8] Luis Vélez de Guevara, in *El diablo cojuelo (The Lame Devil,* 1641*),* pays one of the last tributes made during Mira's lifetime: "Let us not forget Guadix, ancient and celebrated for its melons, and much more for the divine talent of Dr. Mira de Amescua, its son and archdeacon."[9] As has been noted in the section on his biography, Mira was praised by Nicolás Antonio in 1672 for his poetic and dramatic talents, "in which he was exceeded only by the great Lope de Vega."[10] Perhaps the last favorable judgment of the century was registered in 1689-90 by Francisco Bances Candamo in his *Theatro de los theatros,* a work considered by Edward Wilson to be one of the best early studies of Golden Age theater.[11] Following a harsh indictment of Lope, Bances numbers Mira among a small group of dramatists who, thanks largely to their theological training, contributed to a healthy advancement of the *comedia*.[12]

Mira's eclipse early in the eighteenth century is hinted by the total absence of his name in the ambitious but heavily subjective critical work which Alberto Lista dedicated to Golden Age theater.[13] When we turn from contemporary praise and critical comment to the actual performance record of Mira's plays, we find that surprisingly complete documentation is available on the works of Golden Age dramatists which have been produced in theaters in Spain and in the New World through the years. Both the presence and the absence of Mira's titles in this documentation is helpful in assessing the pattern of his popularity.

The exportation of the Spanish *comedia* to the New World, in printed texts and in stage presentations, is documented well enough to corroborate the assertion of Dorothy Schons: "Mexicans were fond of the drama. During the colonial period they imported large numbers of plays from Spain."[14] Irving A. Leonard, who in several publications has studied the shipment of books to the New World, mentions royal prohibitions against the dissemination of secular literature: "By command of the kings of Spain the colonists of America were forbidden under the severest penalties from reading what were called books of fiction, poetry, novels, plays, etc."[15] Leonard theorizes, however, that in spite of such prohibitions, the forbidden works were imported and widely read. He speaks of "the flood of dramatic works which poured into the colonies in the seventeenth and eighteenth centuries, and far exceeded in quantity any other single class of profane literature."[16] He adds: "It is interesting to note that the plays of Lope de Vega and Calderón average a little higher than those of most other dramatists, but they do not dominate the list."[17] A shipment of *comedias* which left Seville on May 16, 1713 contained *El esclavo del demonio, El ejemplo mayor de la desdicha,* a third title falsely attributed to Mira, and *El conde Alarcos,* which could be Mira's or Guillén de Castro's.[18]

Although no productions of Mira's plays are documented in the studies of Lafayette Silva,[19] Emilio Julio Pasarell,[20] or J. R. Spell,[21] Trenti Rocamora reports that the company of Juan Grisóstomo performed *El arpa de David* for Corpus Christi in 1619 in Lima, where *Mujer, ingenio y amor* [sic] was also staged in 1623.[22] In his study of the theater in Lima, 1790–93, Leonard reports that Mira's

El rico avariento was performed on Christmas Day, 1790.[23]
Guillermo Lohmann Villena informs us that ten titles attributed to
the sole or partial authorship of Mira de Amescua were presented
in Lima during the period 1612–1798 and adds the interesting note
that *El esclavo del demonio* premièred in Lima in 1612, the year of
its first publication in Spain.[24] José Juan Arrom documents a performance of Mira's *La Judía de Toledo* [*La desgraciada Raquel*] in
Havana on Sunday, September 4, 1791.[25] Ortega Ricaurte reports
the performance of *El conde Alarcos* in Bogotá in 1793, but no
indication is given as to whether this is Mira's or Guillén de
Castro's.[26] Before returning from the New World to Spain, it is
interesting to note José Mariano Beristain de Souza's report that *El
animal profeta* was translated into Nahuatl.[27]

Impressive documentation is also available on the plays of Mira
de Amescua which have been produced in several cities of Spain
through the years. In Ada Coe's cataloguing of plays announced in
Madrid's newspapers from 1661 to 1819, for example, one notes
with surprise the total absence of *El esclavo del demonio* and the
fact that of the six entries attributed to Mira, four appear to be
variant titles of the same play, *El más feliz cautiverio. El ejemplo
mayor de la desdicha* and *El rico avariento* are included, although
not attributed to Mira.[28] In Valladolid, however, for which Alonso
Cortés has documented play production from 1681 to 1798, Mira's
leading titles were *El esclavo del demonio* and *El ejemplo mayor de
la desdicha.*[29] The same two titles, with six and four stagings
respectively, were among Mira's most popular plays in Valencia
during the first half of the eighteenth century, as is documented in
the ambitious study of Juliá Martínez, who notes that *Los
carboneros de Francia,* staged sixteen times, was Mira's leader in
Valencia for this period. Also staged there were *Las lises de
Francia, El rico avariento,* and *No hay burlas con las mujeres.*[30]

Theatrical performances in Barcelona during the period 1719–94
are documented by Alfonso Par. His use of variant titles and the
absence of authors' names makes a statistical analysis difficult, but
El ejemplo mayor de la desdicha and Diamante's plagiarism of *La
desgraciada Raquel* appear to be the most frequently mentioned
plays connected with Mira's name.[31] Cotarelo, in his monograph
on Isidoro Máiquez, Madrid's leading actor from 1783 to 1819, includes several of Mira's titles in a catalogue of plays produced in
the capital during that period.[32] On the basis of the eleven perfor-

mances of one play, Charlotte Lorenz ranks Mira nineteenth of a
list of twenty-four dramatists whose plays were produced in
Madrid's three theaters, the *Príncipe, Cruz,* and *Caños del Peral*
from 1808–18.[33] For the period 1820–50 in Madrid, however, as
studied by Nicholson B. Adams,[34] there is no mention of even a
single play by Mira.

In recent years there has been a surge of interest in diffusing
information about the available holdings of Spanish plays found in
the collections of institutional or private libraries. Paul P. Rogers,
in 1940,[35] catalogued three Mira entries which are found in the
Oberlin College Library. In 1959, J. A. Molinaro, J. H. Parker, and
Evelyn Rugg[36] catalogued eleven Mira entries in the University of
Toronto Library. In 1965, two more important catalogues
appeared: In B. B. Ashcom's,[37] the Wayne State University Library
and the private library of the compiler were shown to possess
twelve Mira entries; twenty-six Mira titles in the collection of the
University of North Carolina Library were catalogued by William
A. McKnight with the collaboration of Mabel Barrett Jones.[38]

Following a lifetime in which he was held in high esteem by his
contemporaries, Mira de Amescua has been the victim of centuries
of neglect. The neglect may be explained in part by the relative
inaccessibility of several of his better plays, as well as by the assignment to other authors of some of his plays of highest quality.
Thanks to the diligent work of modern editors and critics, interest
in Mira has reawakened. We conclude these pages with the hope
that much new and exciting scholarship related to Mira will be
forthcoming. It is our firm conviction that such new contributions
will cause Mira's star to rise higher and higher. We urge general
reader and scholar alike to reap the rich rewards available through
acquaintance with the best efforts of this neglected but important
Golden Age dramatist.

Notes and References

Chapter One

1. Fructuoso Sanz, "El doctor don Antonio Mira de Amescua. Nuevos datos para su biografía," *Boletín de la Real Academia Española,* I (1914), 551–72. The same document was earlier used, although not as fully exploited, by Torcuato Tárrago, "El doctor Mira de Amescua," *El museo universal,* VIII (1864), 114–15, and in a slightly revised reprint which appeared in *La ilustración española y americana* (Madrid, 1888), p. 307.

2. Nicolás Antonio, *Biblioteca hispana sive Hispanorum* (Romae: ex Officina Nicolai Angell Tinaffii, 1672), p. 114. The same account is found on p. 145 of the more accessible eighteenth-century edition, Madrid: J. de Ibarra, 1783.

3. Ramón de Mesonero Romanos, "El teatro de Mirademescua," *Semanario pintoresco español* (1852), 82–83. See also his introduction to *Dramáticos contemporáneos de Lope de Vega,* in *Biblioteca de Autores Españoles,* XLV (1858), vii–x. Hereafter, this collection will be referred to as the *BAE.*

4. Cayetano Alberto de la Barrera, "Mira de Amescua," in *Catálogo bibliográfico y biográfico del teatro antiguo español, desde sus orígenes hasta mediados del siglo XVIII* (Madrid, 1860; Edición facsímil, Madrid, 1969), pp. 255–60.

5. Torcuato Tárrago, *loc. cit.*

6. Francisco Rodríguez Marín, in *Pedro Espinosa — Estudio biográfico, bibliográfico y crítico* (Madrid, 1907), pp. 91–96; and "Nuevos datos para las biografías de algunos escritores españoles de los siglos XVI y XVII: 'Antonio Mira de Amescua'," *Boletín de la Real Academia Española,* V (1918), 321–32.

7. Narciso Díaz de Escovar, "Siluetas escénicas del pasado: Autores dramáticos granadinos del siglo XVII — El doctor Mira de Amescua," *Revista del centro de estudios históricos de Granada y su reino,* I (1911), 122–43.

8. In *Mira de Amescua, Teatro,* I, Prólogo, edición y notas de Ángel Valbuena Prat (Madrid, 1926; *Clásicos Castellanos,* LXX, Madrid, 1943), ix–xviii.

9. Emilio Cotarelo y Mori, *Mira de Amescua y su teatro — Estudio biográfico y crítico* (Madrid, 1931), pp. 5–43. The material of this book

171

was first published as an article in the *Boletín de la Real Academia Española,* XVII (1930), 467–505, 611–58; XVIII (1931), 7–90.

10. Karl Curtiss Gregg, "A Critical Edition of Antonio Mira de Amescua's *La mesonera del cielo."* Unpublished Ph.D. dissertation, Syracuse University, 1968, pp. 1–19.

11. Karl C. Gregg, "A Brief Biography of Antonio Mira de Amescua," *Bulletin of the Comediantes,* XXVI (Spring, 1974), 14–22.

12. Although Bartolomé José Gallardo, *Ensayo de una biblioteca española de libros raros y curiosos,* III (Madrid: Imprenta y Fundición de Manuel Tello, 1888), 810, stated that Mira "fue hijo natural: su madre se llamó Juana Pérez," Tárrago, *loc. cit.,* had, in 1864, already claimed the modern discovery of the names of Mira's parents, and of his illegitimacy.

13. Tárrago, *loc. cit.,* mentions a fruitless attempt to find Mira's birth or baptismal certificates in Guadix. Undaunted by similar failures of subsequent scholars, we made our own attempt in the spring of 1968. Unsuccessful in the Cathedral of Guadix, we were introduced to don Carlos Asenjo Sedano, Profesor Mercantil and Jefe de la Agencia del Instituto Nacional de Previsión, who was said to possess a document related to Mira's birth. In an interview, Sr. Asenjo claimed to have been given a page torn from the Cathedral records which carried the date of Mira's birth. The loose page, he added, had been lost during a change of residence; he made a promise, to this day unfulfilled, that he would forward a copy of its text if it ever reappeared. With no documentary evidence, the guesses of scholars have ranged widely: Mesonero, *Semanario pintoresco,* p. 82, and *BAE,* XLV, vii, proposes "hacia 1570"; Barrera, *Catálogo,* p. 255, "por los años de 1578"; Tárrago, *loc. cit.,* "por los años de 1580 a 1581"; Rafael Carrasco, *Lope de Vega y Mira de Amescua* (Guadix, 1935), p. 122, "por el año 1570 a 1574, aunque Mesonero da como fija la primera fecha." The testimony of witnesses that Mira was between 54 and 57 years old in 1631 (Sanz, p. 559) suggested a birthdate between 1574 and 1577. Cotarelo, *Mira de Amescua,* p. 10, on the basis of the fact that Mira had attained the legal age of 25 in 1600, narrows the period to 1573–75 and states his preference for 1574.

14. Rodríguez Marín, "Nuevos datos," p. 325.

15. *Ibid.,* pp. 322–23.

16. *Ibid.,* p. 322.

17. *Ibid.,* pp. 321–22. The letter is headed by the date May 8, 1600; we have chosen to use the date included in the text of the document.

18. Carrasco, p. 9.

19. Cotarelo, *Mira de Amescua,* p. 13. Mira's request is discussed, and the document itself is published, by Rodríguez Marín, "Nuevos datos," pp. 322–23.

20. Rodríguez Marín, "Nuevos datos," pp. 323–24.

21. Otis H. Green, "The Literary Court of the Conde de Lemos at

Naples, 1610-1616," *Hispanic Review,* I (1933), 293.

22. Otis H. Green, "Mira de Amescua in Italy," *Modern Language Notes,* XLV (1930), 319, n. 3.

23. See Sanz, p. 564.

24. *Ibid.,* p. 563.

25. Otis H. Green, "Mira de Amescua in Italy," pp. 317-18.

26. Otis H. Green, "The Literary Court...," pp. 300-302.

27. Ruth Lee Kennedy, *Studies in Tirso,* I: *The Dramatist and His Competitors, 1620-26* (Chapel Hill: North Carolina Studies in the Romance Languages and Literatures, 1974), 38.

28. Edward M. Wilson, "Nuevos documentos sobre las controversias teatrales: 1650-1681," *Actas del segundo congreso internacional de hispanistas* (Nijmegen, 1967), p. 156.

29. See Cotarelo, *Mira de Amescua,* pp. 22-24 for details.

30. See Rodríguez Marín, "Nuevos datos," pp. 324-28.

31. *Ibid.,* p. 328.

32. See Kennedy, *Studies in Tirso,* I, 166, n. 23.

33. See Agustín G. de Amezúa, *Epistolario de Lope de Vega Carpio,* IV (Madrid: Aldus, 1943), 53-54.

34. See N. D. Shergold, *A History of the Spanish Stage from Medieval Times Until the End of the Seventeenth Century* (Oxford: The Clarendon Press, 1967), p. 257.

35. Cristóbal Pérez Pastor, *Bibliografía Madrileña, Parte tercera: 1621 al 1625* (Madrid: Tipografía de la Revista de Archivos, 1907), pp. 427-31.

36. Lope Félix de Vega Carpio, *Obras escogidas,* II (Madrid: Aguilar, 1953), p. 135.

37. José Alfay, *Poesías varias de grandes ingenios españoles* (Zaragoza, 1654).

38. *BAE,* XX, xxxii-xxxiii, and *BAE,* LII, 587-88.

39. Luis de Góngora y Argote, *Obras completas,* ed. Juan and Isabel Millé y Giménez (Madrid: Aguilar, 1951), pp. 1049-50.

40. Sanz, p. 565.

41. Rodríguez Marín, *Pedro Espinosa,* pp. 94-95.

42. Ángel Valbuena Prat, *Historia de la literatura española,* II [1st edition, 1937], 4th edition (Barcelona: G. Gili, 1953), 421.

43. Rodríguez Marín, "Nuevos datos," pp. 331-32.

44. George Ann Huck, "A Critical Edition of Mira de Amescua's *La tercera de sí misma.*" Unpublished Ph.D. dissertation, Tulane University, 1968, p. 22.

45. Rodríguez Marín, *Pedro Espinosa,* p. 95.

46. Mesonero Romanos, *BAE,* XLV, vii, affirmed in 1858 that Mira died in Madrid in 1635, the year of Lope's death; Barrera, *Catálogo,* p. 256, suggests 1640; and Tárrago, *loc. cit.,* p. 114, offers a range from 1640-1645.

47. Pedro Suárez, *Historia del obispado de Guadix y Baza* (Madrid: Antonio Román, 1696), p. 314. [Reprint, Madrid: Artes Gráficas Arges, 1948.]

48. Gregg, "A Brief Biography," p. 21.

49. Miguel Herrero García, "En el tricentenario de Mirademescua," *Ecclesia, órgano de Acción Católica*, No. 171 (1944), 18.

Chapter Two

1. Ludwig Pfandl, *Historia de la literatura nacional española de la Edad de Oro*, Spanish translation by Jorge Rubió Balaguer (Barcelona: Editorial Gustavo Gili, S.A., 1952), p. 441.

2. *BAE*, XLV, viii–ix.

3. Rodríguez Marín, *Pedro Espinosa*, p. 93.

4. Lope Félix de Vega Carpio, *Obras dramáticas publicadas por la Real Academia Española*, III (1893). We use the modern reprint in *BAE*, CLVIII, 241.

5. Margaret Wilson, *Spanish Drama of the Golden Age* (Oxford: Pergamon Press, 1969), p. 145.

6. Albert E. Sloman, *The Dramatic Craftsmanship of Calderón* (Oxford: Dolphin Book Co., 1958), p. 294.

7. See Mario N. Pavia, *Drama of the Siglo de Oro. A Study of Magic, Witchcraft, and Other Occult Beliefs* (New York: Hispanic Institute in the United States, 1959), pp. 47, 133, 137–38.

8. C. E. Anibal, *Mira de Amescua: I. "El arpa de David," Introduction and Critical Text; II. Lisardo — His Pseudonym* (Columbus, 1925), p. 181.

9. *BAE*, XLV, viii.

10. Mesonero Romanos, *Semanario pintoresco* (1852), p. 82.

11. Edward M. Wilson and Duncan Moir, *A Literary History of Spain: The Golden Age Drama, 1492-1700* (London: Ernest Benn, 1971), pp. 82–83.

12. Ludwig Pfandl, *Historia*, p. 464.

13. Vern G. Williamsen, "The Dramatic Function of *cuentecillos* in Some Plays by Mira de Amescua," *Hispania*, LIV (1971), 62-67.

14. Vern G. Williamsen, "The development of a *décima* in Mira de Amescua's Theater," *Bulletin of the Comediantes*, XXII (Fall, 1970), 32-36.

15. C. E. Anibal, *"Voces del cielo* — A Note on Mira de Amescua," *Romanic Review*, XVI (1925), 57-70.

16. *Ibid.*, p. 58.

17. Wilson, *Spanish Drama*, p. 144.

18. Ruth Lee Kennedy, *"La prudencia en la mujer* and the Ambient That Brought It Forth," *Publications of the Modern Language Associa-*

tion, LXIII (1948), 1131-90.

19. Sister Mary Austin Cauvin, "The *comedia de privanza* in the Seventeenth Century." Unpublished Ph.D. dissertation, University of Pennsylvania, 1957, p. xxv.

20. *Ibid.,* p. 10.

21. *Ibid.,* p. 12.

22. *Comedias nuevas escogidas de los mejores ingenios de España* [Published in 48 *Partes* in Madrid, from 1652 to 1704].

23. Francisco Medel del Castillo, *Índice general alfabético* (Madrid, 1735) [Reprint published by John M. Hill, *Revue Hispanique,* LXXV (1929), 144-369].

24. The "Catálogo alphabético" is volume XVI of *Theatro hespañol* (Madrid: Imprenta Real, 1785).

25. Mesonero Romanos, *Semanario pintoresco* (1852), p. 83.

26. Barrera, *Catálogo,* pp. 258-60.

27. Cotarelo, *Mira de Amescua y su teatro — Estudio biográfico y crítico.*

28. *El arpa de David,* p. 1.

29. *Ibid.*

30. S. Griswold Morley and Courtney Bruerton, *The Chronology of Lope de Vega's 'Comedias', with a Discussion of Doubtful Attributions, the Whole Based on a Study of His Strophic Versification* (New York: The Modern Language Association of America; London: Oxford University Press, 1940).

31. Agustín G. de Amezúa, *Una colección manuscrita y desconocida de comedias de Lope de Vega* (Madrid: Centro de Estudios sobre Lope de Vega, 1945).

32. *Cronología de las comedias de Lope de Vega,* Spanish version by María Rosa Cartes (Madrid: Gredos, 1968).

33. Alan Paterson, "Tirso de Molina: Two Bibliographical Studies," *Hispanic Review,* XXXV (1967), 64-68.

34. S. Griswold Morley, "The Use of Verse-Forms (strophes) by Tirso de Molina," *Bulletin Hispanique,* VII (1905), 406-07.

35. Morley, "El uso de las combinaciones métricas en las comedias de Tirso de Molina," *Bulletin Hispanique,* XVI (1914), 185, 195.

36. Menéndez Pelayo, *Estudios y discursos de crítica histórica y literaria,* III (Santander: Aldus, S.A., 1941), 201.

37. *El arpa de David,* pp. 174-76.

38. Lidia Santelices, "Probable autor de *El condenado por desconfiado,*" *Anales de la Facultad de Filosofía y Educación,* I, Nos. 2-3 (Santiago: Universidad de Chile, 1936), 48-56.

39. M. A. Zeitlin, *"El condenado por desconfiado y El esclavo del demonio,"* *Modern Language Forum,* XXX (1945), 1-5.

40. Ruth Lee Kennedy, "Tirso's *La república al revés:* Its Debt to

Mira's *La rueda de la fortuna,* Its Date of Composition, and Its Importance," *Reflexión 2,* II (1973), 47.

41. Williamsen, "Some Odd *Quintillas* and a Question of Authenticity in Tirso's Theatre," *Romanische Forschungen,* LXXXII (1970), 488–513.

42. Cotarelo, *Mira de Amescua,* pp. 167–69.

43. *Ibid.*

44. Medel, *Índice,* pp. 178, 319.

45. See J. A. Molinaro, J. H. Parker, and Evelyn Rugg, *A Bibliography of Comedias Sueltas in the University of Toronto Library* (Toronto, 1959), p. 42.

46. Barrera, *Catálogo,* p. 303.

47. Adolfo de Castro, in his 1857 anthology, *Poetas líricos de los siglos XVI y XVII,* II, in *BAE, XLII,* 421–28, includes nine extracts from *comedias* attributed to Mira in the total of fifteen poems which he publishes.

48. *Ibid.,* p. lxxiii.

49. Barrera, *Catálogo,* p. 257.

50. Valbuena Prat, *El teatro español en su Siglo de Oro* (Barcelona: Editorial Planeta, 1969), p. 168.

51. *BAE, XLII,* lxxiii.

52. Gregg, "A Brief Biography," p. 15, indicates that the poem's first line is "Delfines verdinegros y lascivos." In the version published by Adolfo de Castro, *BAE, XLII,* 19–20, the verse cited by Gregg is the initial verse of the sixth strophe.

53. Cotarelo, *Mira de Amescua,* p. 11.

54. Carrasco, *Lope de Vega y Mira,* p. 10.

55. Díaz de Escovar, "Siluetas escénicas," p. 123.

56. Entitled "Canción real. A la instabilidad de las cosas de la vida" by Adolfo de Castro, *BAE, XLII,* 421.

57. In Baltasar Gracián, *Obras completas,* ed. Arturo del Hoyo (Madrid: Aguilar, 1960), p. 277.

58. Mira de Amescua, "Canción real a una mudanza," ed. R. Foulché-Delbosc, *Revue Hispanique,* XVI (1907), 288–94.

59. Milton A. Buchanan, ed., *Spanish Poetry of the Golden Age* (Toronto: University of Toronto Press, 1942), pp. 90–93.

60. *Ibid.,* p. 144.

61. Its new call sign is 3888.

62. Díaz de Escovar, "Siluetas escénicas," p. 126, mentions a poem entitled *El Anteón* and wonders if it is actually *Acteón y Diana.* Actually, the poem found in the codex, on fols. 165r-174v, is entitled *La fábula de Anteón* and it is identical to *Acteón y Diana.*

63. Barrera, *Catálogo,* p. 257.

64. John J. Reynolds, "Mira de Amescua's *Octavas al Príncipe de Gales,*" *Renaissance Quarterly,* XXII (Summer, 1969), 128–39.

65. José Simón Díaz, "Textos dispersos de clásicos españoles: VIII. Mira de Amescua," *Revista de Literatura,* Nos. 35–36 (1960), 169–80.

66. Cotarelo, *Mira de Amescua,* p. 32. n. 1.

67. Francisco de Quevedo Villegas, *Obras completas,* ed. Luis Astrana Marín (Madrid: Aguilar, 1952), pp. 666–710.

68. Reynolds, "Mira de Amescua's *Octavas,*" p. 131.

69. *BAE,* XLII, 423–24.

70. *BAE,* XXXVIII, 153.

71. See Cotarelo, *Mira de Amescua,* p. 172.

72. Poem available in *BAE,* XLII, 425.

73. Simón Díaz, "Textos dispersos,"169–80.

Chapter Three

1. James A. Castañeda, *A Critical Edition of Lope de Vega's "Las paces de los reyes y Judía de Toledo"* (Chapel Hill: University of North Carolina Press, 1962), pp. 5–30.

2. Another play with an equal number of collaborators is *La luna africana,* written before 1643. For a short discussion of this play, see our *Agustín Moreto* (New York: Twayne, 1974), pp. 94–95.

3. Cotarelo, *Mira de Amescua,* p. 47.

4. *BAE,* XX, 487–508. We have used this version for our analysis.

5. Guillén de Castro, *Obras,* ed. E. Juliá Martínez, III (Madrid: Tipografía de la Revista de Archivos, 1927), 593–639.

6. Medel, *Índice,* pp. 164, 319.

7. Barrera, *Catálogo,* p. 259.

8. Cotarelo, *Mira de Amescua,* p. 56.

9. Adolf Schaeffer, *Geschichte des spanischen Nationaldramas,* I (Leipzig, 1890), 320.

10. By letter of October 6, 1966, the Biblioteca Nacional informed us that it neither had this rare volume nor knew where a copy could be found. We are grateful for a typescript of the play which was kindly lent to us by Professor Vern G. Williamsen.

11. Cotarelo, *Mira de Amescua,* pp. 67–68.

12. A. T. Pickering, "Mira de Amescua, *El Conde Alarcos:* A Critical Edition with Introduction and Notes." Unpublished Ph.D. dissertation, Ohio State University, 1951.

13. Ruth Lee Kennedy, "Tirso's *La vida y muerte de Herodes:* Its Date, Its Importance, and Its Debt to Mira's Theatre," *Revista de Archivos, Bibliotecas y Museos,* LXXVI (1973), 144, n. 33.

14. No. 365 in the collection of Agustín Durán, "Romancero general o colección de romances castellanos anteriores al siglo XVIII," *BAE,* X, 224–27.

15. Gladys Wallach, "The Conde Alarcos Theme in Spanish Literature

— A Preliminary Study of Its Poetic and Dramatic Versions." Unpublished M.A. thesis, New York University, 1944.

16. Vernon A. Chamberlin, "Dramatic Treatments of the Conde Alarcos Theme Through Jacinto Grau," *Hispania,* XLII (1959), 517–23.

17. Guillén de Castro, *Obras,* II, 1–39.

18. See Courtney Bruerton, "The Chronology of the *Comedias* of Guillén de Castro," *Hispanic Review,* XII (1944), 95.

19. In *BAE,* CCXLVI, 11–78. According to Morley and Bruerton, *Cronología,* p. 245, the play may be dated with certitude 1595–1603.

20. *El Conde Alarcos. Drama caballeresco en tres actos y en verso...* (Habana: Imprenta del Gobierno y Capitanía General por S.M., 1838). Also published in José J. Milanés, *Obras,* III (Habana: Imprenta del Faro Industrial, 1846), 1–99.

21. *El Conde Alarcos — tragedia romancesca en tres actos* (Buenos Aires: Editorial Losada, S.A., 1944). See José M. Osma, "*El Conde Alarcos* — Tragedia de Jacinto Grau," *Hispania,* XII (1929), 179–84.

22. George Ticknor, *History of Spanish Literature* (1849), p. 116.

23. *Op. cit.,* p. 70.

24. Cotarelo, *Mira de Amescua,* p. 68.

25. James A. Castañeda, "Renacimiento romántico en Cuba del tema del Conde Alarcos," in *Estudios de Literatura Hispanoamericana en honor a José J. Arrom* (Chapel Hill: University of North Carolina Press, 1974), pp. 99–108.

26. In Juan Bautista Diamante,*Parte XXVII* of *Comedias escogidas* (Madrid: Andrés García de la Iglesia, 1667).

27. Comedia Famossa *La desgraciada Raquel, i Rei D^n Alphonso el 8°* Del Doctor Mirademescua [Ms. D. 22, George Ticknor Collection, Boston Public Library].

28. Donald Alan Murray, "Mira de Amescua's *La desgraciada Raquel.*" Unpublished Ph.D. dissertation, Stanford University, 1951.

29. Cotarelo, *Mira de Amescua,* pp. 72–74. On page 72, the play's title is erroneously given as *La desgracia de Raquel,* but the error is noted in the Index, p. 175, n. 1.

30. Hugo A. Rennert, "Mira de Mescua et *La judía de Toledo,*" *Revue Hispanique,* VII (1900), 132–33.

31. Ticknor, *Catalogue of the Spanish Library and of the Portuguese Books Bequeathed by George Ticknor to the Boston Public Library,* Compiled by James Lyman Whitney (Boston: Printed by Order of the Trustees, 1879), p. 231.

32. Rennert, "Mira de Mescua . . . ," pp. 125–26.

33. *Ibid.,* pp. 124–36.

34. *Ed. cit.*

35. Menéndez Pelayo, *Estudios sobre el teatro de Lope de Vega,* IV (Santander: Aldus, 1949), p. 97. See A. Valbuena Prat, *Historia de la*

literatura española, II (Barcelona: C. Enrique Granados, 1953), 429: "*La desdichada* [sic] *Raquel,* although notably improved by Diamante, is of interest in the evolution of the legend of 'The Jewess of Toldeo' — which extends from Lope to Grillparzer—.'' Such an affirmation would indicate that this important legend, which neither began with Lope nor ended with Grillparzer, has not received from Valbuena Prat the attention it deserved from such a conscientious scholar. It also shows the great influence of Menéndez Pelayo on modern criticism. Valbuena repeats the error in his *Historia del teatro español* (Barcelona: Editorial Noguer, 1956), pp. 413, 452.

36. Castañeda, ed., *Las paces de los reyes,* pp. 1–128.
37. Cotarelo, *Mira de Amescua,* p. 77.
38. *Las desgracias del rey don Alfonso.*
39. Fols. 25r–52v.
40. Cotarelo, *Mira de Amescua,* pp. 93–94.
41. Karl Ludwig Selig, "An Edition with Introduction and Notes of *La hija de Carlos Quinto,* comedia famosa del doctor Mira de Amescua.'' Unpublished M. A. thesis, Ohio State University, 1947.
42. Tomás Magallón Antón, then director of the Photographic Laboratory of the Biblioteca Nacional, in a letter dated October 6, 1966, speaking first of *Amor, ingenio y mujer,* states: "la misma desapareció con otras muchas durante la guerra, y aun antes de ella. La misma suerte ha corrido también la comedia *La hija de Carlos V.*''
43. Cotarelo, *Mira de Amescua,* p. 96.
44. Madrid: Antonio Sanz, 1748.
45. *BAE,* XLV, 39–56.
46. Mira de Amescua, *No hay dicha ni desdicha hasta la muerte,* with Introduction and Notes by Vern G. Williamsen (Columbia, 1970).
47. Vern G. Williamsen, "Poetic Truth in Two *Comedias: No hay mal que por bien no venga* and *No hay dicha ni desdicha hasta la muerte,*'' *Hispanófila,* No. 45 (1972), 39–47.
48. Referred to as Porcellos throughout Williamsen's edition.
49. Anibal, ed., *El arpa de David,* pp. 155–57.
50. *Ibid.,* pp. 157–58.
51. Williamsen, ed., *No hay dicha,* p. 2.
52. *BAE,* XLV, pp. 57–71.
53. Castañeda, ed., *Las paces de los reyes,* pp. 70–71.
54. See *Nueva Biblioteca de Autores Españoles,* IV (1906), lix. Hereafter, this collection will be referred to as the *NBAE.*
55. Santiago Montoto, "Una comedia de Tirso, que no es de Tirso,'' *Archivo hispalense,* VII (1946), 99–107.
56. Anibal, ed., *El arpa de David,* pp. 161–76.
57. E. Juliá Martínez, "Rectificaciones bibliográficas: *La adversa fortuna de don Álvaro de Luna,*'' *Revista de Bibliografía Nacional,* IV

(1943), 147–50.

58. *Comedias de Tirso de Molina,* I, *NBAE,* IV: *La próspera fortuna,* 263–85; *La adversa fortuna,* 286–310.

59. Doctor Mira de Amescua, *La segunda de don Áluaro* [*Adversa fortuna de don Álvaro de Luna*], Estudio preliminar y edición crítica por Nellie E. Sánchez-Arce (Mexico, 1960).

60. Mira de Amescua, *Adversa fortuna de don Álvaro de Luna,* Introduzione, Testo Critico e Note a cura di Luigi de Filippo (Firenze, 1960).

61. Mira de Amescua, *Comedia famosa de Ruy López de Ávalos,* notas preliminares y nueva edición revisada por Nellie E. Sánchez-Arce (Mexico, 1965).

62. Tirso de Molina, *Obras dramáticas completas,* I (Madrid: Aguilar, 1946), 1949–59.

63. Luis Fernández-Guerra, *Don Juan Ruiz de Alarcón y Mendoza* (Madrid, 1871), p. 299.

64. William C. McCrary, "The Authorship of *Próspera y adversa fortuna de don Álvaro de Luna,*" *Bulletin of Hispanic Studies,* XXX (1958), 44.

65. Sandra Brown, "A Reconsideration of the Authorship of the *Don Álvaro de Luna* Plays," *Hispania,* LVII (1974), 422–27. Clifford Smith, in a letter to the editor of *Hispania,* LIX (1976), 289–90, proposes several corrections to Sandra Brown's article.

66. Sister Mary Austin Cauvin, "The *comedia de privanza,*" pp. 48–59, 86–107.

67. I. L. McClelland, Chapter IV, "Juan II and His Constables," in *Tirso de Molina. Studies in Dramatic Realism* (Liverpool: Institute of Hispanic Studies, 1948), pp. 90–128.

68. Courtney Bruerton, review of *Tirso de Molina. Studies in Dramatic Realism,* in *Hispanic Review,* XVII (1949), 347.

69. Margaret Wilson, "*La próspera fortuna de don Álvaro de Luna:* An Outstanding Work by Mira de Amescua," *Bulletin of Hispanic Studies,* XXXIII (1956), 36.

70. Sister Mary Austin Cauvin, "The *comedia de privanza,*" p. 88.

71. Raymond R. MacCurdy, "Tragic *Hamartia* in *La próspera y adversa fortuna de don Álvaro de Luna,*" *Hispania,* XLVII (1964), 82–90.

72. Raymond R. MacCurdy, *Francisco de Rojas Zorrilla and the Tragedy* (Albuquerque: University of New Mexico Press, 1958), p. 18.

73. *NBAE,* IX (1907), i.

74. Ruth Lee Kennedy, "*La prudencia en la mujer* and the Ambient That Brought It Forth," *Publications of the Modern Language Association,* LXIII (1948), 1157.

75. *Tirso de Molina,* pp. 99–100.

76. Medel, *Índice,* p. 148.

77. *Ibid.,* p. 230: "*Próspera fortuna* — de Lope; *Próspera fortuna* —

(sic) Don Bernardo de Cabrera." It is impossible to know from these confused entries if Medel intended to parallel his entries for *La adversa fortuna.*

78. Barrera, *Catálogo,* pp. 524, 575.

79. Anibal, ed., *El arpa de David,* pp. 150–58.

80. *Obras de Lope de Vega,* III (Madrid, 1917), 61–99.

81. *Ibid.,* VIII (Madrid, 1930), xli–xliv. The play's pagination is 636–73.

82. Cotarelo, *Mira de Amescua,* p. 166.

83. Anibal, ed., *El arpa de David,* p. 158.

84. See Williamsen, ed., *No hay dicha ni desdicha hasta la muerte,* pp. 2–3.

85. *Obras de Lope de Vega,* III, xii.

Chapter Four

1. Mary Marshall Borelli, "A Tentative Edition, with Introduction and Notes, of Mira de Amescua's *Ero y Leandro.*" Unpublished M..A. thesis, Ohio State University, 1951.

2. Francisca Moya del Baño, *El tema de Hero y Leandro en la literatura española* (Murcia: Publicaciones de la Universidad de Murcia, 1966), pp. 151–211.

3. Lope de Vega includes a similar title in *El peregrino en su patria,* and Agustín Durán (according to Moya del Baño, p. 132) cites two plays entitled *Hero y Leandro,* one by Pajaz, and the other by D.D.S.S., but none of the three appears to be extant.

4. The passage (Act I, vv. 23–36), ed. *Clásicos Castellanos,* CXXXVII, page 4, praises Mira "for having given to the theaters / such a well-written *comedia.*"

5. For the original text and English translation, see *Renaissance and Baroque Poetry,* ed. Elias Rivers (New York: Dell Publishing Co., 1966), p. 38.

6. Cited in Moya del Baño, *op. cit.,* p. 252.

7. *Ibid.,* pp. 175–76.

8. The *suelta* is Número 119 (Sevilla: Francisco de Leefdael); it has 32 numbered pages.

9. Medel, *Índice,* pp. 195, 319.

10. *Obras,* III, xxvi–xxviii, 354–92.

11. *Ibid.,* p. xxviii.

12. Cotarelo, *Mira de Amescua,* p. 111.

13. *Ibid.,*

14. *Ed. cit.,* p. xxviii.

15. *BAE,* XIV, 413–28.

16. The relationship of these two plays is studied by Albert E. Sloman

in *The Dramatic Craftsmanship of Calderón* (Oxford: Dolphin Book Co., 1958). pp. 128–58.

17. See Cotarelo, *Mira de Amescua,* pp. 59–61, for detailed bibliographic data. For a study of other treatments of the theme, see Richard W. Tyler, "Algunas versiones de la leyenda de la 'Reina Sevilla' en la primera mitad del Siglo de Oro," *Actas del segundo congreso internacional de hispanistas* (Nijmegen, 1967), 635–41.

18. For an interesting thesis that the name "Zumaque" may be an anagram for "Mezqua," see Milton A. Buchanan, "Notes on the Spanish Drama: Lope, Mira de Amescua, and Moreto," *Modern Language Notes,* XX (1905), 38–39.

19. Francisco Rojas Zorrilla, *Entre bobos anda el juego,* in *Clásicos Castellanos,* XXXV, see especially pp. 136–41.

20. Anibal, *"Voces del cielo,"* 58–60.

21. See Cotarelo, *Mira de Amescua,* pp. 78–81, for bibliographic data.

22. *Clásicos Castellanos,* LXXXII, 127–250.

23. Carol Louise Krumm, "A Partial Edition of *Las lises de Francia* de Antonio Mira de Amescua." Unpublished M.A. thesis, Ohio State University, 1946.

24. Anibal, *"Voces del cielo,"* pp. 57, 60–63.

25. Cotarelo, *Mira de Amescua,* p. 100.

26. *Ibid.,* p. 101.

27. Hugo A. Rennert, "Notes on the Chronology of the Spanish Drama," *Modern Language Review,* III (1907–08), 55.

28. *Obras de Lope de Vega,* VIII (1930), 1–31.

29. *Ibid.,* p. vii.

30. Morley and Bruerton, *Cronología,* pp. 518, 607.

31. *Obras de Lope,* VIII, p. vii.

32. Cotarelo, *Mira de Amescua,* p. 136.

33. *Ibid.,* p. 139.

34. In *Parte V* of *Flor de las comedias de España de diferentes autores* (Alcalá, 1615).

35. *Epistolario de Lope de Vega Carpio,* ed. Agustín G. de Amezúa, III (Madrid: Aldus, S.A., 1941), 4–5.

36. *BAE,* LII, pp. 222c–223a.

37. Morley and Bruerton, *Cronología,* p. 269.

38. *BAE,* XLV, pp. 1–22.

39. Edward Warren Hopper, "A Critical and Annotated Edition of Mira de Amescua's *La rueda de la fortuna.*" Unpublished Ph.D. dissertation, University of Missouri, 1972.

40. Raymond R. MacCurdy, "Notes on the Fateful Curse in Golden Age Drama," *Kentucky Romance Quarterly,* XXI (1974), 331, notes, having commented on the rare instances in which a son strikes his mother — and a queen at that — in Golden Age theater, that Teodosio is "a foster

son of humble birth."
41. Cotarelo, *Mira de Amescua*, p. 143.
42. *BAE*, XLV, viii.
43. Kennedy, "Tirso's *La república al revés*," 39–50.
44. Kennedy, "Tirso's *La vida y muerte de Herodes*," 121–48.

Chapter Five

1. See Cotarelo, *Mira de Amescua*, pp. 48–50.
2. *Ibid.*, p. 48.
3. Barrera, *Catálogo*, p. 259.
4. Anibal, ed., *El arpa de David*, p. 189. The same mistaken identification of the two titles may also be seen on p. 160.
5. See the edition of George Ann Huck, vv. 440, 1247, 1714, 2296, and 3514.
6. Cotarelo, *Mira de Amescua*, pp. 48–50.
7. Joanne Irene Limber, "A Partial Edition of *Amor, ingenio y mujer, comedia famosa del doctor Mira de Amescua*." Unpublished M.A. thesis, Ohio State University, 1946.
8. Cotarelo, *Sebastián de Prado y su mujer Bernarda Ramírez* (Madrid, 1916), p. 18.
9. John C. Fameli, "*La casa del tahur* de Antonio Mira de Amescua, edición paleográfica anotada." Unpublished Ph.D. thesis, University of Southern California, 1970.
10. *La casa del tahur*, con introducción y notas de Vern G. Williamsen. *Estudios de Hispanófila*, No. 26 (Madrid, 1973). Williamsen's preliminary remarks are dated February 23, 1971, which undoubtedly explains his lack of reference to Fameli's dissertation.
11. Cotarelo, *Mira de Amescua*, p. 63.
12. *Ibid.*, pp. 70–71. We have used the manuscript copy for our analysis.
13. Ruiz de Alarcón, *Teatro*, ed. Alfonso Reyes, *Clásicos Castellanos*, XXXVII, 116–18. Compare even the reactions of the disillusioned suitors: Mira's Captain claims "Yo adoraba esa belleza, / ¿qué importa que yerre el nombre?" (p. 23) and Alarcón's García, "Si el nombre / erré, no erré la persona" (vv. 3079–80).
14. Anibal, ed., *El arpa de David*, p. 180.
15. See Cotarelo, *Mira de Amescua*, p. 85, for bibliographic data.
16. *Ibid.*, p. 85, note 1.
17. *Ibid.*, p. 20.
18. XLV, 73–94.
19. LXXXII, 3–126.
20. Cotarelo, *Mira de Amescua*, p. 86.
21. See M. Romera-Navarro, "Las disfrazadas de varón en la come-

dia," *Hispanic Review,* II (1934), 273-74.
22. Medel, *Índice,* pp. 188, 319.
23. *Ibid.,* pp. 244, 325.
24. Barrera, *Catálogo,* p. 260.
25. *BAE,* XXXIX, xlii.
26. *Ibid.,* pp. 563-81.
27. Cotarelo, "La bibliografía de Moreto," *Boletín de la Real Academia Española,* XIV (1927), 490.
28. Cotarelo, *Mira de Amescua,* p. 88.
29. Mira de Amescua, *Galán, valiente y discreto.* Edición, prólogo y notas por Edward Nagy. *Clásicos Ebro,* 110 (Zaragoza, 1969).
30. *BAE,* XLV, 23-37.
31. Antonio Mira de Amescua, *Galán, valiente y discreto.* Estudio y edición crítica por F. William Forbes. *Colección Scholar* (Madrid, 1973).
32. *Ibid.,* p. 33.
33. Cotarelo, *Mira de Amescua,* p. 90.
34. Pedro Calderón de la Barca, *Obras completas,* I (Madrid: Aguilar, 1951), 927.
35. In *Obras completas de Juan Ruiz de Alarcón,* II (Mexico: Fondo de Cultura Económica, 1959), 916-1004.
36. Mabel Harlan, "The Relation of Moreto's *El desdén con el desdén* to Suggested Sources," *Indiana University Studies,* XI (1924), pp. 80-84.
37. Ruth Lee Kennedy, *The Dramatic Art of Moreto* (Northampton, 1932), pp. 72, n. 58, 165-67.
38. Barbara Matulka, "The Feminist Theme in the Drama of the *Siglo de Oro,*" *Romanic Review,* XXVI (1935), 222.
39. The play is in a volume entitled *Spanish Plays,* V, fols. 326-372.
40. John Lihani, "A Tentative Edition, with Introduction and Notes, of Mira de Amescua's *No hay burlas con las mujeres.*" Unpublished M.A. thesis, Ohio State University, 1950.
41. Cotarelo, *Mira de Amescua,* p. 128.
42. Ralph Edward Angelo, "An Edition, with Introduction and Notes, of Mira de Amescua's *No hay reinar como vivir.*" Unpublished M.A. thesis, Ohio State University, 1949.
43. Cotarelo, *Mira de Amescua,* p. 132.
44. In Henri Mérimée, "*El ayo de su hijo,* comedia de Don Guillén de Castro," *Bulletin Hispanique,* VIII (1906), 378.
45. *Obras de Lope de Vega,* VIII (1930), 324-58.
46. *Ibid.,* p. xxvi.
47. Cotarelo, *Mira de Amescua,* pp. 133-34.
48. *Lope de Vega's "El palacio confuso"* (New York: Instituto de las Españas, 1939), pp. xl-xlviii.
49. *Op. cit.,* lxxv-xci. John M. Hill, in his review of Stevens' edition, *Hispanic Review,* VIII (1940), 364-67, agrees on the proposed dates but

feels "that the case for Lope is not conclusively proved."

50. Morley and Bruerton, *Chronology,* p. 321 (updated *Cronología,* pp. 524-25).

51. Raúl Moglia, *"El palacio confuso no es de Lope de Vega,"* *Revista de Filología Hispánica,* V (1943), 51-56.

52. "Lisardo: Mira de Amescua's Pseudonym," Part II of Anibal's edition of *El arpa de David,* pp. 124-90. On p. 160 Anibal judges the play to be Mira's but surprisingly does not mention the inclusion of a Lisardo in the *dramatis personae.*

53. Cotarelo, *Mira de Amescua,* pp. 48-50, 148.

54. Mesonero Romanos, *Semanario pintoresco,* p. 83.

55. Medel, *Indice,* pp. 319, 320.

56. George Ann Huck, "A Critical Edition of Mira de Amescua's *La tercera de sí misma."* Unpublished Ph.D. dissertation, Tulane University, 1968.

57. *Ibid.,* p. 31.

58. *Ibid.* Schack, *Historia,* III, 275-76, does not specify a Tirsian title; he merely states that, for this play, Mira "imitates Tirso de Molina, but only in his most crude traits."

59. A. Restori, *Piezas de títulos de comedias* (Messina, 1903), p. 134.

60. Buchanan, "Notes on the Spanish Drama," p. 41.

61. Originally published in Lope de Vega, *Obras dramáticas publicadas por la Real Academia Española,* ed. M. Menéndez Pelayo, II (Madrid, 1892). We quote from the reprinting in *BAE,* CLVII (1963), 225-39. In his preliminary observations, p. lii, after citing the passage in question, Menéndez Pelayo affirms categorically that it contains "alusión al título de otra comedia de Lope."

62. Anibal, ed., *El arpa de David,* pp. 177-78.

63. *Chronology,* p. 353 (revised Spanish version, pp. 576-77).

64. Buchanan, "Notes on the Spanish Drama," p. 39.

65. Anibal, ed., *El arpa de David,* pp. 177, 178-82.

66. Anibal, "Mira de Amescua and *La ventura de la fea," Modern Language Notes,* XLII (1927), 106.

Chapter Six

1. Ángel Valbuena Prat, *Historia de la literatura española,* II, 424-25.

2. Valbuena Prat, *El teatro español en su Siglo de Oro,* p. 167.

3. *El arpa de David,* ed. C. E. Anibal (Columbus, 1925).

4. Medel, *Índice,* p. 156.

5. García de la Huerta, *Catálogo alphabético.*

6. Cotarelo, *Mira de Amescua,* pp. 54-56.

7. Anibal, *ed. cit.,* pp. 124-90.

8. *Ibid.,* p. 187.

9. Ed. Rodríguez Marín (Madrid: C. Bermejo, 1935), Chapter III, p. 43, v. 218.

10. In *BAE*, XXXVIII, 195.

11. Anibal, *ed. cit.*, p. 8.

12. Barrera, *Catálogo*, p. 260.

13. Cotarelo, *Mira de Amescua*, p. 66.

14. Barrera, *Catálogo*, p. 260.

15. Cotarelo, *Mira de Amescua*, p. 147.

16. Ada M. Coe, *Catálogo bibliográfico y crítico de las comedias anunciadas en los periódicos de Madrid desde 1661 hasta 1819*. The Johns Hopkins Studies in Romance Literatures and Languages, Extra Volume IX (Baltimore, 1935), 144–45.

17. A. Paz y Melia, *Catálogo de las piezas de teatro que se conservan en el departamento de manuscritos de la Biblioteca Nacional*, I (Madrid, 1934), 339.

18. See Leo Spitzer, "Soy quien soy," *Nueva Revista de Filología Hispánica*, I (1947), 113–127.

19. In *Autos sacramentales con cuatro comedías nuevas y sus loas y entremeses* (Madrid: María de Quiñones, 1655), fols. 165r–185v.

20. Although Cotarelo, *Mira de Amescua*, p. 151, claims that the longer title was the more widely known subsequent to 1657, we have chosen to use *El rico avariento*, which both represents the first known form and also renders more accurately, in our opinion, the main thrust of Mira's play.

21. "A Tentative Edition of Mira de Amescua's *La vida y muerte de San Lázaro*." Unpublished M.A. thesis, Ohio State University, 1951.

22. Anibal, ed., *El arpa de David*, p. 159.

23. See Williamsen, "The Development of a *décima*," p. 33.

24. Karl Gregg, "A Metaphor in Mira de Amescua," *Bulletin of the Comediantes*, XIX (Fall, 1967), 36–38.

25. Wilfred Wilenius, "A Tentative Edition, with Introduction and Notes, of Mira de Amescua's *El amparo de los hombres*." Unpublished M.A. thesis, Ohio State University, 1951.

26. J. M. Bella, "Las fuentes de dos comedias de Mira de Amescua: *El amparo de los hombres* y *El mártir de Madrid*," *Revista de Filología Española*, LI (1968), 139–50.

27. Cotarelo, *Mira de Amescua*, p. 51.

28. *Ibid.*

29. Anibal, ed., *El arpa de David*, p. 182; Bella, "Las fuentes de dos comedias," pp. 149–50.

30. For full bibliographic data, see Cotarelo, *Mira de Amescua*, p. 104. We have a microfilm of Ms. 17.394, transcribed early in the eighteenth century. It is one of the most carefully and beautifully transcribed *comedia* manuscripts we have seen.

31. Adrian Timothy Pickering, "An Edition, with Introduction and Notes, of Mira de Amescua's *Lo que puede el oír misa.*" Unpublished M.A. thesis, Ohio State University, 1947.

32. See Spencer and Schevill, *The Dramatic Works of Luis Vélez de Guevara. Their Plots, Sources, and Bibliography* (Berkeley, 1937), pp. 269–70, for speculation on the date of Vélez' *comedia.*

33. Rennert, "Notes on the Chronology," p. 333.

34. See Cotarelo, *Mira de Amescua,* p. 166.

35. IV (1894), 395–427. Modern version, *BAE,* CLVIII (1965), 179–224.

36. José Mariano Beristain de Souza, *Biblioteca hispano-americana septentrional,* I (Mexico: A. Valdés, 1816), 64.

37. Shirley Tock, "A Critical Edition of Mira de Amescua's *El animal profeta.*" Unpublished Ph.D. dissertation, University of Missouri, 1973.

38. Bonnie Wilds, "A Critical Edition of *El animal profeta.*" Unpublished Ph.D. dissertation, University of Pittsburgh, 1973.

39. *Ibid.,* p. 8.

40. Calderón, *Autos sacramentales,* I, ed. Ángel Valbuena Prat, *Clásicos Castellanos,* LXIX, xviii.

41. Kennedy, *The Dramatic Art of Moreto,* p. 155.

42. For a documented comparison, see Ángel Valbuena Prat, ed., *El esclavo del demonio, Clásicos Castellanos,* LXX, 125–28.

43. See our article, *"El esclavo del demonio y Caer para levantar:* reflejos de dos ciclos," in *Studia Hispanica in Honorem R. Lapesa,* II (Madrid, 1974), 181–88, and our comments on *Caer para levantar* in *Agustín Moreto,* pp. 42–43.

44. Cotarelo, *Mira de Amescua,* p. 81, n. 1, states that the volume was actually published in Zaragoza in 1654, although the handwritten title page of the copy in the Biblioteca Nacional carries a spurious 1649 date.

45. *Comedia famosa del Esclavo del demonio,* compuesta por el doctor Mira de Mesqua, ed. Milton A. Buchanan (Baltimore, 1905).

46. In *Letras españolas. Colección de obras selectas de nuestros autores clásicos.* Publicada bajo la dirección de Juan Hurtado y J. de la Serna y Ángel González Palencia (s.a.).

47. In *Mira de Amescua, Teatro* I, *Clásicos Castellanos,* LXX (Madrid, 1926); in the series of Compañía Iberoamericana de Publicaciones (Madrid, 1931); and in *Clásicos Ebro,* XLI.

48. *El esclavo del demonio,* "Letras hispánicas," Ediciones Cátedra (in press). James A. Castañeda, ed.

49. José Sánchez Arjona, *El teatro en Sevilla en los siglos XVI y XVII* (Madrid: A. Alonso, 1887), pp. 193–99.

50. Chapter LXXII, fols. 343r–346v.

51. Vida 173, fols. 2r–3v. The earliest edition cited by Valbuena Prat, *Clásicos Castellanos,* LXX, lix, is 1589; Cotarelo erroneously states that

editions prior to 1591 did not contain the legend of Fray Gil.

52. Anibal, *"Voces del cielo,"* p. 64, claims this scene to contain a variation of the *voces del cielo* device which might more properly be termed *voces del infierno*.

53. A dissenting vote is cast by Judith Rauchwarger, "Principal and Secondary Plots in *El esclavo del demonio," Bulletin of the Comediantes,* XXVIII (Spring, 1976), 49–52, who detects "yielding to a superior power (father, king, God)" as an aspect of the play which unifies its two plots.

54. Henry A. Linares, "A Paleographic Edition of Mira de Amescua's *El mártir de Madrid."* Unpublished Ph.D. dissertation, University of Missouri, 1974.

55. Cotarelo, *Mira de Amescua,* pp. 114–15.

56. R. L. Kennedy, "Manuscripts Attributed to Moreto in the Biblioteca Nacional," *Hispanic Review,* IV (1936), 320–23. See also Kennedy's *Dramatic Art of Moreto* (Philadelphia, 1932), pp. 185–86.

57. See Castañeda, *Agustín Moreto,* p. 53.

58. Bella, "Las fuentes de dos comedias," pp. 150–53.

59. Karl Curtiss Gregg, "A Critical Edition of Antonio Mira de Amescua's *La mesonera del cielo."* Unpublished Ph.D. dissertation, Syracuse University, 1968.

60. *Mira de Amescua, Teatro,* III, *Clásicos Castellanos,* CLXXI (1972).

61. Cotarelo, *Mira de Amescua,* pp. 115–16.

62. Gregg, *ed. cit.,* p. 44.

63. Cotarelo, *Mira de Amescua,* p. 118, erroneously states: "Abrahán ... niega a Alejandro la mano de su sobrina."

64. *Clásicos Castellanos,* LXX, xxxiv.

65. Valbuena Prat, *Historia,* II, 425, 426.

66. Medel, *Índice,* pp. 241, 320.

67. *Ibid.,* pp. 244, 321.

68. Cotarelo, *Mira de Amescua,* p. 147.

69. Pp. 165–200.

70. In his *Catálogo,* p. 88 — reference found in Cotarelo, *Mira de Amescua,* p. 149.

71. Cotarelo, *Mira de Amescua,* p. 150, n. 1, informs us that a manuscript copy of the inquisitorial trial is found in the Biblioteca Nacional.

Chapter Seven

1. Bruce W. Wardropper, "The Search for a Dramatic Formula for the *Auto Sacramental," Publications of the Modern Language Association,* LXV (1950), 1196.

2. Schack, *Historia,* III, 277–80.

3. Jaime Mariscal de Gante, *Los autos sacramentales desde sus*

orígenes hasta mediados del siglo XVIII (Madrid: Biblioteca Renaci-miento, 1911), p. 98.

4. Pfandl, *Historia,* pp. 485–87.

5. Valbuena Prat, *Historia,* II, 423.

6. Wardropper, "The Search for a Dramatic Formula," p. 1209. See also Wardropper's *Introducción al teatro religioso del Siglo de Oro* (Madrid: Revista de Occidente, 1953), p. 317.

7. See the abstract of her 1963 thesis, "Contribución al estudio del teatro de Antonio Mira de Amescua: los autos sacramentales," in *Revista de la Universidad de Madrid,* XII (1963), 755–56.

8. Phyllis Irene Patteson Mitchell, "The *autos sacramentales* of Mira de Amescua." Unpublished Ph.D. dissertation, Johns Hopkins University, 1971.

9. James Charles Maloney, "A Critical Edition of Antonio Mira de Amescua's *El monte de la piedad, La fe de Hungría,* and *La jura del príncipe.*" Unpublished Ph.D. dissertation, University of Arizona, 1973.

10. Medel, *Índice,* p. 320.

11. Mesonero Romanos, *Semanario pintoresco,* p. 83.

12. Barrera, *Catálogo,* pp. 259–60.

13. Cotarelo, *Mira de Amescua,* pp. 152–65 for individual analyses; p. 176 for a list of Mira's *autos.*

14. Jean-Louis Flecniakoska, *La Formation de l' "Auto" religieux en Espagne avant Calderón (1550–1635)* (Montpellier, 1961), pp. 64–71.

15. Barrera, *Catálogo,* p. 259.

16. Jenaro Alenda, "Catálogo de autos sacramentales, historiales y alegóricos," *Boletín de la Real Academia Española,* IV (1917), 644.

17. *Ibid.,* V (1918), 495–96.

18. Cotarelo, *Mira de Amescua,* p. 156.

19. N. D. Shergold and J. E. Varey, *Los autos sacramentales en Madrid en la época de Calderón, 1637–1681. Estudio y documentos* (Madrid, 1961), p. 32 [reference found in Shergold, *History,* p. 75]. See also Alenda, "Catálogo," *BRAE,* VIII (1921), 277.

20. Mitchell, "The *autos sacramentales* of Mira," pp. 38–42.

21. Paz y Melia, *Catálogo de las piezas de teatro,* p. 422.

22. Mitchell, "The *autos sacramentales* of Mira," p. 46.

23. Probable date supplied by Cotarelo, *Mira de Amescua,* p. 163. This is the version we use for our analysis.

24. Sister M. Carmel Therese Favazzo, "An Edition and Study of Mira de Amescua's *Nuestra Señora de los Remedios.*" Unpublished Ph.D. dissertation, St. John's University, 1970. The text of the *auto* appears on pp. 124–83.

25. *Lo que le toca al valor y Príncipe de Orange;* see pp. 76–78.

26. Flecniakoska, *La Formation de l' "Auto,"* p. 66.

27. *Ed. cit.,* pp. 41–119.

190 MIRA DE AMESCUA

28. *A Critical Edition of Mira de Amescua's "La fe de Hungría" and "El monte de la piedad."* Tulane Studies in Romance Languages and Literature, VII (1975), 93–143.
29. Earl J. Hamilton, *American Treasure and the Price Revolution in Spain, 1501–1650.* Harvard Economic Studies, XLIII (Cambridge: Harvard University Press, 1934). See particularly pages 73–82 of his chapter "Vellon Inflation in Castile, 1598–1650."
30. *Ibid.,* p. 74.
31. Cotarelo, *Mira de Amescua,* p. 157.
32. Maloney, "A Critical Edition" (1973), p. 10; (1975), p. 26.
33. *Op. cit.,* p. 123.
34. Medel, *Índice,* p. 320.
35. *Ed. cit.* (1973), pp. 120–94; (1975), pp. 43–92.
36. John J. Reynolds, "The Source of Moreto's Only *Auto Sacramental,*" *Bulletin of the Comediantes,* XXIV (Spring, 1972), 21–22.
37. See J.-L. Flecniakoska, "A propos d'un rôle de sacristain," *Revue des langues romanes,* LXXVIII (1966), 123–30.
38. Cotarelo, *Mira de Amescua,* p. 153.
39. Flecniakoska, *La Formation de l' "Auto,"* p. 520.
40. Cotarelo, *Mira de Amescua,* p. 165.
41. *Clásicos Castellanos,* LXX, xxvi, n. 2.
42. Cotarelo, *Mira de Amescua,* p. 155.
43. In 1971, we read the transcription in the Institut Hispanique; it is in manuscript and undated.
44. As reported in *Revista de la Universidad de Madrid,* XII (1963), 765–66.
45. In *Mira de Amescua, Teatro,* III, ed. José M. Bella, *Clásicos Castellanos,* CLXXI (1972), pp. 161–207.
46. Maloney, "A Critical Edition" (1973), pp. 195–257.
47. Flecniakoska, *"La jura del príncipe,* auto sacramental de Mira de Amescua," *Bulletin Hispanique,* LI (1949), 39–44.
48. Ed. Bella, vv. 211–20. A similar list of heretical sects may also be found in *La fe de Hungría* (ed. Maloney, vv. 580–84).
49. Maloney, "A Critical Edition" (1973), pp. 29–30.
50. Pp. 32–53.
51. For some other examples see our *Agustín Moreto,* pp. 51–52.
52. Mitchell, "The *autos sacramentales* of Mira," p. 69.
53. Schack, *Historia,* III, 277–78.
54. Cotarelo, *Mira de Amescua,* p. 156.
55. Medel, *Índice,* p. 320.
56. García de la Huerta, *Catálogo alphabético,* p. 202 ff.
57. Barrera, *Catálogo,* p. 260.
58. Cotarelo, *Mira de Amescua,* p. 159.
59. Mitchell, "The *autos sacramentales* of Mira," p. 27.

60. *Autos sacramentales desde su origen hasta fines del siglo XVII,* ed. Eduardo González Pedroso, *BAE,* LVIII (1865), 191-201.

61. Originally published in Lope de Vega, *Obras dramáticas publicadas por la Real Academia Española,* II (1892). We have used for our analysis the reprinting in *BAE,* CLVII (1963), 321-37.

62. *Ibid.,* p. lix.

63. *Ibid.*

64. Sánchez Arjona, *El teatro en Sevilla,* p. 309.

65. In 1972, José M. Bella published *La jura del príncipe* in *Clásicos Castellanos,* CLXXI, pp. 161-207.

66. Medel, *Índice,* p. 320.

67. *Clásicos Castellanos,* LXX, 155-95.

68. Wardropper, *Introducción al teatro religioso,* pp. 316-20.

69. Cotarelo, *Mira de Amescua,* pp. 160-61, is particularly harsh on this point: "Sólo al final se recuerda que es obra sacramental al descubrirse, como de costumbre, el cáliz y la hostia."

70. *Clásicos Castellanos,* LXX, lxxiv.

71. *Ibid.,* p. lxxv.

72. Wardropper, *Introducción al teatro religioso,* p. 318.

73. *Ibid.,* p. 317.

74. *Ibid.*

75. José M. Bella, "Origen y difusión de la leyenda de Pedro Telonario y sus derivaciones en el teatro del Siglo de Oro (Mira de Amescua y Felipe Godínez)," *Revista de Filología Española,* LV (1972), 51-59.

76. Pedro Salvá y Mallen, *Catálogo de la biblioteca de Salvá,* I (Valencia: Ferrer de Orga, 1872), 551.

77. Medel, *Índice,* p. 320.

78. García de la Huerta, *Catálogo alphabético,* p. 202.

79. In Lope de Vega, *Obras dramáticas,* III. We use the modern edition, *Obras de Lope de Vega,* VII, in *BAE,* CLVIII, 439-57.

80. *Ibid.,* 240.

81. Flecniakoska, *La Formation de l' "Auto,"* pp. 70-71.

82. Number 77 in the *Romancero general,* ed. Agustín Duran, *BAE,* X, 504.

83. Wardropper, *Introducción al teatro religioso,* pp. 98-99, convincingly refutes the Neo-Classical rejection of the use of anachronism in the *autos* and states that it is, with allegory, an essential ingredient in the universality to which the genre aspires.

84. Mitchell, "The *autos sacramentales* of Mira," pp. 77-81.

85. See the poem and its English prose translation in *Renaissance and Baroque Poetry of Spain,* ed. Elias L. Rivers (New York: Dell Publishing Co., 1966), pp. 148-49.

86. Sánchez Arjona, *El teatro en Sevilla,* p. 311.

87. Mitchell, "The *autos sacramentales* of Mira," p. 111.

88. Cotarelo, *Mira de Amescua*, p. 162.

89. Mitchell, "The *autos sacramentales* of Mira," p. 176.

90. Barrera, *Catálogo*, p. 457.

91. For bibliographic details, consult *BAE,* CLVIII, p. 241; Cotarelo, *Mira de Amescua,* pp. 154–55; and Flecniakoska, *La Formation de l' "Auto,"* pp. 66–70.

92. Sánchez Arjona, *El teatro en Sevilla*, p. 295.

93. In the reprint of the 1893 Academy edition, *BAE,* CLVIII, 459–75.

94. *Ibid.,* p. 241.

95. Flecniakoska, *La Formation de l' "Auto,"* pp. 66–69.

96. *BAE,* LVIII, p. 62. See also *BAE,* CLVIII, 241.

97. Examples are found in *La jura del príncipe* and *El erario.*

98. Mitchell, "The *autos sacramentales* of Mira," pp. 111–12.

99. Cotarelo, *Mira de Amescua,* p. 165.

Chapter Eight

1. See Hugo A. Rennert and Américo Castro, *Vida de Lope de Vega* (Madrid: Anaya, 1968), p. 142, n. 38.

2. Ed. M. Menéndez Pelayo, *NBAE,* XXI (1915), 496.

3. *Ed. cit.,* p. 43, vv. 205–19.

4. See Díaz de Escovar, "Siluetas escénicas," p. 125.

5. Miguel de Cervantes Saavedra, *Obras completas* (Madrid: Aguilar, 1952), p. 180.

6. Lope Félix de Vega Carpio, *Relación de las fiestas que la insigne Villa de Madrid hizo en la Canonización de su Bienaventurado Hijo y Patrón San Isidro...* (Madrid: Viuda de Alonso Martín, 1622), fol. 150v.

7. *BAE,* XXXVIII, p. 195.

8. See Barrera, *Catálogo,* p. 256; Díaz de Escovar, "Siluetas escénicas," p. 128.

9. Ed. Adolfo Bonilla y San Martín (Vigo, 1902), pp. 63–64.

10. *Biblioteca hispana,* p. 114.

11. *Actas del Segundo Congreso,* II, p. 170.

12. Francisco Bances Candamo, *Theatro de los theatros de los passados y presentes siglos,* ed. Duncan W. Moir (London: Tamesis, 1970), p. 30.

13. Alberto Lista y Aragón, *Ensayos literarios y críticos* (Sevilla: Calvo-Rubio y Compañía, 1844) and *Lecciones de literatura española* (Madrid: José Cuesta, 1853).

14. Dorothy Schons, "Alarcón's Reputation in México," *Hispanic Review,* VIII (1940), 139.

15. Irving A. Leonard, *Books of the Brave. Being an Account of Books and of Men in the Spanish Conquest and Settlement of the Sixteenth Century New World* (Cambridge: Harvard University Press, 1949), p. 79.

16. Irving A. Leonard, "A Shipment of *Comedias* to the Indies," *His-*

panic Review, II (1934), 41.

17. *Ibid.,* p. 45.

18. *Ibid.,* pp. 45-50.

19. Lafayette Silva, *Historia do Teatro Brasileiro* (Rio de Janeiro: Serviço Gráfico do Ministerio da Educaçâo e Saude, 1938).

20. Emilio Julio Pasarell, *Orígenes y desarrollo de la afición teatral en Puerto Rico* (Río Piedras: Editorial Universitaria, 1951).

21. J. R. Spell, "The Theater in Mexico City, 1805-1806," *Hispanic Review,* I (1933), 55-65.

22. J. Luis Trenti Rocamora, *El teatro en la América colonial* (Buenos Aires: Editorial Huarpes, 1947), pp. 367, 369.

23. "El teatro en Lima, 1790-1793," *Hispanic Review,* VIII (1940), p. 102.

24. Guillermo Lohmann Villena, *El arte dramático en Lima durante el virreinato* (Madrid: Estades, Artes Gráficas, 1945), pp. 125, 149, 174, 328, 330, 331, 390, 412, 513.

25. José Juan Arrom, *Historia de la literatura dramática cubana* (New Haven: Yale University Press; London: Oxford University Press, 1944), p. 23.

26. José V. Ortega Ricaurte, *Historia crítica del teatro en Bogotá* (Bogotá: Ediciones Colombia, 1927), p. 26.

27. José Mariano Beristain de Souza, *Biblioteca hispano-americana septentrional,* I, 64.

28. Ada M. Coe, *Catálogo bibliográfico,* pp. 35, 87, 95, 127, 197, 254.

29. Narciso Alonso Cortés, *El teatro en Valladolid* (Madrid: Tipografía de la Revista de Archivos, 1923).

30. E. Juliá Martínez, "Preferencias teatrales del público valenciano en el siglo XVIII," *Revista de Filología Española,* XX (1933), 113-59.

31. Alfonso Par, "Representaciones teatrales en Barcelona durante el siglo XVIII," *Boletín de la Real Academia Española,* XVI (1929), 326-46, 492-513, and 594-614.

32. Emilio Cotarelo y Mori, *Isidoro Máiquez y el teatro de su tiempo* (Madrid: Imprenta de José Perales y Martínez, 1902).

33. Charlotte M. Lorenz, "Seventeenth Century Plays in Madrid from 1808-1818," *Hispanic Review,* VI (1938), 324-31. Lorenz does not name the play in question. She also documents three performances of *El capitán belisario* and four of *La Judía de Toledo,* neither of which is she willing to attribute to Mira.

34. Nicholson B. Adams, "Siglo de Oro Plays in Madrid, 1820-1850," *Hispanic Review,* VII (1936), 342-57.

35. Paul P. Rogers, *The Spanish Drama Collection in the Oberlin College Library — A Descriptive Catalogue. Author List* (Oberlin: Oberlin College, 1940).

36. J. A. Molinaro, J. H. Parker, and Evelyn Rugg, *A Bibliography of*

'Comedias Sueltas' in the University of Toronto Library (Toronto: University of Toronto Press, 1959).

37. B. B. Ashcom, A Descriptive Catalogue of the Spanish 'Comedias Sueltas' in the Wayne State University Library and the Private Library of Professor B. B. Ashcom (Detroit: Wayne State University Libraries, 1965).

38. William A. McKnight and Mabel Barrett Jones, A Catalogue of 'Comedias Sueltas' in the Library of the University of North Carolina (Chapel Hill: University of North Carolina Library, 1965).

Selected Bibliography

PRIMARY SOURCES

1. Collections

Comedias escojidas del doctor D. Antonio Mira de Mescua. Tomo primero [*Galán, valiente y discreto* and *La Fénix de Salamanca*]. Madrid: Imprenta de Ortega, 1830.

MIRA DE AMESCUA, ANTONIO. *Teatro,* I [*El esclavo del demonio* and *Pedro Telonario*]. Prólogo, edición y notas de Ángel Valbuena Prat. Madrid: Ediciones de "La Lectura," 1926; *Clásicos Castellanos,* LXX, Madrid: Espasa-Calpe, S.A., 1943.

———. *Teatro,* II [*La Fénix de Salamanca* and *El ejemplo mayor de la desdicha*]. Edición y notas de Ángel Valbuena Prat. Madrid: Ediciones de "La Lectura," 1928; *Clásicos Castellanos,* LXXXII, Madrid: Espasa-Calpe, S.A., 1957.

LUGO APONTE DE LUIS, ELBA. "Contribución al estudio del teatro de Antonio Mira de Amescua: los autos sacramentales." Unpublished doctoral dissertation, Universidad de Madrid, 1963. As reported in *Revista de la Universidad de Madrid,* XII (1963), 765–66, this dissertation contains transcriptions of 13 *autos.*

MIRA DE AMESCUA, ANTONIO. *Teatro,* III [*La mesonera del cielo* and *Auto sacramental de la jura del príncipe*]. Edición y notas de José M. Bella. *Clásicos Castellanos,* CLXXI, Madrid: Espasa-Calpe, S.A., 1972.

MALONEY, JAMES CHARLES (ed.). "A Critical Edition of Antonio Mira de Amescua's *El monte de la piedad, La fe de Hungría,* and *La jura del príncipe.*" Unpublished Ph.D. dissertation, University of Arizona, 1973.

———. *A Critical Edition of Mira de Amescua's "La fe de Hungría" and "El monte de la piedad."* Tulane Studies in Romance Languages and Literature, No. 7. New Orleans: Tulane University, 1975.

2. Individual Plays

La adversa fortuna de don Álvaro de Luna, Introduzione, Testo Critico e Note a cura di Luigi de Filippo. Firenze: Felice le Monnier, 1960.

La segunda de don Áluaro [*Adversa fortuna de don Álvaro de Luna*]. Estudio preliminar y edición crítica por Nellie E. Sánchez-Arce. Mexico: Editorial Jus, S.A., 1960.

195

Amor, ingenio y mujer, ed. Joanne Irene Limber. "A Partial Edition of . . . , comedia famosa del doctor Mira de Amescua." Unpublished M. A. thesis, Ohio State University, 1946.

El amparo de los hombres, ed. Wilfred Wilenius. "A Tentative Edition, with Introduction and Notes, of Mira de Amescua's. . . ." Unpublished M. A. thesis, Ohio State University, 1951.

El animal profeta, ed. Shirley Tock. "A Critical Edition of Mira de Amescua's. . . with an Introduction." Unpublished Ph.D. dissertation, University of Missouri, 1973.

El animal profeta, ed. Bonnie Wilds. "A Critical Edition of . . . with an Introduction and Notes." Unpublished Ph.D. dissertation, University of Pittsburgh, 1973.

El arpa de David, ed. C. E. Anibal. *The Ohio State University Studies,* II (1925). [Full entry under *Secondary Sources.* Originally a Ph.D. dissertation, Indiana University, 1922.]

La casa del tahur, ed. John C. Fameli. ". . . de Antonio Mira de Amescua, edición paleográfica anotada." Unpublished Ph.D. dissertation, University of Southern California, 1970.

La casa del tahur, con introducción y notas de Vern G. Williamsen. *Estudios de Hispanófila,* No. 26. Madrid: Editorial Castalia, 1973.

El conde Alarcos, ed. A. T. Pickering. ". . . : A Critical Edition with Introduction and Notes." Unpublished Ph.D. dissertation, Ohio State University, 1951.

La desgraciada Raquel, "Mira de Amescua's. . . ." by Donald Alan Murray. Unpublished Ph.D. dissertation, Stanford University, 1951.

El esclavo del demonio, ed. Milton A. Buchanan. *Comedia famosa del . . . ,* compuesta por el doctor Mira de Mesqua. With an Introduction and Notes. Baltimore: J. H. Furst Co., 1905. [This printing, with a new title page, served as a Ph.D. dissertation, University of Chicago, 1906.]

El esclavo del demonio, ed. Ángel Valbuena Prat. Madrid: Compañía Iberoamericana de Publicaciones, 1931.

El esclavo del demonio, ed. Ángel Valbuena Prat, *Clásicos Ebro,* 41. Zaragoza, 1942.

El esclavo del demonio, "Letras hispánicas" Ediciones Cátedra (in press). James A. Castañeda, ed.

Galán, valiente y discreto. Edición, prólogo y notas por Edward Nagy. *Clásicos Ebro,* 110. Zaragoza, 1969.

Galán, valiente y discreto. Estudio y edición crítica por F. William Forbes. *Colección Plaza Mayor Scholar.* Madrid: Playor, S.A., 1973. [Originally a Ph.D. dissertation, University of Arizona, 1971.]

Hero y Leandro, ed. Mary Marshall Borelli. "A Tentative Edition, with Introduction and Notes, of Mira de Amescua's *Ero y Leandro.*" Unpublished M. A. thesis, Ohio State University, 1951.

La hija de Carlos Quinto, ed. Karl Ludwig Selig. "An Edition with Introduction and Notes of..., comedia famosa del doctor Mira de Amescua." Unpublished M. A. thesis, Ohio State University, 1947.

"Auto sacramental famoso de la Jura del Príncipe del Doctor Mira de Amescua." Edition critique et notes par J.-L. Flecniakoska: s.l.n.d. Texte manuscrit, xv–41 pp., fac.sim. See *Bulletin Hispanique,* LI (1949), 39–44. This ms. ed. may be read in the Institut Hispanique, Paris.

Las lises de Francia, ed. Carol L. Krumm. "A Partial Edition of ... de Antonio Mira de Amescua." Unpublished M. A. thesis, Ohio State University, 1946.

Lo que puede el oír misa, ed. Adrian Timothy Pickering. "An Edition, with Introduction and Notes, of Mira de Amescua's...." Unpublished M. A. thesis, Ohio State University, 1947.

El mártir de Madrid, ed. Henry A. Linares. "A Paleographic Edition of Mira de Amescua's...." Unpublished Ph.D. dissertation, University of Missouri, 1974.

La mesonera del cielo, ed. Karl Curtiss Gregg. "A Critical Edition of Antonio Mira de Amescua's...." Unpublished Ph.D. dissertation, Syracuse University, 1968. Contains an excellent biography of Mira.

No hay burlas con las mujeres, ed. John Lihani. "A Tentative Edition, with Introduction and Notes, of Mira de Amescua's...." Unpublished M. A. thesis, Ohio State University, 1950.

No hay dicha ni desdicha hasta la muerte, with Introduction and Notes by Vern G. Williamsen. *University of Missouri Studies,* No. LII. Columbia: University of Missouri Press, 1970. [Originally a Ph.D. dissertation, University of Missouri, 1968.]

No hay reinar como vivir, ed. Ralph Edward Angelo. "An Edition, with Introduction and Notes, of Mira de Amescua's...." Unpublished M. A. thesis, Ohio State University, 1949.

Nuestra Señora de los Remedios, ed. Sister M. Carmel Therese Favazzo. "An Edition and Study of Mira de Amescua's...." Unpublished Ph.D. dissertation, St. John's University, 1970.

El palacio confuso, ed. Charles Henry Stevens. *Lope de Vega's "El palacio confuso," Together with A Study of the Menaechmi Theme in Spanish Literature.* New York: Instituto de las Españas en los Estados Unidos, 1939. [Originally a Ph.D. dissertation, New York University, 1938.]

Comedia famosa de Ruy López de Ávalos (Primera parte de don Álvaro de Luna) [*Próspera fortuna de don Álvaro de Luna y adversa de Ruy López de Ávalos*], Notas preliminares y nueva edición revisada por Nellie E. Sánchez-Arce. Mexico: Editorial Jus, S.A., 1965.

La rueda de la fortuna, ed. Edward W. Hopper. "A Critical and Annotated Edition of Mira de Amescua's...." Unpublished Ph.D. dissertation, University of Missouri, 1972.

La tercera de sí misma, ed. George Ann Huck. "A Critical Edition of Mira de Amescua's...." Unpublished Ph.D. dissertation, Tulane University, 1968.

La vida y muerte de San Lázaro [*El rico avariento*], ed. Robert Jeffers Bininger. "A Tentative Edition of Mira de Amescua's...." Unpublished M. A. thesis, Ohio State University, 1951.

3. Poetry

BUCHANAN, MILTON A. (ed.) *Spanish Poetry of the Golden Age.* Toronto: University of Toronto Press, 1942. Contains Mira's "Canción real a una mudanza," pp. 90–93.

MIRA DE AMESCUA. "Canción real a una mudanza," ed. R. Foulché-Delbosc, *Revue Hispanique,* XVI (1907), 288–94.

MIRA DE AMESCUA, ANTONIO. "Poesías," in *Poetas líricos de los siglos XVI y XVII,* edited by Adolfo de Castro, *Biblioteca de Autores Españoles,* XLII. Madrid: M. Rivadeneyra, 1857; reprinted, 1951, 421–28. Contains fifteen poems attributed to Mira, of which nine have been anthologized from the plays in which they were first used.

SIMÓN DÍAZ, JOSÉ. "Textos dispersos de clásicos españoles: VIII. Mira de Amescua," *Revista de literatura,* Nos. 35–36 (1960), 169–80. Contains twelve of Mira's poems and four of his *aprobaciones.*

SECONDARY SOURCES

ANIBAL, C. E. "*Voces del cielo* — A Note on Mira de Amescua," *Romanic Review,* XVI (1925), 57–70. Anibal finds in seven of Mira's plays, but nowhere else, a device which he designates *voces del cielo* (or, in one of the seven plays, *voces del infierno*). It consists of turning into a mysterious warning, for the protagonist, words or phrases casually uttered by persons (frequently minor characters) who are quite innocent of their dramatic significance.

———. *Mira de Amescua:* I. *"El arpa de David," Introduction and Critical Text;* II. *Lisardo — His Pseudonym.* Ohio State University Studies, II. Columbus, Lancaster Press, 1925. Following his edition of the autograph manuscript of *El arpa de David,* Anibal presents a strong case for accepting Lisardo as Mira's pseudonym and, on the basis of its use in five plays of doubtful authenticity, claims or reclaims them for Mira. Review by José F. Montesinos, *Revista de Filología Española,* XIII (1926), 183–86, contains an attempted refutation of Anibal's theory that Mira dictated the non-autograph portions of the manuscript.

———. "Another Note on the *voces del cielo,*" *Romanic Review,* XVIII (1927), 246–52. Reacting to Krappe's article (*Romanic Review,* XVII [1926], 65–68), Anibal adduces several examples of kledonomancy in

Spanish literature in order to show that Mira could easily have "obtained his material from first-hand observation of his fellows rather than from second-hand information of the ancients."

————. "Mira de Amescua and *La ventura de la fea*," *Modern Language Notes,* XLII (1927), 106. As further support for Anibal's contention that Mira authored *La ventura de la fea,* verses from this play are shown to be almost identical to others in *El esclavo del demonio.*

BARRERA, CAYETANO ALBERTO DE LA. "Mira de Amescua." In *Catálogo bibliográfico y biográfico del teatro antiguo español, desde sus orígenes hasta mediados del siglo XVIII.* Madrid: M. Rivadeneyra, 1860; Edición facsímil — Madrid: Editorial Gredos, 1969, pp. 255-60. The biographic account contains erroneous dates of birth and death.

BELLA, JOSÉ MARÍA. "Las fuentes de dos comedias de Mira de Amescua: *El amparo de los hombres* y *El mártir de Madrid*," *Revista de Filología Española,* LI (1968), 139-53. A pious legend of the thirteenth century seems to have served as Mira's principal source for *El amparo de los hombres.* Mira's *El mártir de Madrid* follows closely a story of martyrdom recounted by the historian Antonio de Herrera in 1601.

————. "Origen y difusión de la leyenda de Pedro Telonario y sus derivaciones en el teatro del Siglo de Oro (Mira de Amescua y Felipe Godínez)," *Revista de Filología Española,* LV (1972), 51-59. Both *Pedro Telonario* and the subsequent *El premio de la limosna y Rico de Alejandría,* by Felipe Godínez, follow closely the earliest account of the frequently retold medieval story of San Juan el Limosnero, patriarch of Alexandria, who died in his native Cyprus around 620 A. D.

BLECUA, JOSÉ MANUEL. "La canción: *Ufano, alegre, altivo, enamorado*," *Revista de Filología Española,* XXVI (1942), 80-89. While not really challenging Mira's authorship of the *Canción real,* Blecua points out that attribution to Mira in seventeenth-century manuscripts of the poem is very infrequent.

BUCHANAN, MILTON A. "Notes on the Spanish Drama: Lope, Mira de Amescua and Moreto," *Modern Language Notes,* XX (1905), 38-41. The name Zumaque, found in the *Entremés del Doctor Carlino* and elsewhere, is discussed as a possible anagram for Mezqua, one of the spellings of Mira's name. Also, *La ventura de la fea* is discussed as a possible attribution to Mira.

————. "Short Stories and Anecdotes in Spanish Plays," *Modern Language Review,* IV (1908-09), 178-84; V (1910), 78-89. Several references to plays of Mira.

CARRASCO, RAFAEL. *Lope de Vega y Mira de Amescua.* Guadix: Imprenta de Flores, 1935. Carrasco traces a congenial relationship which spanned the period which began with their meeting in Guadix around

1602 and extended until 1632. The two were frequently contributors of laudatory poems to the same volume, and each served from time to time as ecclesiastic censor of the other's writings.

CASTAÑEDA, JAMES A. *"El esclavo del demonio* y *Caer para levantar:* reflejos de dos ciclos," *Studia Hispanica In Honorem R. Lapesa,* II. Madrid: Editorial Gredos, 1974, 181–88. Structural cohesiveness and verisimilitude are enhanced by Matos, Cáncer, and Moreto at the expense of much of Mira's poetic and dramatic energy. Qualities clearly characteristic of their respective cycles are found in the source play and its recasting.

―――. "Renacimiento romántico en Cuba del tema del Conde Alarcos," in Andrew Debicki and Enrique Pupo-Walker (eds.), *Estudios de literatura hispanoamericana en honor a José J. Arrom.* Chapel Hill: University of North Carolina Press, 1974, pp. 99–108. A study of the popular theme treated by Lope de Vega, Guillén de Castro, Mira de Amescua, and several others, with special emphasis on the nineteenth-century version of José Jacinto Milanés.

CAUVIN, SISTER MARY AUSTIN, O.P. "The *comedia de privanza* in the Seventeenth Century." Unpublished Ph.D. dissertation, University of Pennsylvania, 1957. Seven of the plays which we have included in Mira's canon are studied in this treatment of the popular theme of the *privado.*

COTARELO Y MORI, EMILIO. *Mira de Amescua y su teatro — Estudio biográfico y crítico.* Madrid: Tipografía de la Revista de Archivos, 1931. First published in *Boletín de la Real Academia Española,* XVII (1930), 467–505, 611–58; XVIII (1931), 7–90. The most useful compendium available on the life and works of Mira de Amescua.

DÍAZ DE ESCOVAR, NARCISO. "Siluetas escénicas del pasado: autores dramáticos granadinos del siglo XVII — el doctor Mira de Amescua," *Revista del centro de estudios históricos de Granada y su reino,* I. Granada: Imprenta de El Defensor de Granada, 1911, 122–43. The most ambitious effort devoted to Mira prior to Cotarelo's book. Sketchy biographic comments are followed by bibliography on several of Mira's poems and on seventy dramatic titles, some of which are false attributions derived from Mesonero Romanos.

FLECNIAKOSKA, JEAN-LOUIS. *"La jura del príncipe,* auto sacramental de Mira de Amescua," *Bulletin Hispanique,* LI (1949), 39–44. Mira is shown to have utilized the historic oath of allegiance sworn by the provinces to the young Baltasar Carlos, son of Philip IV, on March 7, 1632, as a thematic nucleus for his *auto sacramental,* probably represented in Madrid on June 13, 1632.

―――. "A propos d'un rôle de sacristain," *Revue des langues romanes,* LXXVIII (1966), 123–30. Damián, in Mira's *La fe de Hungría,* is the only sacristan known by Flecniakoska to appear in a pre-Calderonian *auto.* Damián's similarity to the sacristans who abound in *entremeses* is cited as proof of the mixing of genres which occurred in the *autos.*

GREEN, OTIS H. "Mira de Amescua in Italy," *Modern Language Notes,* XLV (1930), 317–19. Green adduces documentary proof to dispel Fructuoso Sanz' doubt that Mira actually did take up residence in Naples. He also confirms the fact that Mira held high ecclesiastic office while in Italy.

GREGG, KARL C. "A Metaphor in Mira de Amescua," *Bulletin of the Comediantes,* XIX (Fall, 1967), 36–38. Three passages of *La vida y muerte de San Lázaro [El rico avariento]* are studied to show the use made by Mira of the life-river equation immortalized in the third stanza of Jorge Manrique's *Coplas.*

———. "A Brief Biography of Antonio Mira de Amescua, *Bulletin of the Comediantes,* XXVI (Spring, 1974), 14–22. This excellent biographic account represents but a slight revision of the introductory section on Mira's biography which Gregg includes on pages 1–19 of his edition of *La mesonera del cielo.*

HERRERO GARCÍA, MIGUEL. "El monólogo de Segismundo en *La vida es sueño,*" *Correo Erudito,* III (1943–46), 90–91. Demonstrates the relationship between the soliloquy and a passage from *La adversa fortuna de don Álvaro de Luna.*

———. "En el tricentenario de Mirademescua," *Ecclesia, órgano de Acción Católica,* No. 171 (1944), 18. To our knowledge, this brief reminiscence is the only anniversary tribute ever paid to Mira de Amescua.

JULIÁ MARTÍNEZ, EDUARDO. "Rectificaciones bibliográficas: *La adversa fortuna de don Álvaro de Luna,*" *Revista de Bibliografía Nacional,* IV (1943), 147–50. Report of the discovery of the manuscript of *La adversa fortuna,* signed by Mira de Amescua and attributed to him by Pedro de Vargas Machuca, whose *censura* is dated October 17, 1624.

KENNEDY, RUTH LEE. "Tirso's *La vida y muerte de Herodes:* Its Date, Its Importance, and Its Debt to Mira's Theatre," *Revista de Archivos, Bibliotecas y Museos,* LXXVI (1973), 121–48. Tirso is here shown to be indebted to details which stem from three of Mira's plays: *La rueda de la fortuna, El conde Alarcos,* and *La adversa fortuna de don Álvaro de Luna.*

———. "Tirso's *La república al revés:* Its Debt to Mira's *La rueda de la fortuna,* Its Date of Composition, and Its Importance," *Reflexión 2,* II (1973), 39–50. Tirso is shown to be indebted to Mira for the basic theme of the wheel of fortune and for various details of characterization and action. Kennedy postulates that Tirso was inspired by the 1615 printing of *La rueda de la fortuna* and not by performances known to have been held in 1604 and 1616. This is one of a series of studies undertaken by Kennedy for the purpose of resolving, if possible, the perplexing question of the authorship of *El condenado por desconfiado.*

KRAPPE, ALEXANDER HAGGERTY. "Notes on the *voces del cielo,*" *Romanic Review,* XVII (1926), 65–68. Kledonomancy, the technical designation for the method of divination represented by *voces del cielo,* is briefly traced from Homeric Greece through Italy, Egypt, North Africa, India, and Israel. Since medieval documents are silent about kledonomancy in Spain, Krappe suggests that Mira was familiar with the device through references in the ancient authors, perhaps even through a specific passage in Aristophanes' *Birds.*

———. "More on the *voces del cielo,*" *Romanic Review,* XIX (1928), 154–56. This second article on Anibal's theory concerning Mira's *voces del cielo* reaffirms Krappe's belief that kledonomancy would not have been employed by Spanish Golden Age authors if they had not been aware of having behind them the authority of the ancients.

MACCURDY, RAYMOND R. "Tragic *Hamartia* in *La próspera y adversa fortuna de don Álvaro de Luna,*" *Hispania,* XLVII (1964), 82–90. Having previously classified *La adversa fortuna* as "one of the finest tragedies of the Golden Age, and . . . the best tragedy written in Spain on the theme of the fallen favorite," MacCurdy here convincingly documents the *hamartia* which McClelland was unable to find in her otherwise splendid analysis. Although MacCurdy takes no stand on the authorship of the plays, he mentions scholarship which "seems to offer incontrovertible evidence" that they should be assigned to Mira.

MESONERO ROMANOS, RAMÓN DE. "El teatro de Mirademescua," *Semanario pintoresco español* (1852), 82–83. Sketchy biographic comment and a list of 52 works attributed to Mira which contains several inaccuracies.

MITCHELL, PHYLLIS IRENE PATTESON. "The *Autos Sacramentales* of Mira de Amescua." Unpublished Ph.D. dissertation, Johns Hopkins University, 1971. Excellent study which throws new light on Mira's place as an important writer of *autos.*

MÖLLER, WILHELM. *Die Christliche Banditen-Comedia.* Hamburg: Ibero-Amerikanisches Institut, 1936. Pp. 31–77 deal with *El esclavo del demonio.*

PALLS, BYRON P. "Una justificación hermafrodita del título de la comedia de Mira de Amescua *La fénix de Salamanca,*"*La palabra y el hombre,* 48 (México, 1970), 499–509. "Justifies" Mira's title by pointing out numerous references which relate Mencía, its protagonist, to the mythic phoenix. Palls' speculations regarding bisexuality which might even suggest lesbianism seem farfetched and "unjustified."

———. "Una justificación del título de la comedia de Mira de Amescua *La fénix de Salamanca,*" *Hispanófila,* 47 (1973), 59–71. Represents but a slight revision, both in title and content, of Palls' 1970 article.

PÉREZ PASTOR, CRISTÓBAL. *Bibliografía madrileña. Parte tercera: 1621 al 1625.* Madrid: Tipografía de la Revista de Archivos, Bibliotecas y Museos, 1907. Eight documents related to Mira are included in the Appendix, pp. 427–31.

RAUCHWARGER, JUDITH. "Principal and Secondary Plots in *El esclavo del demonio*," *Bulletin of the Comediantes,* XXVIII (Spring, 1976), 49–52. Yielding to a superior power (father, king, God) is seen as an aspect of the play which unifies its two plots.

RENNERT, HUGO A. "Mira de Mescua et *La judía de Toledo,*" *Revue Hispanique,* VII (1900), 119–40. Comments on the manuscript of *La desgraciada Raquel;* also notes that *Obligar contra su sangre* is, to a degree, a sequel to Mira's main treatment of the Jewess of Toledo theme.

REYNOLDS, JOHN J. "Mira de Amescua's *Octavas al Príncipe de Gales,*" *Renaissance Quarterly,* XXII (Summer, 1969), 128–39. Only modern edition of Mira's poetic homage to Charles Stuart, Prince of Wales, on the occasion of the latter's visit to Spain in 1623.

———. "The Source of Moreto's Only *Auto Sacramental,*" *Bulletin of the Comediantes,* XXIV (Spring, 1972), 21–22. Moreto's *La gran casa de Austria y divina Margarita* is shown to be an adaptation of Mira de Amescua's *La fe de Hungría,* of which Reynolds is preparing an edition.

RODRÍGUEZ MARÍN, FRANCISCO. *Pedro Espinosa — Estudio biográfico, bibliográfico y crítico.* Madrid: Tipografía de la Revista de Archivos, 1907, pp. 91–96. This early biographic account follows Gallardo's erroneous statement that Mira was the illegitimate son of Juana Pérez. His death certificate, published here for the first time, shows that Mira died on September 8, 1644.

———. "Nuevos datos para las biografías de algunos escritores españoles de los siglos XVI y XVII: Antonio Mira de Amescua," *Boletín de la Real Academia Española,* V (1918), 321–32. Contains the texts of nine sets of documents, dealing primarily with ecclesiastical matters, and dated from May 8, 1600 to August 27, 1638. A reproduction of Mira's signature is also provided.

SANZ, FRUCTUOSO. "El doctor don Antonio Mira de Amescua. Nuevos datos para su biografía," *Boletín de la Real Academia Española,* I (1914), 551–72. In reconstructing the most complete biographic account then available, Sanz makes extensive use of the file compiled on July 20, 1631 for the *prueba de sangre* to which Mira had to submit prior to being named Archdeacon of Guadix. In 1864, Tárrago used these same documents to claim the modern discovery of Mira's illegitimacy, but he did not exploit their contents systematically.

SCHACK (ADOLPHE FRIEDRICH VON), COUNT. *Historia de la literatura y del arte dramático en España,* I–V. Translation of E. de Mier. Madrid:

M. Tello, 1885-87. The German original was published in 1845-46. The section devoted to Mira (III, 262-80) contains brief analyses of four *comedias* and two *autos*. The plot summaries are plagued with errors, and many of the harsh, negative evaluations of Mira do not seem justified.

SCHAEFFER, ADOLF. *Geschichte des spanischen Nationaldramas,* I-II. Leipzig: F. A. Brockhaus, 1890. In the section devoted to Mira (I, 303-23), Schaeffer comments on thirty titles, only one of which, *El negro del mejor amo,* has been subsequently excised from Mira's canon.

SUÁREZ, PEDRO. *Historia del obispado de Guadix y Baza.* Madrid: Imprenta de Antonio Román, 1696. Reprinted in an expanded and revised edition, Madrid: Artes Gráficas Arges, 1948. Until the publication by Rodríguez Marín in 1907 of Mira's death certificate, biographers had little more to go on than Pedro Suárez' assertion, in 1696, that Mira "murió ahora cincuenta años con poca diferencia."

TÁRRAGO, TORCUATO. "El doctor Mira de Amescua," *El museo universal,* VIII (1864), 114-15. Takes credit for the modern discovery of Mira's illegitimacy and suggests that this stigma may account for the absence of baptismal and death certificates in Guadix. His source was the same 1631 *prueba de linaje* which Sanz more fully exploited in 1914.

―――. "El doctor Mira de Amezcua," *La ilustración española y americana* (Madrid, 1888), p. 307. Essentially an edited-down version of Tárrago's 1864 article.

WALLACH, GLADYS. "The Conde Alarcos Theme in Spanish Literature — A Preliminary Survey of Its Poetic and Dramatic Versions." Unpublished M. A. Thesis, New York University, 1944. In the section devoted to Mira (pp. 63-74), Wallach detects more polish, logic, and character development than in the versions written by Castro and Lope.

WILLIAMSEN, VERN G. "Some Odd *Quintillas* and a Question of Authenticity in Tirso's Theatre," *Romanische Forschungen,* LXXXII (1970), 488-513. Further corroboration, based largely on a study of *quintillas* in *El condenado por desconfiado,* of the generally accepted view that the play's versification is very atypical of Tirso.

―――. "The Development of a *décima* in Mira de Amescua's Theater," *Bulletin of the Comediantes,* XXII (Fall, 1970), 32-36. After briefly outlining scholarship which has dealt with possible sources for Segismundo's famous first soliloquy, Williamsen cites passages from ten of Mira's plays which evidence a demonstrable progression in thought and technique toward the masterful expression attained in Calderón's *La vida es sueño.*

————. "The Dramatic Function of *cuentecillos* in Some Plays by Mira de Amescua," *Hispania,* LIV (1971), 62–67. While most dramatists used incrusted stories for ornamentation or for didactic purposes related to the specific scene in which they appear, Mira's *cuentos* underscore the play's thesis, foreshadow the conclusion, and serve as a unifying device.

————. "Poetic Truth in Two *Comedias: No hay mal que por bien no venga* and *No hay dicha ni desdicha hasta la muerte,*" *Hispanófila,* No. 45 (1972), 39–47. An illustration of Alarcón's "imitative" and Mira's "creative" handling of the same historical background.

WILLIAMSEN, VERN G. and HENRY A. LINARES. "Two Plays from One Source: *La fianza satisfecha* and *El mártir de Madrid.*" *Bulletin of the Comediantes,* XXVII (Fall, 1975), 81–90.

WILSON, MARGARET. *"La próspera fortuna de don Álvaro de Luna*: An Outstanding Work by Mira de Amescua," *Bulletin of Hispanic Studies,* XXXIII (1956), 25–36. Perceptive study which leads to the conclusion that this play is "undoubtedly one of the best historical dramas of the period."

ZEITLIN, M. A. *"El condenado por desconfiado* y *El esclavo del demonio,"* *Modern Language Forum,* XXX (1945), 1–5. First concurs with critics who suggest Mira's authorship of *El condenado,* but then adduces comparisons with *El esclavo* which, according to Zeitlin make the attribution difficult.

Index

Lisardo; reared by father and two aunts, Isabel and María de Amescua, 14; relatives, 13-14; religious theater, 31-32, 109-38; 139-64; residence in Madrid, 14, 15, 16, 17, 19; residence in Naples, in entourage of Count of Lemos, 16, 78, 107, 120, 201; secular theater, 29-31, 36-108; studies: in Guadix, 14; in Granada, 14; subplots, 23, 121, 127, 128; surname, different forms of (Mescua, Amezcua, Mezqua, Mirademescua), 14; only known use of surname in his theater, 118; *teatro menor*, 32, 139-65; witchcraft, 22, 174; women in male disguise, 21, 87, 93, 94, 105-106, 125, 129, 133, 183

WORKS — *COMEDIAS:*